# Deeper Shades of Purple

RELIGION, RACE, AND ETHNICITY
General Editor: Peter J. Paris

*Public Religion and Urban Transformation: Faith in the City*
Edited by Lowell W. Livezey

*Down by the Riverside: Readings in African American Religion*
Edited by Larry G. Murphy

*New York Glory: Religions in the City*
Edited by Tony Carnes and Anna Karpathakis

*Religion and the Creation of Race and Ethnicity: An Introduction*
Edited by Craig R. Prentiss

*God in Chinatown: Religion and Survival in New York's
Evolving Immigrant Community*
Kenneth J. Guest

*Creole Religions of the Caribbean: An Introduction from
Vodou and Santería to Obeah and Espiritismo*
Margarite Fernández Olmos and Lizabeth Paravisini-Gebert

*The History of the Riverside Church in the City of New York*
Peter J. Paris, John Wesley Cook, James Hadnut-Beumler, Lawrence H.
Mamiya, Leonora Tubbs Tisdale, and Judith Weisenfeld
Foreword by Martin E. Marty

*Righteous Content: Black Women's Perspectives of Church and Faith*
Daphne C. Wiggins

*Beyond Christianity: African Americans in a New Thought Church*
Darnise C. Martin

*Deeper Shades of Purple: Womanism in Religion and Society*
Edited by Stacey M. Floyd-Thomas

# Deeper Shades of Purple

## Womanism in Religion and Society

EDITED BY

*Stacey M. Floyd-Thomas*

*New York University Press*

NEW YORK AND LONDON

NEW YORK UNIVERSITY PRESS
New York and London
www.nyupress.org

Library of Congress Cataloging-in-Publication Data
Deeper shades of purple : womanism in religion and society /
edited by Stacey M. Floyd-Thomas.
p.  cm. — (Religion, race, and ethnicity)
Includes bibliographical references and index.
ISBN-13: 978-0-8147-2752-2 (cloth : alk. paper)
ISBN-10: 0-8147-2752-2 (cloth : alk. paper)
ISBN-13: 978-0-8147-2753-9 (pbk.                )
ISBN-10: 0-8147-2753-0 (pbk.                )
1. Womanist theology.    I. Floyd-Thomas, Stacey M., 1969–  II. Series.
BT83.9.D44 2006
230.082—dc22          2006008042

New York University Press books

Manufactured in the United States of America
c 10 9 8 7 6 5 4 3 2 1
p 10 9 8 7 6 5 4 3 2 1

This anthology is dedicated to our womanist sisters who have gone to prepare another place for us:

Rosemarie Freeney Harding
Prathia Hall Wynn
Halima Dhuhuty Hoover
Annie Ruth Powell

And our honorary womanist mothers

Helen Louise Hayes
Dr. Mary M. Townes
Bertha Ross
Rev. Anne Hargrave Pinn

And all of those known, but unnamed.

# Delving Deeper Shades of Purple

*Cheryl Kirk-Duggan*

Sprung from the Nile
Many thousands coming from the Continent,
Groaning, birthing, giving
Her young, her old into bondage
Their cargo: God's children, of most noble heritage
They stayed their course, despite walking through the doors of no return.

These saints from whom we inherited much:
We honor and celebrate in gratitude
As we delve into the mysteries, the powers, the tenacities
Of these awesome women who traversed death in many ways
So that we might live.

And because they were, we are
because they were we must write
And ruminate, and cogitate, and make inquiry
About who they were and who we are and who we will be:
Womanists, queens, priests; mothers, daughters, sisters, partners;
Ordained to delve to research, probe, ask questions
Posit theory, embody wholeness and wellness
Being outrageous: revolutionary women; not trapped by ugliness.
Anointed in many hues of purple: we give this volume as a testament of
hope and faith
Royally, celebrating dignity, honor, love, and possibility.

# Contents

# Acknowledgments

"I think, therefore I am." ——Cartesian Philosophy

"I am because we are."  —African Proverb

Being a Black woman in the academy necessitates that one knows who she is, whose she is, and how it is that she came to be if remaining sane, safe, and successful are her goals. Learning is not a luxury for Black women, nor is the academy an ivory tower. Our work is an endeavor of head and heart that is done for and with our communities in mind, if not in tow.

My progress and success is not my own. And in keeping with the womanist context of traditional communalism, I would like to thank my people who helped to make this anthology become a part of our reality: my mother, Lillian Floyd; my sister, Janet Floyd; my mentor, Katie Cannon; the wonderful contributors in this volume; my colleagues Carol Duncan, Anthony Pinn, Stephen Ray, and Lynne Westfield who gave valuable feedback; my conscientious student assistant, Jacob Robinson; and my editors, Jennifer Hammer and Peter Paris. I would like to express special thanks to my husband, soulmate, best friend, and colleague, Juan M. Floyd-Thomas.

# Wisdom Rocked Steady

## *Nancy Lynne Westfield*

*Wisdom rocked steady in her mahogany chair*
Purple floral cotton dress draped mid-calf at her varicose veins
Nude-colored support hose rolled just below her knees
Her wide feet tucked neatly into the worn tan-corduroy slippers she
    borrowed from Grand-pa thirty-odd years ago
Her swollen knuckle hands rested softly upon her big belly
Wisdom's silver-gray mane frames her burnished leather face calm with
    compassion & mercy—lament & sorrow
She smells like Nana's salve rubbed on my child-chest to rid me of croup
She tastes like mother's milk—sweetness & warmth
She feels like old/new—then/now & always will be—all rolled up into
    One
Gazing on her beauty I see—my child, Mama n'em, Pooky, Big Mama
& I see myself—ancient & yet-to-be-born
*Wisdom stirs    clears her voice then takes a deep breath*
*rocking back & forth*
I stretch to listen afraid I will miss some bit of truth
Rapt by her soothing voice we begin by singin', hummin', moanin'
    together . . . .
        At the Cross . . . . At the Cross . . . . Where I First Saw the Light
        In Times Like These . . . . . . You Need An Anchor
        Blessed Assurance . . . . . Oh What a Foretaste of Glory . . . . . .
During the singin', hummin' moanin' She looked deeply into my eyes &
    she spoke to me with conviction
        "Our freedom is not out there/it is in here"
        *she lays her hand on her own bosom*
She says with audacity *still gently rocking herself*

"Our freedom does not rest with the good will of Mr. Charlie &
 Miss Anne
Our beauty is not measured by Massa's wife nor his girlchilds
Our salvation is not in the hands of the White Woman's Christ"
*Wisdom narrowed her eyes    balled up her fist & struck her own knee—real
 hard*
Wisdom says in a serious willful tone
"It took a woman to turn dis ole worl' up-side down
It'll take a woman to turn her right-side up"
With a twinkle in her eye she says
"Baby you gotta act grown up
act courageous
even when you feel skirrred"
*Wisdom frowned—her large lips turned down—momentarily like she
 remembered a nightmare then her sad eyes returned to mine—*
*She took a short breath, wiped the tears from her big brown eyes*
With a timbre of determination Wisdom says
"We got to keep expanding, keep moving, keep going to the next
 level
Gathering as we go, including all the folk,
Learning that the journey is home
Baby concern yourself about others & their struggles
But not to the hurt of our own souls"
*Wisdom leaned forward & touched me gently on my cheek*
"Chile we got to love our own strength—our own roundness—our
 own men & children"
*Wisdom smiled at the thought of men & children, then her smile gave way to
 laughter*
Through her own giggle she said
"Sing often, dance furiously, watch the moon & consider her tides,
Above all else—Love"
*Wisdom's voice grew passionate as she spoke*
"Love Spirit, drink deeply, eat often with friends—love yourself—
 inside & out, no matter what, no matter what . . . no matter what
 —love your Self . . .
Baby Girl you got to want to know more
learn to resist & refuse madness
accept the good love of women
dig deeper into our ways & wit"

Sage words pulsed & vibrated 'round the room
*Wisdom sat back in her rocking chair spent & joyful*
She rested her head back against the doily & eased off into her nap
I retrieved her favorite hand sewn quilt from Nana's cedar chest & tucked
    her snuggly in
Her words echoing in my mind
       "Baby Girl, You gotta keep loving—you gotta keep moving . . . . ."

WOMANIST

1. From *womanish*. (Opp. of "girlish," i.e., frivolous, irresponsible, not serious.) A black feminist or feminist of color. From the black folk expression of mothers to female children, "you acting womanish," i.e., like a woman. Usually referring to outrageous, audacious, courageous or *willful* behavior. Wanting to know more and in greater depth than is considered "good" for one. Interested in grown up doings. Acting grown up. Being grown up. Interchangeable with another black folk expression: "You trying to be grown." Responsible. In charge. *Serious.*

2. *Also:* A woman who loves other women, sexually and/or nonsexually. Appreciates and prefers women's culture, women's emotional flexibility (values tears as natural counterbalance of laughter), and women's strength. Sometimes loves individual men, sexually and/or nonsexually. Committed to survival and wholeness of entire people, male *and* female. Not a separatist, except periodically, for health. Traditionally universalist, as in: "Mama, why are we brown, pink, and yellow, and our cousins are white, beige, and black?" Ans.: "Well, you know the colored race is just like a flower garden, with every color flower represented." Traditionally capable, as in: "Mama, I'm walking to Canada and I'm taking you and a bunch of other slaves with me." Reply: "It wouldn't be the first time."

3. Loves music. Loves dance. Loves the moon. *Loves* the Spirit. Loves love and food and roundness. Loves struggle. *Loves* the Folk. Loves herself. *Regardless.*

4. Womanist is to feminist as purple is to lavender.

Definition of a "Womanist" from
*In Search of Our Mothers' Gardens: Womanist Prose*
Copyright © 1983 by Alice Walker,
Harcourt Brace Jovanovich

# Introduction

## *Writing for Our Lives: Womanism as an Epistemological Revolution*

### *Stacey M. Floyd-Thomas*

I am writing to expose and explore the point where racism and sexism meet. I am writing to help understand the full effects of being black and female in a culture that is both racist and sexist. I am writing to try and communicate that information to my sisters first and then to any brothers of good will and honest intent who will take the time to listen. . . . I am writing to allow myself to feel the anger. I am writing to keep from running toward it or away from it or into anybody's arms. . . . I am writing, writing, writing, for my life.

—Pearl Cleage[1]

[O]ur objective is to use Walker's four-part definition as a critical, methodological framework for challenging inherited traditions for their collusion with androcentric patriarchy as well as a catalyst in overcoming oppressive situations through revolutionary acts of rebellion. [Our] overall goal in this project is to recast the very terms and terrain of religious scholarship.

—Katie Cannon[2]

Womanism is revolutionary. Womanism is a paradigm shift wherein Black women no longer look to others for their liberation, but instead look to themselves. The revolutionaries are Black women scholars, who have armed themselves with pen and paper, not simply to dismantle the master's house, but to do the more important work of building a house of their own. As intellectual revolutionaries, womanist scholars undertake praxis that liberates theory from its captivity to the intellectual frames and cultural values of those which cause and perpetuate the marginalization of Black women in the first place. Knowledge is no longer interpreted in light of the gaze of racist and misogynistic "subjectivities" that masquerade as human normativity, but rather taking into consideration a new "Black-woman" consciousness. These women have claimed their turf, reenvisioned history, mined the motherlode of their own wisdom, shared these teachings, and instilled methods for others so that the revolution will continue. What characterizes womanist discourse is that Black women are engaged in the process of knowledge production that is most necessary for their own flourishing rather than being exploited for the enlightenment and entertainment of white psyches and male egos.

Since its inception, the academic study of religion and theology in America has been the domain of white men. The sources and norms of theological study were drawn from their experience and largely served to reinforce the misnomer that objective inquiry and universal truth could only be achieved by answering the questions posed by white male subjectivity. Regrettably, even when liberation movements such as Black theology and feminist theology challenged this hegemony in the late 1960s, the material reality of Black women was still largely ignored. Although black theologians and feminist theologians declared that their theologies and notions of racial justice and women's rights were written for, by, and on behalf of their respective groups, they still operated from myopic perspectives that viewed all Blacks as men and all women as white.[3] While a white male-dominated academy felt threatened at worst and charitable at best for allowing Black men and white women scholars to come into the cracks of the ivory tower, even among the marginalized "undeclared war was waged."[4] Akin to the feuds between Frederick Douglass and Elizabeth Cady Stanton in the late decades of the nineteenth century, Black male theologians and white feminist theologians from the 1960s to the 1980s were often disempowered in the public sphere yet powerbrokers in the subaltern counterpublics of the dispossessed which rendered others who were both Black and female as frontline casualties in a war that was never waged with them in mind. Throughout American history, even in the academy, the interrelationship between racial oppression, gender inequity, and class exploitation reflects that Black women's lives and deaths have been characterized by trying to survive while fighting a battle on *at least* three fronts.

More than a century and a half after Isabella Baumfree changed her name to Sojourner Truth, a small cadre of Black female scholars of religion claimed a similar power of naming and called themselves womanists. In both cases, much more than names changed—minds changed. By various levels of inspiration, Black women could bear witness to the truth of their surroundings and situations. With changed names and changed minds, these Black women took hold of an emerging consciousness that not only provided a new outlook on life but also ushered forth a new epistemology. An epistemology, or way of knowing, that took the experience of Black women as normative. Womanist scholars of religion redefined the term epistemology as the unction to search for truth, interrogating the foundations upon which truth itself is established, and for reimagining truth in a world that denies its existence.[5] Womanist ways of knowing has the audacity to proclaim that truth has been reified thus far within the confines of certain ideological formulations, certain cultural complexities, and certain languages of existence that have kept white supremacist heteropatriarchy intact and omnipresent. However, womanist epistemology was not a "hand-me-down" perspective that was founded upon and validated by the normative gaze of white supremacy and patriarchal domination. Rather, it sought to deal explicitly with moral, spiritual, and political purposes of constructed knowledge to dismantle rather than support the white and patriarchal powers that compromised Black women's integrity and self-determination. This self-avowed standpoint sought to do away with Black women forever feeling forced to be caretakers or surrogates to white men, white women, or Black men. Womanist theological reflection created frames of thinking and ways of being that took Black women being agents of their own destiny as the norm. For many Black women scholars in theology and religion, the emergence of womanist epistemology was a fierce and rigorous intellectual exercise in defining, determining, and defending the Black woman's revolution to be self-actualizing in a death-dealing context.

The year 1985 marked an epoch for Black women scholars of religion in America. It was in that year that the term "womanist," adopted from Alice Walker's definition in her classic text, *In Search of Our Mothers' Gardens*, was utilized, employed, and theorized for the task of analyzing identity politics and faith formation at the intersections of race, class, and gender oppression.[6] Outside of the full version of the term, a common understanding of a womanist is that she is a Black woman committed to defying the compounded forces of oppression (namely, racism, classism, sexism, and heterosexism) that threaten her self-actualization as well as the survival of her community. During the two decades that followed its introduction into the academy, via biblical studies, ethics, theology, history of religion, sociology of religion, and religious education, womanist approaches to religion and society have contributed much to the understanding of Black religious life, scholarly activism, and women's liberation from the perspective of this newfound integrated analysis of oppression. Though the term *womanist* was coined by Walker, *womanism* became a movement when Black women scholars of religion used their *logos*— marked by their intellectual reason and God-given sense—to reconcile theoretical/theological reflection to social transformation which would forever change the way they constructed knowledge and the way knowledge constructed them. Thus, when womanism debuted in 1985 to the American Academy of Religion and the Society of Biblical Literature, womanist approaches to religion and society were introduced as a means of addressing Black women's concerns from their own intellectual, physical, and spiritual perspectives. Although the academy may have initially ignored the particular critique of womanist scholars as little more than a passing fancy, the movement continued to provide the communal and ideological space, in which a small, yet growing, cohort of committed Black women discovered the scholarly means to confront the more painful and unpleasant aspects as well as to celebrate the joys and accomplishments of their lives.

As a result of over two decades of writings, scholarly debate, teaching, and administrative leadership, the development of womanism has been much more than a trend that paid lip service to justice issues in academic or religious circles. As womanist matriarchs like Katie Cannon, Jacquelyn Grant, and Delores Williams introduced this new concept to the academy and birthed a collective enterprise, a first generation of womanist scholars emerged, including Shawn Copeland, Cheryl Townsend Gilkes, Renita Weems, Diana Hayes, Clarice Martin, Toinette Eugene, Jamie Phelps, Emilie Townes, and Marcia Riggs. These scholars' works influenced the second generation of womanists, like Kelly Brown Douglas, Linda Thomas, Karen Baker-Fletcher, Cheryl Kirk-Duggan, Barbara Holmes, Joan Martin, Rosetta Ross, and Daphne Wiggins, who advanced the theological constructions of their predecessors. And now a third generation has emerged as Black women are able to study with first- and second-generation womanists and learn about womanist theories and methodologies in semi-naries and universities throughout North America and extending to the Caribbean and West and South Africa.[7] Much more than a definition or movement and now an epistemology, twenty-first century womanism has been adapted and challenged not only in an effort to more effectively address the interest and exigencies of Black women but also to broaden the limited scope of religious discourse in the academy. Through this long-standing revolution, womanism now has become a touchstone for liberation studies in religion and other interdisciplinary discourses and has become for many the measure by which justice is critiqued. Thus, the claim in this book's title to delve into "deeper shades of purple" is appropriate and authentic.

Intended to celebrate over two decades of womanist epistemology, this anthology is multidisciplinary, reflecting the range of womanist approaches to the study of religion and society from ethics, history of religion, and religious education to sociology of religion and theology. As womanist work has reached beyond Black women's life experiences, several leading nonwomanist scholars are also included as respondents in this volume.

This work is a major contribution and extension of contemporary womanist discourse. In addition to the Protestant and Catholic thought that has dominated womanist discourse for twenty years, this volume recognizes the interfaith diversity of Black women's religious experience as an African diasporic transformation. It formally includes and dialogues with emerging African Derived Religions, African American Muslim, as well as Humanist womanist perspectives. Moreover, African American womanist thought has embraced African and Afro-Caribbean influences. The importance of this new mutuality cannot be overstated because these perspectives speak more specifically and yet broadly to the authentic depth of Black women's cultural, epistemological, and "theological" experience. The implications of this complex dialogue is one that not only deepens religious studies and theological studies, in general, but also demystifies the monolithic assumptions about Black women and their religious formation.

Critical to this anthology on womanist thought is the notion that womanism is neither a "neck-up" (i.e., disembodied) nor an "ivory tower" (i.e., elitist) venture. Womanism and womanist scholars are concerned with the mental, physical, and social dimensions of Black women's real-lived epistemology because knowledge construction that seeks to inform Black women's culture, survival, and liberation must be embodied and multi-sensory. This observation remains beyond the purview of the academy. Moreover, womanist scholars are *real* women (mothers, daughters, sisters, lovers, partners, church women, religious women, spiritual women, working women, educated women, wise women, leaders, and servants) who first and foremost understand what they do not only as a career or profession but also as a calling and vocation. Thus, womanism is a "homegrown" discourse deeply rooted in the concerns and realities of women of African descent. To be a womanist, in turn, is to be a "Blackwoman"[8]—one among the dispossessed, no matter whose house one may work in or visit. In particular, womanism is concerned with how theoretical insights and identity politics concerning the life and work of Black women work to facilitate liberationist scholarship and anti-oppressive social praxis. Womanist knowledge grants epistemological privilege to the lived everyday realities of Black women and the difficult, often marginated, issues they confront.

This volume brings together reflections from an intergenerational group of womanist scholars, ranging from those senior scholars whose works represent the formation of womanist theological discourse (first-generation womanists) to junior scholars whose intellectual formation was nurtured by the first- and second-generation womanists. Each womanist contributor and nonwomanist commentator charts her/his own historical engagement with womanism, both in its earliest inception (or when it was first encountered) and in the present. Each author addresses several questions: When and where do you enter along the womanist trajectory? What has changed about your engagement with womanism over time? What has changed about womanism over time? What are the particular challenges presented by womanism to your particular discipline, and presented by your particular discipline to womanism, both at its nascent stage and in the present? What part(s) of the definition serves as a critical lens or touchstone for your doing or celebrating womanist work? Where must womanism now take us and where must we take it in order to fulfill its task of justice?

This volume takes the bold step to define womanism. As these chapters will show, womanist epistemology, though inspired by the classical four-part definition, represents a shift from Walker's original definition partly because the emphasis of "womanism as an academic enterprise" necessitates that womanist scholars construe its meaning for the work of theological and religious studies. Whereas Walker has defined what it means to be *womanist,* womanist scholars of religion, in turn, have defined what it means to practice *womanism.* Thus, this anthology does not seek to interpret what Walker envisioned in her solo enterprise but rather provides a broadly representative understanding of how womanist scholars ever since have used her definition as a vantage point for apprehending the scholarly context, criteria, and claims of Black women's intellectual development in the academy.

The contributors to this volume reexamine and extend Walker's classic four-part definition of womanist far beyond her original premise. While keeping the elemental parts of Walker's definition intact, this volume defines and explores the four tenets of "womanism"—*radical subjectivity, traditional communalism, redemptive self-love,* and *critical engagement*—in order to illustrate the viability of this academic paradigm for interrogating religious and social phenomena at the dawn of the twenty-first century.[9] Pressing beyond the four-part definition, the volume also adds a fifth part (*appropriation and reciprocity*)[10] that analyzes the ongoing critical dialogue among womanist and nonwomanist scholars regarding theories and practices of justice in religion and society in an effort to demonstrate the far-reaching multidimensionality of womanist theory and praxis.

These chapters all deal centrally with epistemology inasmuch as the various authors articulate their respective evolving engagement (personal, historical, and cultural) in constructing knowledge with womanism in their lives and in their works. They avoid a monolithic view, speaking to the needed expansiveness and diversity within womanism in order to address the intersections in Black women's lives among race, gender, class, sexuality, and environment. Each in its own way stresses the accountability of womanist theology, ethics, sociology of religion, and history to everyday Black women and to everyday issues that impact these women, including sexuality, spirituality, and social status. These authors argue quite convincingly that womanism is a movement with multiple voices, cultures, and experiences, rather than a school or a canon that prefers one voice, culture, or experience of "woman" or of "the Black woman" over others. These scholars also mine their particular experiences as everyday Black women to shed light on the interstructuring of oppressions that affect and distort all people. Together this illustrious, intergenerational group of scholars highlights womanism as a vital and viable epistemology in religion and society.

## Outline Summary

The organization of the volume directly corresponds to the tenets of womanist epistemology: Part 1—Radical Subjectivity; Part 2—Traditional Communalism; Part 3—Redemptive Self-Love; and Part 4—Critical Engagement. Part 5—Appropriation and Reciprocity, contains the reflections of nonwomanist scholars. Each part is prefaced with a definition of the corresponding tenet of womanism for which each part is named and a poetic expression of it.

The essays in part 1, Radical Subjectivity, discuss the formation of Black women's radical subjectivity in light of the racist-sexist-classist oppression that they face and the ways in which they have subverted forced identities and hegemonic truth claims. As the chapters in this part articulate, the radicality of affirming authentic self-hood lies in Black women's ability to speak truth to power even in the face of formidable odds and thus marks the conscious-raising entry point of womanist discourse. Katie Cannon's chapter, "Structured Academic Amnesia: As If This True Womanist Story Never Occurred," discusses the angst suffered by womanist scholars and the imbalance that is struck in the intellectual pursuit of truth when the veracity of Black women's realities are classified as questionable, unreliable anecdotes lacking any authenticity or validity. Cannon mandates that womanist thought must play a critical role in subverting the gaze and the mastermind of "intellectual imperialism" by highlighting Black women's subjective truths. Carol Duncan's "From 'Force-Ripe' to 'Womanish/ist': Black Girlhood and African Diasporan Feminist Consciousness" charts a transatlantic Black woman's journey along a diasporan womanist trajectory. Duncan validates the womanish rite of passage from black girlhood into womanhood as a viable source of knowledge production and feminist consciousness cultivated through multiple migrations. Debra Mubashshir Majeed's "Womanism Encounters Islam: A Muslim Scholar Considers the Efficacy of a Method Rooted in the Academy and the Church" explores an emerging paradigm—Muslim Womanist Philosophy—as an apt framework for explicating the histories of Muslim women. In articulating a womanist theoretical and epistemological perspective, Majeed charts the inroads for womanist thought as an identity politics that must be inclusive of Black women's religious pluralism. In "Standing in the Shoes My Mothers Made: The Making of a Catholic Womanist Theologian," Diana Hayes discusses the meaning of "womanism" from a Black, female, Catholic, and celibate standpoint as a movement which asserts the rights of

Black women to have the freedom and space to define themselves as beings in their own right rather than in response to others who have already been on the playing field for much too long.

The chapters in part 2, Traditional Communalism, speak to the ways of being, doing, and thinking that have nurtured and supported Black women in their individual and collective quest for liberation. Dianne Stewart's "Dancing Limbo: Black Passages through the Boundaries of Place, Race, Class, and Religion" draws upon the author's Caribbean American experiences of migration, hybridity, fragmentation, and memory for the privileging of indigenous sources of cultural knowledge in womanist deconstructions of racist and sexist representations of Black, ethnic identities. Rosemarie Freeney Harding and Rachel Harding's "Hospitality, Haints, and Healing: A Southern African American Meaning of Religion" reflects on the meaning of a grassroots, southern mystic spiritual tradition that arises from a place closely linked to Alice Walker's creative ethics and spiritual aesthetics that informed the context out of which womanism sprang. Rosetta Ross's "Lessons and Treasures in Our Mothers' Witness: Why I Write about Black Women's Activism" is a methodological exploration of Black women's activism as seen in the lives of Pernessa Seele and Ella Baker. In her womanist analysis of these two women, Ross puts the flesh of ethical language on the normative understructure of moral insights, moral wisdom, and moral practices that are a part of Black women's activism and everyday lives for a more thoroughgoing methodological approach to reading the moral texts of Black women's lives. And Nancy Lynne Westfield's "'Mama Why . . . ?': A Womanist Epistemology of Hope" reveals the prophetic mode of epistemology within womanist discourse as a phenomenon that allows Black women to take their past to understand their present and define their future. In so doing, Westfield situates Walker's definition as particularly "shamanic" in its ability to "open spiritual doors and bind up undesirable spiritual forces" in terms of Black women scholars' epistemology, pedagogy, and didactics.

The chapters in part 3, Redemptive Self-Love, follow autobiographical and/or spiritual trajectories in their discussion of individual womanist's paths to self-love, self-acceptance, and the emergence of womanist consciousness and aesthetics. They assert the importance of self-reflexivity and cultural metaphor as a redemptive project of Black womanhood. All four chapters discuss the spiritual import and real life impact of Walker's definition at a crucial crossroads in each author's academic and personal trajectory. In Kelly Brown Douglas's "Twenty Years as a Womanist:

An Affirming Challenge," the author poignantly discusses the role woman-ism plays in her privileging and keeping at the center the real lived expe-riences of Black church women in her role as preacher and scholar of religion. Douglas asserts that womanist epistemological orientation must enable Black women to claim their voices and spaces, as well as to carve out their places from which "true knowledge" (knowledge that liberates rather than oppresses, knowledge that creates moral agents rather than further embeds people in existing power relations) can emerge. Karen Baker-Fletcher's chapter, "A Womanist Journey," celebrates womanism as more than a theoretical orientation but as a "movement of the Spirit" and as an "oasis," where Black women scholars and students come to be revived and rejuvenated in the midst of an academic context which has marginalized Black women's intellectual gifts and contributions. In "Quilt-ing Relations with Creation: Overcoming, Going Through, and Not Be-ing Stuck," Cheryl Kirk-Duggan highlights the relationality indicative of womanist thought and methodology. For her, relationality is the spiritual-ity of womanism, the actual embodiment of the Creator/Spirit that allows Black women the ability to liberate themselves. And finally in "The Sweet Fire of Honey: Womanist Visions of Osun as a Methodology of Emanci-pation," Shani Settles stresses that redemptive self-love may take many forms across Black religious traditions. Within ADRs (African-Derived Religions), redemptive self-love is broadly conceived as deep, expansive, and revolutionary in any context *regardless*. It engenders transformation not only of consciousness, but also of being; it is simply *ashé*.

In part 4, Critical Engagement, the chapters highlight the necessity for womanist thought to remain on the cutting edge of approaches to and discourses on religion and society. Realizing the role that womanism plays in tandem with other feminist, liberationist, and anti-racist scholarly movements and social institutions, the authors mandate that womanism continues to be a fruitful resource for engaging major questions in a vari-ety of disciplines and social contexts that take seriously the interaction of religion and society. Central to the notion of critical engagement is em-bracing the dynamic tensions in what ought to be the meaning and iden-tity politics of womanism itself in the normative field of religious studies, extending especially to the politics of white feminism and Black [male] theological thought in the United States and globally. According to Mel-anie Harris in "Womanist Humanism: A New Hermeneutic," the inclusive nature of womanist discourse mandates that womanist scholars seriously engage issues of religious pluralism. Building on the womanist project of critical engagement that takes inclusivity seriously, Harris invites womanist theological scholars to use Black women's voices representing a variety of religious traditions by introducing womanist humanism as a new hermeneutic that helps to expand the discourse of womanist theological thought beyond traditional Christian categories. In "A Thinking Margin: The Womanist Movement as Critical Cognitive Praxis," M. Shawn Copeland considers how womanism is often pressed to the academic, ecclesial, and social margins and insists that womanist thought is a "serious thinking margin" from which other critical discourses might glean directives for doing thoroughgoing research and analysis "that seek to discover and tell what is true." And in "The Womanist Dancing Mind: Speaking to the Expansiveness of Womanist Discourse," Emilie Townes calls for a more expansive womanism that not only weaves in and out of Africa and the Diaspora, but also welcomes the "messiness" of the enormous intracommunal task in seeking out and building allies, intellectually and practically. Ultimately for Townes, critical engagement underscores the agility of womanism and womanists in managing and negotiating various connections with numerous communities in which womanists are necessarily a part.

Womanist approaches to religion and society have not only been invested in knowledge production and reconstruction for themselves and their mainstreaming disciplines but also for other scholars who remain on the margins and who are committed to extending the epistemological privilege of the oppressed. In part 5, Appropriation and Reciprocity,[11] renowned liberationist scholars offer their responses to womanist thought and its contributions to their analyses of religion and society. While not identifying themselves as womanists, these scholars nevertheless acknowledge the impact that womanist thought has had on their own ways of knowing and scholarly approaches to religion. Their commentaries are an attempt to articulate their evolving engagement (personal, historical, and cultural) with womanism in their lives and in their works. In their own ways, Kwok Pui-lan, Letty Russell, Ada María Isasi-Díaz, Daisy Machado, Anthony Pinn, Dwight Hopkins, and Traci West, attend to the role of partnership and dialogue in womanist scholarship (especially by highlighting when and where "they" enter) in an effort to locate an epistemological position from which to formulate liberation epistemologies of their own that problematizes the invisibility of the many silenced and marginalized "others" from moral and ethical relations and responsibilities. Their inclusion in this anthology demonstrates the variety of dialogues with which womanists engage.

As these chapters brilliantly illuminate, womanist approaches to religion and society will continue to take up an "intracommunal task" for our time in a way that is responsive and responsible to African/African American communities both local and global. But this intracommunal task does not lead to exclusivity, essentialism, or a narrow sense of identity politics as traditionally defined. Womanism for our time is rather a praxis of solidarity and of building relationships and allies, both within Black communities and among womanist, Black, feminist, and other liberationist scholars and communities. And more importantly, it is an epistemology that will continually strive to delve deeper.

This volume is dedicated to the memory of those valiant revolutionary Black women who fought the good fight, laid down to rest, and study war no more. It is also dedicated to the spirit helpers and "home girls"[12] who give me the will to live by providing a refuge of protection and nourishment while prodding me to *"G'on ahead and write, girl, cause what you're writing in that book I just might need!"*

## NOTES

1. Pearl Cleage, *Deals with the Devil: And Other Reasons to Riot* (New York: Random House/Ballantine, 1993), 7.

2. Katie Cannon, *Katie's Cannon: Womanism and the Soul of the Black Community* (New York: Continuum, 1997), 23.

3. With such a normative view, as Gloria Hull et al., state, not only are these respective fields assumed to be all male or an all white domain but, in fact, it might lead one to conclude that in deed *all the women are white, and all the blacks are men!* Gloria Hull, Pat Bell Scott, and Barbara Smith, *All the Women Are White, All the Blacks Are Men, but Some of Us Are Brave* (Old Westbury, NY: Feminist Press, 1982).

4. Rosemary Radford Ruether, "Crisis in Sex and Race: Black Theology vs. Feminist Theology," *Christianity and Crisis* 34 (1974): 67–73.

5. Linda Thomas, "Womanist Theology, Epistemology, and a New Anthropological Paradigm," *Cross Currents: The Journal of the Association for Religion and Intellectual Life* 48 (Winter 1998–1999): 488–499.

6. Alice Walker, *In Search of Our Mothers' Gardens: Womanist Prose* (San Diego: Harcourt Brace Jovanovich, 1983), xi–xii. Walker actually coined the term "womanist" in 1979 when she was invited by Laura Lederer to write the essay, "Coming Apart by Way of Introduction to Lorde, Teish, and Gardner." But 1983 marks her fullest description and formal definition of the term. For a fuller exploration see, Alice Walker, "Coming Apart," in *Take Back the Night: Women on*

*Pornography,* ed. Laura Lederer (New York: William Morrow, 1980), 100n; Alice Walker, "Coming Apart by Way of Introduction to Lorde, Teish, and Gardner," in *You Can't Keep a Good Woman Down* (San Diego: Harcourt Brace Jovanovich, 1981), 41; and Rufus Barrow, "Womanist Theology and Ethics," *Encounter* 59, 1–2 (1998): 158–159.

Katie Cannon's "The Emergence of Black Feminist Consciousness," in *Feminist Interpretation of the Bible,* ed. Letty M. Russell (Louisville, KY: Westminster, 1985), 30–40, provided the first written work announcing womanism as a scholarly orientation of, for, and by Black women that was introduced to the American Academy of Religion and the Society of Biblical Literature.

7. The generational distinctions of womanist scholars have not always been organized in this same way. Some would argue that generations would be marked by decades. Others would argue that one's generational affiliation is based upon the womanist scholars or scholarship that has informed her work. In that case, if someone studied with one of the pioneering womanists, like Katie Cannon, she would be a second-generation womanist. And still again, there are others who would argue that like feminist discourse, womanist discourse has no generational separations but rather is categorized in waves or streams.

8. Here "Blackwoman" is to be understood as an individual who can "legitimately" place a foot in two realities—what one individually and/or collectively may perceive of what it is to be "Black" and what it is to be "woman" simultaneously. Such a multifaceted standpoint enables womanist scholars to move away from narrow or essentialized definitions of Black subjectivity. For the origin of the term, see Joan M. Martin, "The Notion of Difference for Emerging Womanist Ethics: The Writings of Audre Lorde and bell hooks," *Journal of Feminist Studies in Religion* 9, 1–2 (Spring–Fall 1993): 43.

9. A few years after womanist scholars in religion started to use the term "womanist" as a self-referential term and modifier for their work, Cheryl Sanders launched a critical roundtable discussion concerning what she felt could be a misappropriation of "womanism," a secular term that was never meant to be used as a resource for theological reflection and scholarship. In this legendary intellectual debate, several prominent womanist scholars (Katie Cannon, Emilie Townes, Cheryl Townsend Gilkes, and M. Shawn Copeland) and Black feminist, bell hooks, challenged Sanders's strident critique. This anthology joins these defenders of womanism in claiming that womanism is much more than a secular term; it is a resource for theological reflection and scholarship in religion. It has been the works of Black women scholars in religion, rather than Walker's self-referential term, that has proven and continues to demonstrate that the viability of this concept is not limited to one woman's definition or another woman's assertion in limiting its scope. For the full narrative see, Cheryl J. Sanders et al., "Christian Ethics and Theology in Womanist Perspective," *Journal of Feminist Studies in Religion* 9, 2 (Fall 1989): 83–112.

10. For an in-depth treatment of the four tenets of womanism, see Stacey M. Floyd-Thomas, *Mining the Motherlode: Methods in Womanist Ethics* (Cleveland, OH: Pilgrim Press, 2006).

11. For an extensive discussion of "appropriation and reciprocity" as a womanist concern, see Katie G. Cannon, "Appropriation and Reciprocity in the Doing of Womanist Ethics," in *Katie's Canon*, 129–135.

12. For my usage of the word "home girls," see Barbara Smith, *Home Girls: A Black Feminist Anthology* (New York: Kitchen Table Press, 1983).

# Part I

# Radical Subjectivity

RADICAL SUBJECTIVITY—[the first tenet of womanism] 1. a process that emerges as Black females in the nascent phase of their identity development come to understand agency as the ability to defy a forced naiveté in an effort to influence the choices made in one's life and how conscientization incites resistance against marginality

"The power analyses, biotextual specificity and embodied mediated knowledge" of Black women and girls. "The anecdotal evidence" of Black women's lives that reveals truth, "the measure of womanism."   —Cannon

"An intelligence grounded in a wisdom that [comes] from deep within —born of the experiences of being Black and female."   —Hayes

2. an assertion of the real-lived experiences of one's rites of passage into *becoming* a Blackwoman, *being* "womanish"; the audacious act of naming and claiming voice, space, and knowledge

"The 'fresh,' 'fast,' 'facety' (from 'feisty' in Jamaican patois), 'force ripe,' and 'womanish' behavior, attitude, and consciousness found in Black girls and women."   —Duncan

"The empowering assertion of the black woman's voice" or the "voice that speaks when others fear to."   —Majeed

3. a form of identity politics that is not a tangible, static identity that measures and gauges the extent to which one is or is not what others had planned or hoped for one to be

"Feeling a whole lot like God" [Colloq.]   —RevSisRaedorah

# When Mama Was God

## *RevSisRaedorah*

When mama was God
   She made miracles happen
   In the middle of a Houston ghetto
   The center of my universe, indeed.

She walked on water
   In three inch heels, matching bag
   With us five kids in her footsteps.

   She taught us to fear not
   Night lightning, thunderstorms
   Hard work, new things, good success.

When mama was God
She created not one but two
   Fancy Easter dresses and sewed
   Lace on my socks to match.

   She hollered for me from the porch
   Compelling me to come out, come out
   From all of my favorite hiding places.

   She held me close with strong hands
   So close that I would inhale
   Warm fleshy bosom heat for air.

When mama was God
   She laid hands on us
   So the cops wouldn't and trifling men couldn't
Healing bad attitudes and broken hearts.

She stood her ground with white folk
   Those blue-eyed devils of pure evil
   Of the 60s . . . 80s . . . this new millennium.

She made a dollar hollah
   On the occasions of more month than money
   Without robbing anyone of anything.

When mama was God
She blessed two fish and five loaves
   Or was that govm't cheese
   And canned mystery meat?

   She kept an open door policy
   Always meant that somebody else
   Would be sleeping on the living room floor.

   She prayed for us and others
   We eavesdropped listening for our name to be called
   Knowing that no weapon formed against us would prosper.

When mama was God.

*"Girl, you just like your mama,"*
somebody said one day
when I was feeling a whole lot like God.

*Chapter 1*

# Structured Academic Amnesia
## *As If This True Womanist Story Never Happened*[1]

## *Katie G. Cannon*

What does it mean to structure academic amnesia? To whom, then, do we turn when we are told that our truth is a lie? How, it is asked, can Womanist realities be verified in institutions of higher learning where the dailiness of our authentic experiences cannot be proven by scientific methodology? Indeed, there are countless real-life dilemmas that these questions presuppose. And, this is certainly the case for Black women in the theological academy who grapple with the fact that our existential situations are oftentimes classified as questionable, anecdotal evidence; our genuine perceptions and factual registration of cutting-edge issues end up encoded as sporadic wanderings, downloaded as rambling, make-believe, episodic soap operas flowing into the institutional sea of forgetfulness. It is as if this true Womanist story never happened.

Some years ago I was physically assaulted by a man I did not know as I walked down the corridor of a hotel in New York City, on my way to a meeting of Presbyterian women of color. Back in those days I often wore my clergy collar when attending ecclesiastical gatherings. Ah, distinctly I remember that on this particular morning, I caught the number-one IRT train from 116th street and Broadway down to 42nd street, shuttled over to Grand Central Station, moving as fast as I could, putting one foot in front of the other, and I arrived at the appointed meeting place on time.

To be sure, I was caught off guard, completely taken aback, when a white man in a hotel service worker's uniform walked toward me. The man looked at my clergy collar, and in one fell swoop, grabbed me by the shoulders and slammed me into the wall, screaming, "How dare you defy Jesus Christ!" I was startled, shocked, discombobulated, but I did not say one mumbling word about the body slam incident that happened in the hallway when I entered the meeting room of the women of color. I simply kept pace with the order of the day, because part of my survival strategy as a Womanist is what Alice Walker's names as being *traditionally capable.* Walker defines traditional capable, in these words, "Mama I'm walking to Canada and I'm taking you and a bunch of other slaves with me." Reply: "It wouldn't be the first time."[2]

Now, the specificity of what it means for Womanists to be traditionally capable has to do with conscientization, wherein we realize that we are walking to freedom and that we are taking our Mama and a bunch of other enslaved people with us, and that this particular liberating work that we are called to do is more than supplementing malestream theology. This capacity for resistance emerging forth from the core of our beingness moves us beyond serving as superfluous appendages, add-ons to required androcentric knowledge at the bottom of core course syllabi, as endnotes in church publications, or as impotent members, labeled as special consideration, appointed at-large to denominational boards and agencies.

Instead, a Womanist understanding of being traditionally capable focuses on the quintessential skills that are confined in the strictest sense to the collective conscious will of African American women desiring not to repeat oppressive domination in the dailiness of life. Instead, this Womanist version of traditional capability connects our cultural values, oral traditions, and social experiences to our spirit forces in the quest for meaning amid suffering.

Well, several years passed, and an African American woman from the *Wall Street Journal* interviewed me for an article that she was writing about clergywomen. When asked if I had encountered any hardships, any outright vicious, vindictive, violent experiences as a woman minister, for the first time I shared the story about the white man in the hotel in the service worker's uniform who saw my clergy collar, walked over and grabbed me by the shoulders and slammed me into the wall, screaming, "How dare you defy Jesus Christ!"

The newspaper reporter drafted the story, and a few days later the sister-reporter called back to check the facts. The reporter's voice was filled with perplexed hesitation. I sensed that this reporter was locked inside of a precarious, soul-searching quandary, because the hotel where the incident took place no longer exists and according to her fact checking, the truth of my story never happened. The reporter's boss told her that my story was no longer plausible because there was no evidence in recent memory that there was ever such a hotel near Grand Central Station. I detested whole-heartedly, and in my struggle to regain unequivocal, unmistakable, indisputable evidence for the truth of my experience, I made the case, that just because the hotel had been torn down, demolished, scattered to the wind, that did not mean that my truth was a lie. I encouraged the sister-reporter to go to a Manhattan court of law, to the office of records and deeds, and to get the necessary signed and sealed papers for proof of property, to retrieve the rigorous empirical documentation that a particular hotel existed right near Grand Central Station at such a place and during a particular time in history. The bottom line, fundamental point is this, it is as if this true Womanist story never happened.

Thus, this essay is not only a description of some of the trials and tribulations of early Womanist scholars in the academies of religion, but it is also an invitation to all who cast their lot with us. I invite you to measure womanism in the twenty-first century by calling into question the presuppositions operative behind the following soul-searching inquiry: What does it mean that academia is so structured that Black women are severely ostracized when we re-member and re-present in our authentic interest? What does one do when told that our refusal to split, to dichotomize from God's presence in the daily fabric of our communal lives makes us a liability to civilization? What is the role of Womanist intellectuals in institutions of higher learning, where our pedagogical styles and scholarly lexicons are derailed on a daily basis? The point that I am arguing is that anecdotal evidence does a lot to reveal the truth as to how oppressed people live with integrity, especially when we are repeatedly unheard but not unvoiced, unseen but not invisible.

Speaking primarily of Womanist scholars, but expressing an idea that applies equally well to *Mujerista* and Feminist intellectuals, most women can name the exact time and the specific place when the truth of our private lives appears stranger than public fiction. In the capacity to elaborate this dilemma of oversimplified reduction of anecdotal evidence, I often share the story about two white men, one, the president, and the other, the provost, sitting across the room from me, early in my career, during a job interview. These two white men wanted to know how I, a thirty-three-year-old black woman, got my libido needs met. So, I answered saying that I read and write. The majority of people who hear this true story about this type of undressing question, this under-my-clothes kind of talk during a job interview, want to argue how such a question is forbidden, improper, and against the law and therefore, two powerful, tenured white men interrogating a brand new Ph.D. Black woman about her sensual embodiment could not have happened.

Keep in mind that this type of adversarial aggression in academic institutions is also represented by those designated as the golden boy-mindguards in professional learned societies. Such individuals make it their business to announce to colleagues that our scholarship is mediocre because there is no evidence in our publications that we are grounded in the authoritative assumptions of white men. On one occasion, I sent the message back to one of the golden boy-mindguards that no one earns a Ph.D. in the Western hemisphere without knowing a whole lot about the evidential determinism of white men, whether we want to or not.

By this I mean that there are men and women walking among us at the annual meeting of various guilds, who check the footnotes, endnotes, index, and bibliography in each of our publications to see if their names are mentioned, and if they and their peers are not cited in our books and journal articles, then these powerhandlers, wielding tyrannical, experience-distant rationalism, devalue womanist modes of experience-near cognition. In practice, they go to great length to demand that our intellectual concerns and canons of discourse be ignored in all matters of contract evaluation, tenure review, and refereed endorsement for promotions, grants, fellowships, and awards.

From 1983 until now, storms of opposition, bigotry, and suspicion mount. Women intellectuals find ourselves giving pause daily as we reflect upon the socially constructed discursive values implied in androcentric space, a space "that proposes to be gazing from 'human' eyes at 'human' subjects but the 'human' in both instances is always male and masculine."[3] As Black women scholars, in an academy, which structurally excludes women from the formal systematic thinking about religious data, our scholarship is often a scholarship of struggle. In fact, because of pre-established power relations and preconceived cultural stereotypes of women, we often wonder if our experiences of being "exoticized, eroticized, anomalized, masculinized, and demonized"[4] are peculiar to the religious academy or if these are general patterns of misogyny practiced in other fields of study where women have been traditionally barred, such as in medicine and law.

Similarly, when Black women began earning the Doctor of Philosophy Degree in Theological Education and officially entered as full-fledged members of the American Academy of Religion (AAR) and the Society of

Biblical Literature (SBL) in a small, but critical mass, we ha⌷
picture and almost no orientation of what to expect, when w
Our entry into the AAR/SBL is what Nikki Giovanni calls landi⌷
land-mark-less situation, dropping anchor at a place and in a space w⌷
we see very little of anything that is familiar and yet we continue to make ⌷
conscious decision to be human and humane in death-dealing situations.[5]

Yes, a careful, faithful reading of the historical milieu discloses that for more than twenty years, the investigative Womanist projects in our various disciplines of study are punctuated with utter silence in the sacred halls of the majority of the accredited colleges, universities, and seminaries. This type of deafening silence can be compared to competitive absent-mindedness, or repressed, suppressed, compressed brain-fade, wherein hegemonic iconographers, who dictate "the terms under which the world is to be perceived and experienced,"[6] degrade and/or dismiss the scholarship that emerges from our credible living labs of embodied reasoning as a threat to their respective beliefs, and they, in turn, deem us as unnecessary.

Far too many of our professional colleagues, who are defenders of androcentric, heteropatriarchal, malestream, white supremacist culture, experience our very presence as colleagues as a cruel joke. The fragility of some men, especially if they have been indoctrinated all of their lives to believe that women in general are insufficiently intelligent, and Black women in particular are "naturally" inferior, that our mere presence walking down the hall, sitting in the same classroom, offering critical comments in committee meetings around the faculty table, these men, as well as women who have not divested themselves of white supremacy, feel their scholarly homogeneity being threatened, and in turn, they assess all that we say and do as dumbing-down and diluting the very essence of so-called academic rigor.

Law Professor Patricia A. Williams sums up the situation of African American women intellectuals in traditional male space in this way: she says that, as Black women scholars, we are often greeted and dismissed as unreliable, untrustworthy, hostile, angry, powerless, irrational, and probably destitute.[7] Therefore, I contend that even though some of us feel displaced and estranged, we must continue to read and write, even though our journey is littered with nervous confusion and hostile resentment, full of all kinds of intimidating, ossifying professional quagmires.

In the brief commentary that follows—power analyses, biotextual specificity, and embodied mediated knowledge[8]—an attempt has been made to convey the pragmatic strategic work of collective resistance that quali-fies a Womanist as traditionally capable. These three concepts, as we will see, spell out the Womanist work that we are called to do in order to re-dress the inequalities of power and the arbitrariness of violence.[9]

## Power Analyses

First, and most important, traditional capability requires Womanists to assert and demand realistic power analyses in order to tackle the narrow-ness of inherited "modes of standardization and mechanisms of legit-imization."[10] In her classical study *Yurugu: An African-Centered Critique of European Cultural Thought and Behavior*, Marimba Ani states that it is our responsibility to create systematic theoretical formulations which will re-veal the truths that enable us to liberate and utilize the energies in our communities of accountability.

The plausibility of our claim of a valid Black woman-centered religious discourse must first be proven within and around the sacred halls of acad-eme. Seminaries and university departments of religion possess a lot of power in defining when, where, and for whom God-talk will be extended. Furthermore, educational institutions have always been given a principal place in mainline ecclesiastical social order. So for good and substantial reasons, Black women scholars "must throw into question precisely what is assumed to be beyond question,"[11] in order to provide substantial evi-dence of our talk about God as a legitimate, intellectual agenda.

To do power analysis means that we investigate the beliefs, behaviors, and assumptions that are often unspoken and unwritten, but yet they dic-tate institutional culture. Both discreetly and directly, if we succeed in the socialization process, adapting with single-minded devotion to dominant norms of individualistic autonomy, then those responsible for making de-cisions, dispersing funds, and bestowing privileges will identify us among the respected personage. Reading power dynamics means that we excavate the pipelines of good-faith-efforts that often empty into workplace terri-tories that are uninviting, unappealing, trivialized token assignments with limited opportunities for decision-making. Whenever the status quo at our academic institutions proves to be a formidable and intractable force, it simply means that Womanists must dig deeper in order to uncover the methodological biases, contradictory priorities, and inconsistencies in performance evaluations. In situations of structured academic amnesia, powerbrokers encourage allegiance to their self-defined interests. Any other loyalty is considered disingenuous.

In other words, the way to measure traditional capability of Womanist scholars in the twenty-first century means that we know how to debunk seamless histories; that we unmask the deadly onslaught of stultifying intellectual mystification; and that we continue to disentangle the ordinary absence of women of color in whole bodies of literature.

## Biotextual Specificity

Second, if we do not want to be set aside, excluded from the production of knowledge, dismissed as a passing phase, fad, trend, or fly-by-night operation, then it is important that we bring the specificities of our autobiographical context into play. Using concise but lively, uncompromising language we must tell our stories. Anecdotal evidence suggests that this type of straightforwardness will enable us to communicate in suitable language the theoethical issues born in our living.

Sometimes the gist of the creative ideas in the mining of our biotexts comes from negotiating difficult personal experiences. At other times, it is the echoing of communal realities against the deadly onslaught of stultifying intellectual mystification that grab us as participant-observers in our family and community. In one way or another, at the center of our life-led narratives we must take a clear-eyed look at the immediate irregularities that relegate our truth to falsehood. And simultaneously, we must consciously grasp our historical struggle for authentic self-determination, so that the organic, sentient, living myths of our spiritual existence as a holistic people will continue to serve as resources in the ongoing development of successful strategies against intellectual colonization.

The specificities of our autobiographical context require that we plumb the depths of both death-dealing and life-giving experiences. The internal logic for the examination of both sobbing heartbeats and soulful loving is that it enables us to wrestle with time-tested ethical questions until we gain an understanding of present circumstances. In this sense, the core dilemmas mediated via Black women's real-life embodiment are repeated generation after generation. Therefore, when we interface the inner struggles of our personal narratives that evolve out of and remain inextricably tied to our ancestral worldview, we begin to see interpretive possibilities for creative change in our contemporary social locations.

## Embodied Mediated Knowledge

Third, and finally, it is also important to be aware that in order to be flexible in our construction and cogent in our articulation of the generative themes comprising our religious landscape, womanism cannot be measured by those who hide behind abstract screens of disinterested explorations or fixed ideas of dispassionate objectivity. Nor can we, as Womanists, idealize the detached, disembodied, mathematically calculated professional persona of armchair academicians, working only from the neck up. Instead, as scholars of religion, we beg the macroquestion "who is God?" and the microquestion "how is God acting in the social fabric of our lives?"[12]

Within learned institutions, structured academic amnesia is relentless. Intellectual rank and scholarly authority are assessed as unalterable, fixed, mechanical phenomena. By this I mean that when Womanists refuse to play the game of illusive objectivity, a game that is incapable of tolerating ambiguity, ignores emotions, weeds out passion, resists spontaneity, maintains rigid predictability, and celebrates the isolated solo-self, then the prescriptive authorities impose theoretical frameworks categorizing our truth as a lie. Each and every time that we are not willing to dissect people, places, and things; that we stand over against the intellectual propensity to tear apart foundational experiences, meanings, and elements by way of suprarational technical, abstract, referential facts, then we get demoted to the status of second-class thinkers.

With all of this said, whether we find ourselves teaching in a college, seminary, or research university, or any other institution of higher learning, there is a great need to see how overt power and covert force maintain hidden controls of sophisticated notions of academic processes. In order to survive professionally, those with the least amount of academic capital cooperate by making the habits of waddling and shuffling appear as natural choices. An appreciation of Womanist refusal to be banished to the periphery of religious knowledge is essential in understanding African American women's collective resistance. One of the earliest-noted aspects of Womanist traditional capability was how we participated in revolutionary acts so that our life work would not be situated on the bottom rung of the hierarchical order of priorities relevant only to men. Those of us who are serious about not wanting partial and false generalizations about Black women in religion to persist, we have decided to remedy the situation by bringing our best embodied reasoning to the academic venue of scholarly inquiry and publication.

In essence, the major point that I want to contribute to the task of delving deeper is this: whenever the academy fails to take seriously valid bodies of knowledge produced at the intersection of race, sex, and class; whenever the academy desires only to systematically classify the inner workings of our embodied mining of the motherlode as questionable fool's gold; whenever the masterminds of intellectual imperialism encode our candid perceptions and scholarly labor as nothing more than culturally laden idiosyncrasies, then we end up with education that is unbalanced, knowledge that is incomplete, and a worldview that is distorted. "Mama I'm walking to Canada and I'm taking you and a bunch of other slaves with me." Reply: "It wouldn't be the first time." And, it won't be the last.

NOTES

1. This phrase is related to Beryl Gilroy's "it was as if this true story never occurred," in *Stedman and Joanna—A Love in Bondage: Dedicated Love in the Eighteenth Century* (New York: Vantage, 1991), 181.

2. Alice Walker, *In Search of Our Mothers' Garden: Womanist Prose* (San Diego: Harcourt Brace Jovanovich, 1983), xi–xii.

3. Darlene M. Juschka, ed. *Feminism in the Study of Religion: A Reader* (New York: Continuum, 2001), 2.

4. Ann duCille, "The Occult of True Black Womanhood: Critical Demeanor and Black Feminist Studies," in *The Second Signs Reader: Feminist Scholarship, 1983–1996,* ed. Ruth-Ellen B. Joeres and Barbara Laslett (Chicago: University of Chicago Press, 1996), 70–108.

5. Nikki Giovanni's interview on *The Tavis Smiley Show,* National Public Radio, February 14, 2003.

6. Marimba Ani, *Yurugu: An African-Centered Critique of European Cultural Thought and Behavior* (Trenton, NJ: Africa World Press, 1994), 10.

7. Patricia Williams, "Alchemical Notes," cited by Adrien Katherine Wing, "Brief Reflections Toward a Multiplicative Theory and Praxis of Being," in *Critical Race Feminism,* ed. Adrien K. Wing (New York: New York University Press, 1997), 28.

8. See the discussion of my understanding of Beverly Wildung Harrison's concept of *embodied mediated knowledge* in my essay, "Unearthing Ethical Treasures: The Intrusive Markers of Social Class," in the *Festschrift for Beverly Harrison: Union Seminary Quarterly Review (USQR)* 53, nos. 3–4 (1999): 53–64.

9.  Rachel E. Harding, *A Refuge in Thunder: Candomble and Alternative Spaces of Blackness* (Bloomington: Indiana University Press, 2000).

10.  Ani, *Yurugu*, 6.

11.  Ibid., 8.

12.  See Katie G. Cannon, *The Womanist Theology Primer: Remembering What We Never Knew—the Epistemology of Womanist Theology* (Louisville, KY: Women's Ministries Program Area, National Ministries Division, Presbyterian Church (U.S.A.), 2001); and Rachel Lee, "Notes from the (non)Field: Teaching and Theorizing Women of Color," *Meridians* 1, no. 1 (Autumn 2000): 85–109.

# Chapter 2

# From "Force-Ripe" to "Womanish/ist"
## Black Girlhood and African Diasporan Feminist Consciousness

## Carol B. Duncan

*Entering the Womanist Trajectory as a Transatlantic
Diasporan Black Woman: 1983*

In many ways, the 1980s began for me in 1983, the publication year of *In Search of Our Mothers' Gardens* and the subsequent introduction of Alice Walker's womanist definition.[1] My orientation to the definition is rooted in the history of the early 1980s and the year 1983, in particular. This year marked the beginning of young adulthood with the start of my life in the academy as a first-year sociology student at the University of Toronto. The year also marked several turning points in the fabric of black cultural and political life in North America and Western Europe. And 1983 was Hip Hop culture's fourth year in the mainstream after the release of the pioneering rap group Sugar Hill Gang's "Rapper's Delight" in 1979 and the popularization of a particular 1980s black aesthetic signified by the jheri curl hairstyle. This hairstyle and by extension that aesthetic culture out of which it grew was characterized, sympathetically, by black British sociologist and cultural critic, Kobena Mercer,[2] as a practice of "New World black stylization" that emerged out of African-European cultural contact and mutual appropriation and popularized by popular musical entertainment stars such as Michael Jackson and Prince. The jheri curl hair style, circa 1983, was the turning point and cultural sign of a black aesthetic and value system arguably based in economic acquisition which in many ways contravened the radicalism of the 1960s and 1970s Civil Rights and Black Power movements signified by hairstyles such as the afro or "natural," as much as it drew on the gains of these earlier political and social movements.

As a transatlantic diasporan black woman born in mid-1960s London, England, to parents from the Caribbean—my mother is from Antigua and my father is from Guyana—the early 1980s held the promise of a new post–Civil Rights era, in which the victories of my parents' generation's anti-colonialist, anti-racist, and civil rights political, economic, and cultural struggles would guarantee a quality of life unprecedented for generations of black folk. Nineteen eighty-three was also the year that the Grenadian socialist revolution, led by Maurice Bishop, was quashed by a U.S. military invasion. For those of us who were sons and daughters of the Caribbean, by birth or by heritage, some of whom may have served in the armed forces of our adopted North American homelands, this event brought the post–Second World War era of the 1960s and 1970s third world anti-colonialist revolutionary movements to a shattering close with a terrifying moment of cognitive dissonance.[3]

Into this period of flux and change, Alice Walker's collection of essays, *In Search of Our Mothers' Gardens*,[4] represented her own personal recollection and sharing of wisdom developed through her activism in anti-racist and radical social justice movements in the United States as well as her work as a writer. When I read, Alice Walker's definition of "womanist," for the first time, I connected with it immediately for the term on which the definition is based, "womanish," was one with which I was familiar from my own Caribbean girlhood in Antigua and Toronto, Canada.[5] "Womanish," as referenced by Walker, is also a word found in anglo-Caribbean Creoles and it refers to a girl who acts "grown" (forward-thinking and mature) or who is "fast" (not necessarily with the implication of sexual precocity and/or promiscuity but who is self-motivated)[6] or "nuff" (a particularly Antiguan term usually used to imply someone, either male or female, who is unusually and perhaps even intrusively inquisitive). These are all terms pointing to a precocious orientation to social relationships and knowledge acquisition, in which the girl-child insists on speaking up and asking questions rather than being content with the knowledge gained from the position of the passive listener referenced by the phrase: "little donkey have big ears." The latter is a Jamaican Creole expression which acknowledges that even in a cultural context in which children should be "seen and not heard" that quite often children are witnesses if not active participants in social events and forces which shape their lives and those of others in their communities. Thus, when I read Alice Walker's definition of womanist, I related to it through my multiple social locations as a British-born African-Canadian woman of Caribbean heritage.

In the expression, "womanish," I heard an echoing of the admonitions that I myself and other young Caribbean girls had received: "Yuh too womanish." (You are too womanish); "Yuh mus' keep out-ta big people business." (Literally, "Keep out of the business of big people" with the implied meaning, "Keep out of the affairs of adults."); with the aside, "She too love dip she mout' in people business." (Literally, "She likes to dip her mouth in other people's business" meaning "She is always interfering in the affair of others."). In other words, all these phrases are tantamount to: "Min' yuh business; nobody was talkin' to you!" ("Mind your business; no one was talking to you!"). Yet, even with admonitions, as womanish girls, we still minded our own *and* other people's business with alacrity and determination and I dare say the beginning of a burgeoning feminist consciousness grounded in care, concern, and the ability and willingness to step outside of established boundaries and norms of strategies of communication and inquiry.

Walker's radicalism lies in her valuation of this quality of womanishness which was very rarely, if ever, acknowledged as positive during my girlhood, except in the occasional amused, hushed laughter and knowing glances exchanged between "big women"[7] in my family and community. Their occasional concealed laughter and glances seemed to validate the very quality which they saw as somehow simultaneously dangerous but also necessary for survival. In valuing "womanishness," Walker affirmed an important experience in black girlhood, namely, stepping outside of the boundaries of expected gender normative behavior in familial and community contexts, in which obedience (read *silence*) and compliance (read *silence* again) were highly valued and seen as effective child-rearing practices that reflected positively on the child's mother. Important to note here, as Caribbean scholar and novelist Olive Senior observes, in Caribbean cultural contexts, many girls are "raised" and "trained" while boys are allowed much more freedom in their choice of activities within and outside the household.[8] In her assessment of gender and socialization in Caribbean families across class backgrounds, Senior further notes that "[g]irls seem to suffer most from over-strictness of parents, especially with regard to their social lives and friendships."[9] To be womanish, then, encompassed challenging widely accepted gender norms and to rebel against child-rearing practices which restricted young girlhood and female adolescent social relationships.

## Fresh, Fast, and Facety

"Womanish" was also used along with the terms "fresh,"[10] "fast," "facety"[11] and "force-ripe" to indicate behaviors and attitudes in youth and children that should, ideally, lie far beyond their life experiences. "Force-ripe," in particular, referred to a young person who acted in adult ways long before their time as a result of experiences, sometimes by choice and sometimes due to the choices of others, especially adults in their lives as well as wider social and political circumstances beyond their control, which forced them to grow up too fast and enter the world of adulthood without adequate preparation. The metaphor is ostensibly taken from plant cultivation and conjures images of the practice of forcibly ripening fruit after it has been prematurely plucked from the tree or vine by placing it in artificially created situations such as a brown paper bag at a warm room temperature. These circumstances subsequently "force" the fruit to ripen well before its time of maturation. Force-ripe fruit is notable in that no matter the beauty of the "forced" fruit, including its unblemished surface and smooth skin, it is never as sweet as that which is vine ripened, "naturally" through a longer process of maturation. So, how do we then, as scholars, teachers, parents, family, and community members, engage black sons and daughters who are forcibly ripened by the circumstances of their birth and the choices that they then subsequently make? What kinds of subjectivities do force-ripe experiences engender? And are they always negative? "Womanish" as utilized by Walker in her definition of womanist honors those life choices and circumstances, as difficult as they may be, chosen or imposed, as part of the continuum and range of black girls and women's life experiences. It is this capacity of womanism to encompass diversity and contradiction that informs my work in sociology and cultural studies.

## Womanist Perspectives and Caribbean Religion and Culture

Womanism was an important part of my intellectual formation as an undergraduate in the 1980s and then a graduate student in the 1990s in sociology of religion. While some of its central texts were not included, formally, in my course work, I found these books through references from other black women graduate students, writers, and scholars and in women's bookstores. There were at least two curricula which shaped my formation as a scholar, the formal, organized one as dictated through course syllabi and program requirements, as well as an informal network of artists, scholars, and cultural workers who shared books and references. The intersection of these two networks proved to be a fertile grounding for my intellectual growth and creative and artistic imagination.

Womanism resonated with me powerfully, for it gave credibility not only to my own personal experiences as a Caribbean-descent black woman in Canada, but also to those of other black women whose experiences were vastly varied culturally, linguistically, and geographically. As a sociologist concerned with immigrant Caribbean women's everyday religious life experiences in Canada, especially in the Toronto Spiritual Baptist community, womanism opened a space for me to infuse a concern with wider social relations of power and individual black women's life experiences.[12] In the academic discipline of sociology, which grew out of trying to come to terms with the angst of late-nineteenth- and early-twentieth-century industrial capitalism, the sociological subject, as in other social science and humanities disciplines, was historically, overwhelmingly a generic masculine and almost always normatively white. The critical intervention of feminist sociologists such as Anne Game[13] and Dorothy Smith[14] encouraged a focus on women's everyday life experiences as the locus for analyzing power relations. In her thesis of the "everyday world as problematic," Smith radically proposed that sociological analysis of power not be confined to notions of a wider structure that imposed its logic on women's lives but rather that women have intimate knowledge of the matrixes of power that structure their lives through the relationships in their everyday world. Womanism, in its definition, underscores this premise, for the womanish subject is one who dares to question and, in so doing, is actively engaged in uncovering the contours of her myriad social relationships.

While all parts of the definition are meaningful to me in using cultural studies and sociological perspectives in my study of immigrant Caribbean women's religious lives in Canada, Walker's inclusion of a diasporic impulse and the sensual body as sources of empowerment and touchstones for examining aesthetic culture are particularly salient. The radical inclusivity of the definition in stretching to encompass diasporan origins in Canada, referenced in the second part of the definition in the assertion of "capability" that "Mama, I'm walking to Canada and I'm taking you and a bunch of other slaves with me," made it possible for me to envision womanism as being salient for African-Canadian and transnational diasporan identities and experiences. While Walker's originary moment for African-Canadians remains rooted firmly south of the border, black community formation in Canada is in actuality the result of several migrations from different geographic areas, including the Caribbean, South America, Africa, and western Europe, over a 400-year period. This is a crucial factor in contemporary Canadian academic and cultural criticism, since one of the central predicaments of discourses of blackness and the study of African-Canadian experiences is how frequently these are subsumed under the general rubric of "African-American" so that what results is what George Elliott Clarke terms "African-Canadian African-Americanism."[15] Often, the unspoken epistemological assumption here is that black equals African-American or that African-American peoples and cultures occupy the most legitimate and authentic territory of blackness not only in this hemisphere but also globally, leaving the discernment of African-Canadian identities an ontological tangle.

Alice Walker's definition is also meaningful to me specifically because of the affirmation of transgressive acts rooted in black girlhood experiences as a source of feminist consciousness, creativity, and activism. Womanish she notes is "opp. of "girlish," i.e., frivolous, irresponsible, not serious." Womanish, then, by definition as "opp." is contemplative, responsible, and serious. Walker's definition could thus be read as identifying girlhood, rather than the more typical metaphor of motherhood, as the locus of change and transformation for black women. This dimension of the definition, which affirms girlhood as the site of feminist consciousness, is witnessed by the accounts of black women artists and scholars in their assessment of the development of their craft. Acclaimed African-American science fiction writer Octavia E. Butler,[16] African-American of Grenadian heritage, poet and activist Audre Lorde,[17] African-American cultural critic bell hooks,[18] African-American anthropologist Zora Neale Hurston,[19] Haitian-born, Canadian-raised writer, literary critic, and photographer Myriam Chancy,[20] African-American poet Maya Angelou,[21] storyteller, folklorist, and expert in Jamaican oral traditions Louise Bennett,[22] and Trinidadian calypsonian Calypso Rose[23] in their autobiographical assessments of the origins of their work all site a girlhood in which they dared to transgress normative codes of gendered behavior concerning the place of black female children, as an important origin of their creativity and subjectivity as artists and critical thinkers.

In many ways, this sentiment lies in stark contrast to black girlhood as represented in contemporary popular cultural images which feature rappers such as Li'l Kim and Foxy Brown and R 'n' B and pop music divas such as Ashanti and Beyoncé Knowles as highly eroticized and hypersexualized products of the cultural marketplace endlessly playing out mixed race brown/black girl images of Jezebel in a celluloid fantasy world. Many of these young women entertainers, now in their early to midtwenties, became popular as teenaged girls in marketing campaigns that featured them in highly sexualized images. These sexualized images can be read as riffs—to borrow a term from jazz improvisation—or embellishments on Walker's notion of "girlishness" (as implied in the opp. of womanish) which is "frivolous, irresponsible, not serious." These images conform to popular, long-held, cultural stereotypes of black women as sexually licentious while simultaneously proclaiming the naturalness of the stereotype through providing a kind of celluloid biography of this highly sexualized black girl subject in the myriad images of advertising, music videos, and popular movies.

Though inherently critical of objectifying images of black female subjectivity, Walker's definition, however, is not anti-erotic or anti-sexual. In fact, it is explicitly affirming of sensuality and embodiment for the third part of the definition notes that a womanist "[l]oves music. Loves dance. Loves the moon. Loves the Spirit. Loves love and food and roundness. Loves struggle. Loves the Folk. Loves herself. Regardless." The coda, "regardless" signals the centrality of valuing the sensual, erotic, and aesthetic aspects of black cultures in spite of these aspects of black experiences being the fodder of racialized stereotypical images, particularly those rooted in embodiment. The "regardless" wordlessly signals that even in the face of stereotypes which situate black folk as "naturally" rhythmic, musical people who are good dancers and who like food and eating, the womanist still dares to embrace these parts of herself. This statement is radical in its embrace of the artistic and cultural productions of black people which are linked with the spiritual, even in spite of criticism from dominant cultural perspectives which devalue them and/or use distorted representations as the basis of stereotyping.

## Radical Subjectivity and the Promise of Womanism

Relatedly, as a scholar who is concerned with the expressive culture of Caribbean religions, including representations of the sacred in church dress, sacred space, and cinematic and photographic images, in many instances, I find myself in the paradoxical position of knowing that in exploring black aesthetic culture, that I must necessarily engage the stereotypic since so many of the discriminatory representations of black people take place in the visual terrain.[24] Even if not directly addressing stereotypes, it often seems as if I am in some way speaking back to, or engaging them, implicitly, in talking about visual representations. Walker's definition affirms a valuation of that aesthetic that exists outside of (and in spite of) dominant cultural representations of black women as either desexualized, docile mammies, hypersexual jezebels, or castrating, angry sapphires.

The capacity of womanism to include a variety of black girls' and women's experiences makes it a viable theoretical and methodological framework for critical research and intellectual and creative projects. Indeed, womanism's appreciation of everyday life experience as the grounding for critical approaches bodes well for interdisciplinary academic research that consciously makes links between the academy and black community life experiences. Potentially, there are as many womanist frameworks as there are individual womanist thinkers and writers since subjectivity is so highly valued. What might be interpreted as a lack of specificity and inherent instability of womanism is actually one of its greatest strengths. In discerning the radical subjectivity of our grandmothers, othermothers, and black girlhood selves, Walker outlined a framework for analysis and research methodology which is as forward thinking as it is, simultaneously, backward looking.

NOTES

1. Alice Walker, *In Search of Our Mothers' Gardens: Womanist Prose* (San Diego: Harcourt Brace Jovanovich, 1983).

2. Kobena Mercer, *Welcome to the Jungle: New Positions in Black Cultural Studies* (New York: Routledge, 1994).

3. See Carole Boyce Davies discussion of black women's migratory subjectivity with reference to this military example in *Black Women, Writing and Identity: Migrations of the Subject* (New York: Routledge, 1994).

4. Walker, *In Search of Our Mothers' Gardens*.

5. Ibid., xi–xii

6. "Fast" or "fass" (using a spelling that more closely approximates Jamaican Creole speakers' pronunciation) is defined as "interfering, meddlesome, quick to intrude in other's business" by Honor Ford-Smith, in *Lionheart Gal: Life Stories of Jamaican Women* (Toronto: Sister Vision: Black Women and Women of Colour Press, 1987), 308.

7. The term "big women" in a Caribbean anglo-Creole linguistic context refers

to "grown" women as opposed to young girls or women. The term does not refer to body size but rather to maturity and life experience.

8. Olive Senior, *Working Miracles: Women's Lives in the English-Speaking Caribbean* (Cave Hill, Barbados: Institute of Social and Economic Research, University of the West Indies, 1991).

9. Ibid., 32.

10. The term "fresh" in Antiguan Creole refers to behavior, speech, and attitudes that are deemed haughty, rude, and impertinent. The term can also be used to refer to sexual impropriety or inappropriate sexually suggestive commentary. As used with children, however, it usually referenced the first meaning.

11. Facety, ostensibly based on the standard English word, "feisty," is a Jamaican Creole term for "rude and impertinent" as discussed in Ford-Smith, *Lionheart Gal.*

12. Carol B. Duncan, "Hard Labour: Religion, Sexuality and the Pregnant Body in the African Diaspora," *Journal of the Association for Research on Mothering* 7, 1 (Spring/Summer 2005): 167–173.

13. Anne Game, *Undoing the Social: Towards a Deconstructive Sociology* (Toronto: University of Toronto Press, 1990).

14. Dorothy Smith, *The Everyday World as Problematic: A Feminist Sociology* (New York: Open University Press, 1988).

15. George Elliott Clarke, "Contesting a Model Blackness: A Meditation on African-Canadianité," in *Odysseys Home: Mapping African-Canadian Literature* (Toronto: University of Toronto Press, 2002), 27–70.

16. Octavia E. Butler, *Bloodchild and Other Stories* (New York: Four Walls Eight Windows, 1995).

17. Audre Lorde, *Zami: A New Spelling of My Name* (Tramansburg, NY: Crossing Press, 1982).

18. bell hooks, *Bone Black: Memories of Girlhood* (New York: Henry Holt and Company, 1996).

19. Zora Neale Hurston, *Dust Tracks on a Road* (New York: HarperPerennial, 1991).

20. Myriam J. A. Chancy, "Je suis un negre," in *Miscegenation Blues: Voices of Mixed Race Women,* ed. Carol Campter (Toronto: Sister Vision: Black Women and Women of Colour Press, 1994), 304–305.

21. Maya Angelou, *I Know Why the Caged Bird Sings* (New York: Bantam Books, 1971).

22. Nesha Z. Haniff, *Blaze a Fire: Significant Contributions of Caribbean Women* (Toronto: Sister Vision: Black Women and Women of Colour Press, 1988).

23. Ibid.

24. Carol B. Duncan, "Aunt/y Jemima in Spiritual Baptist Experiences in Toronto: Spiritual Mother or Servile Woman?" *Small Axe: A Caribbean Journal of Cultural Criticism* 9 (March 2001): 97–122.

# Chapter 3

# Womanism Encounters Islam

## A Muslim Scholar Considers the Efficacy of a Method Rooted in the Academy and the Church

### Debra Mubashshir Majeed

African American Muslim voices—as scholars and subjects—have largely been absent from womanist conversations. Perhaps the black female religious scholars who spearheaded womanist thought unconsciously held the belief that the language of "God-talk" sufficiently speaks to the realities of Muslim women. Like many Christian women, the lived experiences of African American Muslim women "arise out of specific contextual locations." Certainly our Christian sisters do not employ the terminology of *gender jihad* but, like us, they do endeavor personally and publicly to negotiate the politics of gender discourse within and without the religious and societal spaces which they traverse, and like us they fight for the inclusion of their experiences and their voices. We differ from non-Muslim women, however, in regards to issues of marriage, identity, and the means by which we are both situated and situate ourselves in the United States and the world. Thus, our attention to reconstructed knowledge encompasses Islam and our religious self-identity as Muslim women.

In this essay, I will articulate my womanist theoretical and epistemological orientation and journey as a Muslim and American of African ancestry who, like other American Muslim women, strives to "actualize the Qur'anic mandate of social justice" and, concomitantly, survive in a racist and patriarchal society. I will explicate a journey which reflects the complexities and nuances of womanist discourse and draws attention to narratives and praxis that both accentuate and challenge the interdisciplinary approaches of scholars whose socioethical analysis first concretized a womanist agenda. In the process, I will explore an emerging paradigm—

Muslim Womanist Philosophy—as an apt framework for explicating the histories and life journeys of Muslim women. Ultimately, I hope to accomplish four goals: (1) encourage further scholarly attention to African American Muslim—as well as other non-Christian Diaspora—women as producers and "gatherers" of knowledge who embody the essence of what it means to be Muslim in a non-Muslim nation and whose perceived *womanish* presence is actually a more authentic expression of their divinely crafted nature; (2) extend consideration of womanist discourse to include the ways in which varied cultural, religious, and historical experiences of black women enable a creative tension to exist in postmodern explorations of gender, religion, race, and/or sexualities beyond the bounds of colonialism; (3) solicit critical responses to my Muslim-centered theoretical methodology; and (4) challenge other African American Muslim scholars to more intentionally engage womanist discourse as a field ripe for the sowing and harvesting of metalevels of dialogue—a postmodern reclamation, if you will—which reclaims the trajectory of our own scholarship as we endeavor to define and refine disciplinary ways to understand, interpret, and teach the lived experiences of African American peoples and African American women. In the process, I hope to convey the realization that womanist discourse in all its embodied forms enables African American scholars to be about the business of celebrating our beingness and intellectual gifting as we endeavor to "move towards the betterment of our own humanity, as representatives or trustees or agents of the divine."[1]

I first encountered "womanism" as articulated by first-generation African American female womanists in 1995 as a first-year doctoral student at Garrett-Evangelical Theological Seminary and Northwestern University.[2] With the zeal that many graduate students strap to their book bag-carrying backs, I caught hold of the term and never looked back. I scoured the library and internet for every piece of literature on the concept. As a financially struggling student, I celebrated my free find of Alice Walker's *In Search of Our Mothers' Gardens* while on a trip to Berkeley, California. I was in awe of those first-generation scholars—though embarrassingly, but no less excitedly, I called Emilie Townes "Dr. Cannon" on one too many encounters at my first AAR meeting in 1997. Even then I had no trouble *NOT* characterizing myself as a feminist. I was a second-career student who had survived eleven years in corporate communications as the only African American writer/editor in my department at predominantly white, patriarchal institutions. I also ran an independent communications consulting firm for three years. In the end, I had personally experienced discrimination, marginalization, and patronization because of my race at the hands of both white men and women.

Feminism, even with an introduction to bell hooks's crafting of black feminism, held far too much political currency that excluded my black female experience. To me—and many other African American women—the evolution of the feminist movement in the United States, born in the dust of anti-slavery campaigns, mirrors Margot Badran's observation: "feminisms are produced in particular places and are articulated in local terms."[3] Indeed, early American feminist proclamations for gender equity rarely extended to black women; too often when debates surrounded women's control of their personal physicality and agency, for instance, white women empowered themselves to dictate to black women the utility of a black woman's body as well as where and in what manner black women were to support themselves. Most white female activists also failed to appreciate the communal nature of the African American battle against oppression. As white women fought for their own emancipation, their efforts did not authentically reflect the interface between race and gender and class and power and privilege as these forces shaped the world in which African American and other women of color lived. "Middle class feminists worked for the limited emancipation of well-to-do white women, seeking suffrage and recognition by society," explains Angela Davis. "On the other hand, black women first sought credit as women."[4] In the end, the exclusionary nature of the "feminist movement" rendered the *feminist* label as inauthentic and representative of an experience that I did not share.

Outside of the business world, I was an ordained Christian minister who had served in pastoral ministry, preached, led revivals, facilitated workshops domestically and internationally, and was invited to start a new Methodist congregation. While journeying within independent, Baptist, Pentecostal, Congregational, and United Methodist communities, I became well acquainted with male chauvinism, prejudice against the questioning that my seminary education allowed, as well as the shortsightedness of older female clergy who did not become ordained to do "the work of the ministry" or whose administrative ideology saved little room for a call to both the academy and the church. Institutional patriarchy, gender and racial inequalities, along with the disarming thinking and action those structures can manifest, clearly influenced my "pre-womanist" journey. As a result, by 1997, I was convinced that womanist was a wearable label—one that fit me as close as I used to keep my shaven head.

At first, I did not approach Walker's four-part definition critically in its totality. For instance, homophobia limited my ability and desire to discern how women might authentically love each other and still remain within the divine sanction of behavior. My graduate school small group consisted of myself and four married men, whose spouses shared little interest in our intellectual conversations. Thus, I was not preoccupied with building relationships with female peers with whom I could share analytical and reflective insights. Neither did I feel it necessary to problematize the characterization of a womanist as a feminist of color. I devoted more energy to a contextualization of radical subjectivity. Besides, I was so overwhelmed by the possibility of visibly exercising a modicum of self-definition and self-determination as a budding scholar that I reserved scant attention for aspects of Walker's theorizing that did not fit neatly into my still fundamentally Christian, approval-seeking, other-privileging paradigm.

As a more clearly articulated dissertation proposal became a concrete reality, however, my appropriation of the concept of womanism entered its first in a series of evolutionary stages. Motivated by my own unwanted singleness, the lack of marriageable black men attending Christian churches, and what appeared to be the overwhelming African American male presence in Islamic communities, I chose to focus specifically upon African American formulations of Islam and female agency. To accomplish that task with any sense of authenticity, I needed to assume behavior some considered outrageous, if not audacious. I needed to act *womanish*. I needed to enter onto enemy territory—an environment in which lived those void of the salvation necessary to gain an eternity with our Creator. That is to say, I needed to journey beyond the safety and familiarity of my Christian roots and circumstances to encounter and engage African American Muslims on their turf. I wanted to test my preconceptions, to understand the sensibilities and rationale of people whose fervent piety seemed to contradict all that I had been taught about them and their faith. In other words, I wanted to know more about the religion of one-billion-plus inhabitants of this planet, and particularly its attraction to a growing number of African American men and women. I didn't realize at the time that the academic journey on which I chose to embark would so clearly resonate with a building spiritual odyssey and both serve as challenges to the way I approached the womanist agenda.

I was welcomed by a group of Muslims in Chicago who referred to me as "Sister Debra." The women modeled for me the "do's and don'ts." They were as passionate about their faith as they were of their identity and agency in their local mosques. Both men and women shared—through their walk and talk—the centrality of the Qur'an as the fulfillment of the revelations that preceded it and as a liberatory tool for all humanity. I could embrace what I heard and witnessed. As I moved closer to becoming a Muslim, I committed an act that some might label as responsible, another expression of *womanish* behavior. While serving a United Methodist congregation in Evanston, Illinois, I was invited by my superintendent to start a church in North Chicago. The offer appeared to be an awesome task for any junior clergy person, especially one still in graduate school. Without a doubt, I desired to serve my conference, but I also wanted to complete my doctorate and knew that accepting such a demanding position would not allow me to effectively complete either task. I humbly refused the offer, partly because I knew that my theological position had expanded beyond the boundaries of the brand of Christianity I had been educated to teach and model. Thus, while attending a meeting of Women of Color scholars in Nashville, Tennessee, a few months later, I was compelled to decide against requesting reallocation of the $10,000 renewal scholarship I had been awarded two years earlier. Instead, I rode to a nearby Islamic center and made my *Shahadah* or publicly declared my faith in Islam and the revelation given by Allah to the Prophet Muhammad.[5]

While my Muslim friends celebrated with me, most members of my biological, denominational, and intellectual communities were at best prayerful, and at worst, outraged and confused. My mother, naturally concerned about her progeny through the loins of her eldest child and only daughter, angrily wondered aloud whether I would get a husband, since with my more modest attire, "he can't see your legs." Overseas speaking invitations were rescinded. I had to sever a close relationship with a male colleague and study partner. I assumed additional debt through student loans to replace the Women of Color funding. Couples at whose marriage ceremony I had officiated wondered whether "our vows are still intact." Christians, whom I had led to Christ as a zealous evangelist, asked "am I still saved?" Seminaries once interested in an African American church historian were not so inclined to interview a Muslim to teach Christianity. Thus, the consequences involved in my decision to turn away from denominational support and turn toward a new belief system and way of life resonates with the subversive element of behavior that is courageous, willful, and responsible, or simply *womanist*.

Once a Muslim, I discovered something I had not realized as a Christian—the womanist agenda often made normative the Christian experience of African American women. That is, historiography by and about black women in the United States documented and reinterpreted their experience almost solely through the lens of the black Christian experience.[6] It was clear that the contributions of Muslim scholars, such as Aminah McCloud, were not addressed or cited.[7] Concerned, I approached Katie G. Cannon, a first-generation womanist and at the time a member of the steering committee of the Womanist Approaches to Religion Group of the American Academy of Religion, about what appeared to be a glaring omission and a religious privileging of black women's experience. Her response was akin to: "Debra, you're right, we are missing the Islamic perspective, but few of us know anything about Islam. It would be great to have Muslim scholars share their stories." Cannon's prompting led to the inclusion of Islamic themes in the Womanist Approaches "Call for Papers," an AAR panel in 2000 which drew attention to womanist spirituality and social activism in the lives of African American Muslim women, and consideration of a framework which presupposes the primacy of Islam in the historical experience of some African American women. She and other first-generation womanists understood the need to reject an essentialist womanism which privileged religion or any single spiritually based experience and to allow space for the problematizing of womanist theories so as to acknowledge, differentiate, and reclaim the diverse faith journeys and spiritual influences in the lives of African American women.

One could argue that scholars who called for the inclusion of Muslim female perspectives, in particular, advocated for a type of womanism that maintains a threefold allegiance: to *Islam,* as an essential part of self-determination and identity for Muslim women, men, and children; to *the Qur'an,* as a source of teachings about Allah and about human creation, ontology, sexuality, and marital relationships that challenge sexual inequality and patriarchy; and to *African American Muslim women,* whose struggles and triumphs have largely been ignored in global and local explorations of Muslim women. One methodological attempt to address these concerns is the emerging concept of Muslim Womanist Philosophy.

## *Muslim Womanist Philosophy: The "Voice" of African American Muslim Women*

Before we consider what, to me, Muslim Womanist Philosophy is not—Islamic feminism—let me attempt to articulate what I believe this methodology is. When bell hooks first championed an intellectual and observable move "from margin to center" in her twenty-year-old work of the same name, she articulated the central thrust of Muslim Womanist Philosophy, the developing "voice" of African American Muslim women.[8] This framework removes the scholarly and popular veil from their lived experiences, giving public voice, material expression, and legitimacy to what has long existed privately but misunderstood due to two "parallel structures."[9] The first structure, internal colonialism, as expressed by some male Muslims and others who view the embodied experiences and knowledge of African American Muslim women as inconsequential because of their gender and/or less than authentic because of their race. As Islamic studies scholar Amina Wadud has observed:

> African Americans are very astute to practices of racism and discrimination; it is our history. Immigrant Muslims will come to this country aimed at mainstreaming themselves with regard to American privilege. [This] has sometimes meant, as with other immigrants, that they have assumed the mainstream ideology regarding rights and privileges. They have therefore imbibed some of the prejudices or the stereotypes with regard to oppressed peoples in this country. And instead of alleviating them, especially with Islam as the cause of their alleviation, they have perpetuated them.[10]

Likewise African American Muslim women, who in increasing numbers choose to marry polygynous men, are oppressed in the eyes of their non-Muslim neighbors. Islamic polygyny, the practice of a husband taking up to four wives, is gaining supporters, some argue as a result of the lack of marriageable black men. It is illegal in the United States. Women who enter into the practice do so with a social stigma and often with financial insecurity.

The second structure, external colonialism, creates a hierarchy of black religious expression, suppresses non-Christian traditions, especially Islam, and calls into question the moral agency of Muslim women as a spiritual and social witness. Such a process also can relegate African American Muslim women to the perceived role of "subject without agency."[11] Perhaps the historic absence of articulated Muslim perspectives within womanist conversations in the academy has provided an excuse or rationale for disassociation on the part of Muslim scholars, who feel more comfortable within traditional disciplines such as Islamic studies, where their religious knowledge, experience, and expression may be more overtly validated.

When first-generation womanist Emilie M. Townes writes, for example, "the spirituality that issues from Black women's lives is found in the moral wisdom of African women," her theorizing is guided by a Christian orientation of the Creator and the Creator's relationship to humanity which rarely differentiates the faith experiences of black Christian women and other African American women.[12] Arguably, most African Americans who self-identify themselves with a religious tradition call themselves Christian. Their allegiance supports the "natural" tendency in black America to *speak* of African American religion and *mean* Christianity. Thankfully, Townes, and a number of womanist scholars, are keenly aware of the methodological tensions that arise when Christocentric language and/or symbols are employed universally to speak of worship, G'd, devotion, Spirit, or love, regardless of audience. She wrestles with the resulting disequilibrium and collaborates with non-Christian scholars in drawing attention to changing perspectives and the varieties of womanist discourses that consider categories of survival which African American women encounter every day.

The leadership of Townes and others has been critical to the creation of an academic environment, in which *all* African American women are acknowledged as agents, responsible for contributing to all matters of relevance to human society, and thereby essential to any analysis of the social, spiritual, and intellectual grounds informing our understanding of black life in America. Interestingly, as word has spread about the growing eclectic nature of womanist conversations and new paradigms for the academic study of African American religiosity, American Academy of Religion session organizers have found themselves in competition for the participation and presence of African American Muslim scholars. Perhaps a Muslim-centered consciousness that also critically reflects upon the experiences of African American women can also serve as a bridge to scholarship that is more visibly interconnectedness rather than isolationist or competitiveness.

## Muslim Womanist Philosophy: An Interpretation of Reclamation

Muslim Womanist Philosophy is a perspective created to reclaim, enhance, and produce thoughtful explorations of African American Muslim life. It is grounded in the racist and patriarchal culture of the United States, in the nuances of black struggles for survival, in quests for Islamic legitimacy, the adaptability of the Qur'an, Islam's emphasis on justice and equity, and in the social activism of African American Muslim women. This interpretive methodology challenges scholars to speak holistically about Islam and the diverse experiences of its female adherents by accomplishing for Muslim women what Cannon and other womanists have endeavored to achieved for their Christian subjects: documentation of the agency and moral formulas African American Muslim women construct and pass on to succeeding generations from within the social conditions of membership in both a racial class and religious group that are marginalized in the United States. Muslim Womanist Philosophy engages the structures that oppress and support African American Muslim women, men, and children, sometimes at the risk of alienating African American Muslims who prefer not to render public communal issues that reflect negatively on Islam and/or Muslims. The elasticity of Muslim Womanist Philosophy permits a womanist agenda, in the words of Nigerian literary critic Chikwenye Ogunyemi that "celebrates black roots and the ideals of black life while giving a balanced presentation of black womandom."[13] It takes seriously the contribution and agency of the ancestral quilt bequeathed to African American Muslim women which extends from Eve, the first woman, to Khadijah, the first wife of the Prophet, to Clara Muhammad, the wife of Elijah Muhammad and the Supreme Secretary of the *original* Nation of Islam.[14] The tasks of a Muslim Womanist discourse are to promote a female-inclusive reading of the Qur'an which challenges external articulations of Islam used to justify subjugation and empowers African American women to determine for themselves what it means to be a Muslim. Moreover, Muslim Womanist Philosophy affirms "the experiences and ideas shared by [African American Muslim] women that provide a unique angle of vision on self, community, and society."[15] Clearly it is a redemptive method of intellectual inquiry that can provide insight into the social realities of the larger Muslim community as well.

Womanist discourse as presented by black religious scholars is rooted in the works of Alice Walker, whose explorations of the cultural productions, revolutionary struggles, and social activism of black women led African American female theorists to name womanism as a site of critical inquiry and multidimensional analyzes about black people, and to acknowledge that the lived experience of women of African ancestry is central to the discussion. Thus, Muslim Womanist Philosophy moves beyond the race analyzes of black male intellectuals, the gender analyzes of many feminist (predominantly white female) intellectuals, and the faith analyzes of Christian womanists in its interest in questions of knowledge production, history, and human existence that form African American Muslim family life and the life-world of African American Muslim women.

### *Muslim Womanist Philosophy: A Method of Justice*

I was introduced to the possibilities of fashioning a Muslim Womanist Philosophy through the writings and speeches of Islamic jurist and legal scholar Azizah Y. al-Hibri. This Lebanese American founder and president of KARAMAH: Muslim Women Lawyers for Human Rights, and "a Renaissance woman," celebrates a contextualized notion of womanism as a model that acknowledges the centrality of the Qur'an, is committed to the survival and wholeness of entire communities, and, thus, "provides hope for Muslim societies."[16] Her understanding of womanism as "female- or woman-centered" as demonstrated in one lecture titled, "A Qur'anic Worldview: A Womanist Perspective," guides my approach to a gender-inclusive reappropriation of the Qur'an with the participation of women in the exposition of the Qur'an. To speak of the womanist notion of community is to al-Hibri to consider the relationship of male and female, especially in examinations of Muslim family life. She challenges this African American Muslim scholar to expand my understanding of womanist discourse in a way that makes more visible the concept of justice as reflected in the world *and* in Islam. In this regard, al-Hibri shares womanist sensibilities with Wadud, whose appropriations of her Islamic faith were greatly influenced by her experiences as a black person facing institutional systems of oppression and by the practices of her family's Methodist faith. Both al-Hibri and Wadud promote a Qur'anic hermeneutics that is "inclusive of female experiences and of the female voice" and can "yield greater gender justice to Islamic thought and contribute toward the achievement of that justice in Islamic praxis."[17] Wadud's preoccupation with gender justice and Islamic praxis connects the experiences of African American Muslim women to those of female Muslims across the globe, particularly those of Diaspora Muslim women. She also advises that such a method must privilege the language of the Qur'an—not non-Arabic interpretations—but value as well the different languages African American Muslim women articulate among themselves and with others. As the "voice" of African American Muslim Women, Muslim Womanist Philosophy carves out space for them to articulate their struggles and fears, to question *interpretations* commonly accepted as *revelation*, to shout out their frustrations with being objectified, and to devise for themselves exegetical tools that speak to their complex social conditions and also help draw communal attention to equitable laws.

This Muslim Womanist philosophical method recognizes, as Leila Ahmed has clearly articulated, that different readings of the Qur'an and other primary sources of religious authority may yield "fundamentally different" interpretations of Islam. Yet, Muslim Womanist Philosophy incorporates a womanist ethic of justice that takes exception to interpretations which overlook justice as a mandatory practice in the Qur'an, even as it challenges Muslim women to empower themselves by knowing their faith. "Until and unless we are experiencing justice in our lives as Muslim women," declares Wadud, "then we have not been following the Qur'anic mandate."[18] Consistent with the theorizing of womanism, this framework leads me to consider issues of power, agency, culture, and religion, and their effect on women, children, Muslim communal life, and the larger societies in which African American Muslims live. It permits, in the words of Wadud, a determination as to whether "the experiences of Muslim women in all parts of the world [are] in fact the experiences of Islam towards women."[19]

## Muslim Womanism Is Not Islamic Feminism

First, let me concur with the findings of Hibba Abugideiri that "the terms 'Islam' and 'Muslim' mean different things to different people."[20] That said, Muslim Womanist Philosophy differs from what is commonly referred to as Islamic feminism in regards to considerations of race, religious signification, and politics. I affirm the attempts of many Muslim feminists whose gendered interests also seek a contextualized reinterpretation of the Qur'an that takes seriously the influence of culture and changing social conditions. Feminist scholarship like the challenge Basharat Tayyab makes to "interpret the Qur'an against women's background, skills, procedures, practices and so forth prevalent in existing society" is consistent with my attraction to Wadud above, as is Muslim feminist focuses on gender equity.[21] Still, the limitation of Islamic feminism for the reclamation of African American Muslim female history is grounded in a failure to adequately address the social contradictions in American society. Like all black women, African American Muslim women and their lived experiences are "inherently valuable."[22] For most of them, race and religion are codependent variables that cannot easily be separated. In fact, "the categories of life which [African American Muslim] women deal with daily are intricately woven into the religious space" they occupy.[23] Nor can the categories of gender and race be placed in a hierarchical stratum with gender on top, especially in the absence of concern for the health of the community. African American Muslim women, many of whom came to Islam through the *original* Nation of Islam and survived the covert tactics of the FBI and other law enforcement agents, astutely realize "that we need to pay attention to what happens 'over there to those people,' because 'there' can become 'here' and 'them' can become 'us' rather quickly."[24] They also realize that they have questions that are worth pursuing.

Furthermore, non-Western and sometimes multicultural, Islamic feminism is often closely identified with the legacy of Western (white) feminism, which is informed as much by class and white female privilege as it is by secularism. Indeed, Islamic feminism emerged in the writings of educated, privileged women, as early as the late nineteenth century.[25] The contemporary nature of Islamic feminism is broad enough to encompass the perspectives of a burqa-wearing, radical feminist in Kashmir who prays that her sons grow up "with gun in hand," postmodern feminists who celebrate the wearing of the veil, and a Muslim feminist writer and cowgirl in America. Still, while Islamic feminism is a label often imposed upon the work of African American Muslim scholars like Wadud—who are forced to accept the imposition of the feminist label by others—it is a methodology that rarely speaks to or appears interested in the African American Muslim experience or the significance of *Din*—religion—in the lives of Muslim women. Indeed, the attempts of Muslim feminists to be inclusive can on occasion be exclusive, ultimately racist and manifest issues of domination and oppression—particularly in light of the continued tensions between "immigrant" and "American-born" Muslims.

Naturally, both Muslim Womanism and Islamic feminism seek legitimacy and logical connections to Islamic principles. To employ the term, Islamic, to me suggests validation from within the revelation given to the Prophet Muhammad, or a reference to an act, practice, tradition, or structure maintained/suggested by or reflective of the teachings of our faith. Muslim is a better term for such human endeavors such as social movements and interpretive methodologies as they develop, evolve, and bear witness to the limitations and contradictions that challenge their practitioners.

Finally, politics for African American Muslim women is personal, social, and reflective of identity markers. The battles of these women for
gender equity go hand in hand with community development, the nurturing of shared resources, and the embodiment of their faith. These believ-
ers are rarely passive, at least not behind closed doors, but their activism,
agency, and what some might call subversive behavior are not easily understood or identifiable outside of their communities. The legacy of slavery ensures that African American Muslims do not share the powerless-
ness reflective of the journeys of some white women and other Muslim
women. Often, they had to learn survival skills early and quickly. When
rendered voiceless, it was not because they could not fashion audible
utterance. Rather they were forced into a "silent" mode or entered into one
for their health and/or the health of their loved ones. The struggles of
other Muslim women sometimes differ from those of American Muslim
women whose practice of Islam is not driven by traditions or cultures
cemented on a different shore and still imposed upon the principles of the
faith. In fact, what some Muslim women might characterize as an oppressive manifestation of patriarchal domination, these Muslim women would
celebrate as an authentic expression of their particularity. That is to say, in
few instances can one universalize the African American Muslim female
experience. But Muslim Womanist Philosophy does value the commonali-
ties it shares with African American Womanism, especially its communal
sensitivities, lack of dependence upon dominant culture methodologies,
and its determination to craft a framework that identifies the categories
significant to its practitioners. In the case of Muslim Womanist Philosophy, these three key categories are the centrality of the teachings of Islam
and their effect on the experience of being black and becoming Muslim in
an environment that negates both identities.

## Conclusion

The goals of Muslim Womanist Philosophy are to "interrogate the social
construction" of African American Muslim womanhood in relation to the
realities of African American Muslim life and the global community of
Muslims.[26] It is a methodology of justice, which seeks to reclaim the
embodied experiences of African American Muslim women, significant
contributors to scholarly understandings of the global sphere of Muslim
women and Muslim life in the world. Far from being a divisive tool, this

interpretive framework particularizes the African American Muslim female experience and promotes the excavation of African American Muslim life as a worthy subject of intellectual inquiry. Like Womanist Theology, Muslim Womanist Philosophy assumes a "liberatory perspective" as "the empowering assertion of the black woman's voice" in its consideration of what it means to be black, female, and Muslim in contexts that continue to perpetuate racism, sexism, and religious bias. As womanist scholar Linda Thomas has observed of poor and working class women, the lived experiences of African American Muslim women "arise out of specific contextual locations" that differ from most Christian and other black women particularly in regards to issues of marriage and identity.[27] Thus, our agenda for reconstructed knowledge moves beyond concerns for empowerment along gender, race, class, and sexual orientation lines to encompass religion and religious self-identity. As a theoretical method that mirrors the culture and ethos of African American Muslim life and can benefit scholars of African American Muslim life and practice, Muslim Womanist Philosophy fits comfortably within a diversifying womanist discourse, but it is not restricted to the conversational space crafted in the academy and the black Christian church. Rather, this developing framework draws strength as a reflection of the social and religious dynamics of life for African American Muslim women and others that is free to evolve across time and space in the service of Allah.

NOTES

1. I appropriate the concept of postmodern reclamation from the work of Amina Wadud, an African American Muslim and Islamic studies scholar. See, in particular, "Muslims: Interview: Amina Wadud," *Frontline,* 2002, 29 Sept. 2004 http://www.pbs.org/wgbh/pages/frontline/shows/muslims/interviews/wadud.html.

2. In this essay, all references to womanism refer to the critical analyzes of African American female scholars, whose primary scholarly training and lived experiences occurred in the United States. "First-generation" womanists, thereby, include Katie G. Cannon, Emilie M. Townes, Delores Williams, Jacquelyn Grant, Kelly Brown Douglas, Renita Weems, Clarice Martin, Francis Wood, Karen Baker-Fletcher, Jamie Phelps, Marcia Riggs, Cheryl Townsend Gilkes, Cheryl Kirk Duggan, and Cheryl Saunders.

3. Margot Badran, "Islamic feminism: what's in a name?" Al-Ahram Weekly Online, 17–23 January 2002, 1 Oct. 2004 http://weekly.ahram.org.eg/2002/569/cu1.htm.

4. Angela Davis, *Women, Race, and Class* (London: The Women's Press, 1994), 23, as cited in Eryn Scott, "Differences and Intersections between Feminism in Africa and Feminism in the United States," 17 Aug. 2005 http://www.columbia.edu/cu/sister/Differences.html.

5. The *Shahadah* is the first of five pillars or foundational practices Muslims are taught to observe. The other four hallmarks of the faith are *Salat,* required five daily prayers; *Zakat,* welfare contributions; *Hajj,* pilgrimage to Mecca; and *Sawm,* fasting during the month of Ramadan.

6. Womanist scholar C. S'thembile West provided one of the few exceptions to the practice. See "Revisiting Female Activism in the 1960s: The Newark Branch Nation of Islam," *Black Scholar* 26:3–4 (1996): 41–48.

7. Aminah McCloud, author of *African American Islam,* and Islamic studies scholar at DePaul University, served as the presider for the Afro-American Religious History Group panel, whose theme was "The Legacy of C. Eric Lincoln and the Study of Islam in North America," at the 2004 meeting of the American Academy of Religion. Her presence signifies the rare occasion when Islam has been the focal point of a session of the Afro-American Religious History Group.

8. See bell hooks, *Feminist Theory: From Margin to Center* (Cambridge, MA: South End Press), 1985. I am indebted to mentor and colleague Linda Thomas whose analysis and reconstruction of Womanist Theology serves as a model for my early formulations of Muslim Womanist Philosophy.

9. My theorizing about parallel structures is drawn from a contextualization of the liberatory perspectives of a first-generation womanist. See Marcia I. Riggs, *Awake, Arise & Act: a Womanist Call for Black Liberation* (Cleveland, OH: Pilgrim Press, 1994).

10. "Muslims: Interview: Amina Wadud," *Frontline,* 2002, 29 Sept. 2004 http://www.pbs.org/wgbh/pages/frontline/shows/muslims/interviews/wadud.html.

11. Amina Wadud, *Qur'an and Woman: Rereading the Sacred Text from a Woman's Perspective* (New York: Oxford University Press, 1992), xi.

12. Emilie M. Townes, *In a Blaze of Glory: Womanist Spirituality as Social Witness* (Nashville: Abingdon Press, 1995), 11.

13. Chikwenye Okonjo Ogunyemi, "Womanism: The Dynamics of the Contemporary Black Female Novel in English," *Signs* 11:1 (1985): 72.

14. *Original* distinguishes the movement founded by W. D. Fard in 1930 and built by Elijah Muhammad from the *contemporary* organization to the same name led by Louis Farrakhan.

15. Ogunyemi, "Womanism: The Dynamics," 72.

16. Azizah Y. al-Hibri, "The Quranic Worldview: A Womanist Perspective," Rice Webcast Archive 2003, 1 May 2003 http://www.rice.edu/webcast/speeches/20030421alhibri.html.

17. Wadud, *Qur'an and Woman,* x.

18. "Muslims: Interview: Amina Wadud," *Frontline*, 2002, 29 Sept. 2004 http://www.pbs.org/wgbh/pages/frontline/shows/muslims/interviews/wadud.html.

19. Ibid.

20. Hibba Abugideiri, "The Renewed Woman of American Islam: Shifting Lenses Toward 'Gender Jihad'?" *Muslim World*, 2001, 1 March 2001 http://web9.epnet.com/citation.

21. Barbara Tayyab, "Islam," in *A Companion to Feminist Philosophy*, ed. Alison M. Jaggar and Iris Marion Young (Oxford: Blackwell, 1998), 244.

22. Combahee River Collective, "A Black Feminist Statement," in *Women's Lives: Multicultural Perspectives*, 2nd ed., ed. Gwyn Kirk and Margo Okazawa-Rey (London: Mayfield, 2001), 36.

23. Linda Thomas, "Womanist Theology, Epistemology, and a New Anthropological Paradigm," in *CrossCurrents*, Winter 1998, http://www.crosscurrents.org/thomas.htm.

24. Legal scholar Lani Guinier as quoted in Noliwe M. Rooks, "Like Canaries in the Mines: Black Women's Studies at the Millennium," *Signs* 25:4 (Summer 2000): 1209.

25. Margot Badran, "Competing Agenda: Feminists, Islam, and the State in Nineteenth- and Twentieth-Century Egypt," in *An Introduction to Women's Studies: Gender in a Transnational World*, ed. Inderpal Grewal and Caren Kaplan (New York: McGraw Hill, 2002), 192.

26. Linda Thomas, "Womanist Theology, Epistemology, and a New Anthropological Paradigm."

27. See Linda Thomas, *Under the Canopy: Ritual Process and Spiritual Resilience in South Africa* (Columbia: University of South Carolina Press, 1999).

# Chapter 4

# Standing in the Shoes My Mother Made[1]
## *The Making of a Catholic Womanist Theologian*

### *Diana L. Hayes*

My mother was born in the Old South, before the Civil Rights movement in a small town called St. Elmo, which no longer exists as it was annexed to the much larger city of Chattanooga, Tennessee. The fifth child, the fourth daughter, she spent her formative years in the segregated world of Jim Crow. To be born Black and female in the Old South was to be born into a life of struggle, hardship, and limitation. How did they survive, we wonder today? Her greatest shame was that she had to leave school at the age of 12 to work as a domestic to help her family. Despite that early introduction to a life of labor, my mother survived, and somehow managed to find a joy in life that bore her up until she passed, much too soon, at the age of 79.

I often wonder at the loss of intellect and wisdom that was the result of the discrimination against and prejudice toward persons of African descent in the United States, a loss, a hemorrhage really, that continues to the present day as bright, intelligent women and men of African ancestry are denied the right to study, to pursue graduate education, and to work at meaningful jobs that they choose rather than having them forced upon them, narrowing and eventually destroying the possibilities that dwelled within them.

My mother taught me to read when I was three. She was one of the most intelligent human beings I have ever known. She was intelligent, not because of formal education for, as I noted, she had very little. Her intelligence was that of so many Black women of her time, including her sisters. It was an intelligence grounded in a wisdom that came from deep within them, born of their experiences of being Black and female in the rural South. From that well, my mother drew forth the strength and spirit to hold on to life's precious moments and to build a world and worldview that nurtured and sustained, challenged and taught the young Black women and men coming after her. Like many women unable because of their limited circumstances to live the lives they would choose for themselves, she prepared her daughters and countless others, again male and female, for a future she knew nothing about. She, and our other sheroes of faith, somehow prepared us and provided us with whatever it was that we needed to survive. As Jean Toomer noted, these named and nameless Black women "dreamed dreams and had visions" of a world unlike that which they themselves lived in. Somehow, they wove a tapestry of strength and protection and constructed shoes made for walking in unknown worlds. They constructed a support system, made of equal parts love, strength, fearlessness, wonder, faith, and hope in the unseen and as yet realized future. Somehow they knew what we needed to exist and persist in the new world aborning even though they themselves would more than likely never see that world.

I stand today in the shoes my mother made, wrapped from head to toe in that wondrous tapestry she created that protects but also encourages me to challenge the status quo and keep movin' on up a little higher. These shoes are strong, firm, and supportive. They have enabled me to stand tall on a foundation of faith, in myself, my family, and my God, and to enter into worlds that historically were off limits to Black women. I, and my brothers and sisters in the Black community, owe our mothers, our grandmothers, our godmothers, and othermothers, our play mothers and aunties, our foremothers stretching back through the centuries to Africa a great debt as we attempt in our daily lives to live up to their dreams and our own. They stand, a great cloud of witnesses, sending us forth, urging us forward, naming and claiming us as their own in whom they have great faith.

I am a Catholic womanist theologian. When I make this claim, I do so based on several assumptions. First, that to be a womanist is to be Black, that is, of African ancestry.[2] Second that to name myself Catholic is to call upon 2000 years of African and African American history, claiming the Roman Catholic Church as Black and African long before the existence of the English, Irish, Polish, Germans, or Italians as Catholic and catholic.[3] Third, I lay claim to myself as a woman, equal in grace and beauty to those of European ancestry, "Black *and* Beautiful" as the unnamed lover of King Solomon proclaims in her song.[4] I make these claims in the face of centuries of denial of my womanhood, my femininity, my faith, and my race in the United States and its Christian churches.

As a womanist, I am concerned about and committed to the survival of an entire people, male and female, rich and poor, gay, lesbian, and straight, physically and/or mentally challenged, and of every race and ethnicity. I believe that my rights as an African American, as a Black woman are guaranteed only when the rights of all people are guaranteed; that my liberty is restricted when that of another is restricted; that my human dignity and thus my creation by God is denied when that of others is trampled into the dirt for any reason. I believe that no one can be free until all are free.

Part of my struggle is to name and affirm myself and my sisters as women of African descent who have been denied their rightful place in the history of humanity. We speak a new and challenging word, born out of centuries long struggles to be free women created in the image and likeness of a loving God, as all women and indeed all of humanity have been created. Our words well forth from centuries of denigration and dehumanization, from the denial of our female persons and the right to control our own bodies, minds, and souls. We speak words of love, of passion, of anger, and of frustration; words that cut but also heal; words that challenge yet also affirm; words that call for new ways of being and seeing in our communities and throughout the world.

I am a Catholic celibate female womanist theologian and attorney; an affirmative action dream to some. That dream, however, can quickly turn nightmarish as I attempt to hurdle the obstacles laid before me and my brothers and sisters who have been schooled to be "better than" but are interpreted by those seeking to obstruct if not overturn our progress as "less than" those with whom we compete in the white world outside the communities that have nurtured and sent us forth. But, as noted above, we did not come unprepared. To be an affirmative action baby, for me and many like myself who insist upon self rather than "othered" definition, is to wear a Black badge of coverage that we use to pin up, and hold tightly around us, that protective tapestry woven for us as shield and goad so long ago.

Standing in my mother's shoes has provided me with the courage to look back to where she and so many other Black women paved the path I walk today. These shoes allow me to also look forward to a time when I shall pass them on to a daughter not of my own womb but certainly of my own convictions and faith. They are shoes meant for endless walking; for long-distance running; for standing patiently in hope and defiance; they lift me up to heights unexpected and carry me over the traps and snares that beset my path. They are womanist shoes, made by and for strong, centered, courageous, defiant, responsible, faith-filled Black women who seek to have a positive impact on the world and people around them. They were my mother's shoes and her mother's before her, and now they are mine. I wear them with pride as well as awe at the faith and courage of my mother and foremothers who challenged me to dream my own dreams and make them come true through my own efforts, but never forgetful of those upon whose shoulders and in whose shoes I now stand.

I am a womanist. Inspired by Alice Walker's defiant definition of a re-newed understanding of Black womanhood, I, and many others like my-self, found in the term "womanist" a home where we could be comfortable and find peace and rest. My understanding of womanist is very simple and relates intimately to my own experiences of living as a Black woman in the United States. I define it theologically, for the first women to take Walker's powerful statement and use it for self-definition were Black women seek-ing to survive the masculine and patriarchal worlds of the seminary, divin-ity schools, and theologates. Thus, for me, a womanist is a female African American Christian theologian. I use these terms deliberately, not to ex-clude other women of color or of other religious beliefs, nor to narrow or restrict Walker's definition, but simply to recognize the historical develop-ment of womanism as well as, because of my own circumstances, which I will discuss in greater detail below, to be specific in my self-naming. I honor Walker's definition but have, like many other Black women, moved beyond it. Therefore, I deliberately drop her first sentence: "a womanist is a black feminist or feminist of color." I do so because I believe that it is long past time that we of African ancestry in these United States and else-where in the African Diaspora, name and claim ourselves as the unique individuals we are without having to resort to placing color before a term that has already been defined and overdefined. I do this while affirming, at the same time, solidarity with my feminist sisters, and all women, of what-ever race or ethnicity, recognizing that as women we share a great deal in terms of the oppression of sexism and heterosexism but that as women of African descent, we have experiences that are uniquely our own, oppres-sions that sadly our sisters of other races and ethnicities have too often participated in to our detriment.

Womanist theologians use the "stuff" of women's lives to spin a narra-tive of their persistent effort to rise above and beyond those persons and situations, which attempt to hold them down. Their sources are social, political, anthropological and, especially, literary, seeing Black women's literary tradition is a "valid source for the central rubrics of the Black woman's odyssey"[5] for it is in her literary writings that she sets forth the documentation of the "living out of Black lives in a world confronted daily by racism, sexism, and poverty."[6]

Alice Walker's classic dictionary definition of womanist is both expansive and pointed. The first section reveals that a womanist is grown-up, daring, responsible, and self-reliant. This necessarily negates the historically stereotyped image of Black women (and their men) as irresponsible, careless, shiftless, child-like beings needing care by others. It reflects the reality I discussed earlier, of girl children being required to leave school early, giving up cherished dreams in order to help support their families; of young women raising both their children and those of others, as my mother did, in order to supplement the income their husbands brought in. It is a recognition and affirmation of a Black womanhood that allowed little time for playing childhood games, for partying, or living out one's dreams. Zora Neale Hurston placed in the mouth of Janie's grandmother the prayer of many Black mothers for their daughters: "The nigger woman is the mule of the world. I been praying it will be different for you, Lawd, Lawd."[7]

Growing up in the 1950s and '60s, young women usually began mirroring their mothers at an early age, preparing themselves for love, marriage, and the inevitable baby carriage. I did not. At the age of 10, I consciously rejected the idea of marriage, committing myself to a celibate lifestyle, which I did not fully understand, however, until I converted to the Roman Catholic faith. As the second of four girls born to loving parents but whose father was also an abusive alcoholic, I was the one on whom the responsibilities of protecting and supporting my mother and sisters fell. That commitment is one I have kept to this day. But it pushed me, like my mother, into a life of responsibility at an early age. My way to escape was through books and education, access to which my mother did not have in the South but which, in the more integrated Northeast, became increasingly available to young Black women and men. I was determined to find a better way by going to college and further if possible. As in Walker's definition, I was bold, daring, audacious, and outrageous, a woman long before I reached adulthood.

In other words, like my mother before me, I was modeling what it means to be a womanist without consciously knowing it. My first encounter with the term did not come until I returned to graduate school to study theology in 1980, after having practiced law for a number of years. As an attorney, I was familiar with NOW and had supported the Equal

Rights Amendment. I had begun to hear of the term "feminist" but did not feel particularly drawn to it. My response was the same as that of a group of Black churchwomen in an effort to explain the feminist movement: "There isn't enough fabric in that dress to fit me."[8]

## The Language of Womanism

Although I empathized deeply with feminists and their issues, I found myself disconnected, especially in response to their constant assertions that I must be a feminist as I was a woman studying theology. I refused to be stuffed into the boxes others built for me as I had done all of my life, daring to be different in whatever ways I could. There were too many issues in feminism that did not affect me or my Black sisters who were trying to find our voices during this time. We wanted to speak a language created from our lives and experiences of humanity and God, not a language others had written. Although I have had my differences (what woman hasn't?) with my Black brothers, we have been through too much together as persons of African descent for me to exclude them from my life.[9] Additionally, the problem of overemphasizing the experiences and concerns of white middle-class women to the exclusion of women of color and working class women, although more acknowledged by white feminists, still in many ways remains, despite the valiant and persistent efforts of Black and other feminists of color to draw attention to issues of race and class within the feminist movement. Sexism is not and cannot be the only concern as we who are Black acknowledge our triple and often quadruple oppression in today's world.

As well, the issue of inclusive language, although it sounded a stronger chord of affinity, especially with regard to the overmasculinized language of the Roman Rite of the Catholic liturgy, was not as critical to my understanding of Jesus as Lord and King and God as Father. To me, these were not negative but positive statements. They were and are, quite simply, a recognition and affirmation of Jesus as the one who overcame all obstacles and suffered greatly in order to do so as my people had done. Jesus' maleness just is not an issue of division in the Black community or should not be as the man Jesus is seen in so many ways, as brother, lover, friend, helpless child; one who earned his kingship as a bringer of peace and overturner of the oppressive status quo. Language is, indeed, critical but as a womanist, I see and use it very differently.

I find the work of Delores Williams, in her seminal articles on womanist theology, as well as in *Sisters in the Wilderness,* very important to this
discussion. As the experiences of Black women are often radically different
from those of other women, especially white women, so too must our language be different. As a critical aspect of her womanist theological methodology, Williams proclaims "a commitment both to reason and to the
validity of female imagery and metaphorical language in the construction of theological statements."[10] Calling for the creation of a theological
language grounded in both imagery and reason, one which brings "black
women's history, culture, and religious experience into the interpretive
circle of Christian theology and into the liturgical life of the Church,"[11]
she, thereby, reveals how womanist theological language must and can
serve as an instrument for social and theological change in both church
and society.[12]

Williams especially questions the language of surrogacy that has been
so prevalent in Christian tradition, seeing it as a way of restricting the
freedom of women, especially, and Black women, in particular.

> Two kinds of social-role surrogacy have negatively affected the lives of
> African American women and mothers: coerced surrogacy and voluntary
> surrogacy. Coerced surrogacy, belonging to the ante-bellum period, was a
> condition in which people and systems more powerful than black people
> forced black women to function in roles that ordinarily would have been
> filled by someone else. . . . Slave women could not exercise the choice of
> refusing surrogacy roles.
>
> After emancipation, the coercion associated with antebellum surrogacy
> was replaced by social pressures that influenced many black women to con-
> tinue to fill some surrogacy roles. . . . The difference was that black women,
> after emancipation, could exercise the choice of refusing the surrogate role,
> but social pressures often influenced the choices black women made as they
> adjusted to life in a free world. Thus post-bellum surrogacy can be referred
> to as voluntary (though pressured) surrogacy.[13]

Her critique of Anselm's doctrine of salvation via atonement is critical
in today's world, where so many "have-nots" sacrifice years of their lives
and health for the benefit of those who "have" and constantly want more.
How do we move away from this masculine language of subservience and
subordination to a liberating language of inclusive humanity? Just as Anselm and others used the language of the sociopolitical thought of their

times to render Christian ideas and principles understandable, thought which took for granted a patriarchal worldview with its accompanying hierarchical order, womanist theologians today are "empowered" to do the same.

> [T]he womanist theologian uses the sociopolitical thought and action of the African-American woman's world to show black women their salvation does not depend upon any form of surrogacy made sacred by traditional and orthodox understandings of Jesus' life and death. Rather their salvation is assured by Jesus' life of resistance and by the survival strategies he used to help people survive the death of identity caused by their exchange of inherited cultural meanings for a new identity shaped by the gospel's ethical world view. This death of identity was also experienced by African women and men brought to America and enslaved. They too relied upon Jesus to help them survive the forging of a new identity. This kind of account of Jesus' salvific value—made compatible and understandable by use of African-American women's sociopolitical patterns frees redemption from the cross and frees the cross from the "sacred aura" put around it by existing patriarchal responses to the question of what Jesus' death represents.[14]

Jesus' death was, indeed, liberative for all. His life and death brought renewed life for all, a new vision of life, one Williams declares as ministerial because it is a vision of life which seeks to right relations between body (individual and community), mind (of humans and tradition) and spirit.[15] This ministerial life is one available to all of humanity, both male and female, because of Jesus' own life of relationship and community. It is incumbent upon women and all who are oppressed, especially Black American women, historically the "mules of the world," to drop that burden and come down from the cross of surrogacy, rejoicing in their long overdue liberation.

> Jesus came for life, to show humans a perfect vision of ministerial relation that humans had very little knowledge of. As Christians, Black women cannot forget the cross, but neither can they glorify it. To do so is to glorify suffering and to render their exploitation sacred. To do so is to glorify the sin of defilement.[16]

As Williams and other womanist theologians acknowledge, for centuries, a life of surrogacy has been the experience of African American women. Womanist Theology provides us with a foundation upon which to critique not only the masculinized, self-serving language of Christian theology but also its embodiment in the Christian churches themselves, cleansing them of their sexism, racism, classism, and homophobia by creating a language that speaks of life, hope, equality, and love; a language that builds, rather than destroys, communities of affirmation. To do so, however, we must first come to grips with our own selves, recognizing who we are and how the women we are today have come into existence.

## Becoming Catholic, Becoming Womanist

Finding myself in a predominately white religious institution, the Roman Catholic Church, after growing up in a historically Black community, the African Methodist Episcopal Zion Church, was a shock in every way. Initially, although believing, as I still do, that God for God's own reasons called me into this church, I feared that the words of my younger sister when I first told her of my conversion were true: "You've finally become white!" Thank God, when I moved to Washington, D.C., I encountered "cradle" (born into the faith) Black Catholics who could trace their Catholic heritage back over many generations.

I began to learn a history that, for the most part, was unknown and untaught, the history of persons of African descent in Christianity. I was astounded to learn of the African origins of and influence on Christianity from its earliest beginnings, as well as the significant role that Africans played in preserving and passing on the Christian faith in North and East Africa. Like most Christians, I had assumed that African Americans became Christians only in the colonies of North America. It was exhilarating to learn of not just East and North African Christianity but of the Christian and Catholic King Afonso whose son became the first indigenous Central African Bishop. The role that Africans like St. Moses the Black played in establishing monasticism in the Egyptian desert was an additional revelation.

It was less exhilarating, however, to learn of the role that Christianity, as a whole, and the Catholic Church, in particular, had played in beginning and sustaining the African Slave Trade as well as the institution of Black slavery in the Americas. Learning this history and at the same time encountering the liberation theology of James Cone, I began to explore Black Theology with an eye toward developing a Black Catholic perspective. I was excited about the prospect of developing a theology that brought forth the particular experiences of Catholics of African descent but became increasingly perplexed at the absence of the historical experience and voices of Black women, Catholic and Protestant, in Cone's and others' early writings. It is at this point that I encountered the term "womanist" in Alice Walker's essay collection, *In Search of Our Mothers' Gardens.*[17] My entire world shifted. As did other Black women, I recognized in Walker's definition a voice like my own which spoke of my own particular experiences as a Black woman. Walker's definition fit me! It described my experience and the journey I had been on for most of my life, one of naming and claiming myself as a Black woman, boldly, proudly, and loudly. Thus, unlike many of my Protestant sisters, my encounter with both feminism and womanism, as well as with Black Liberation, came at almost the same time as I was beginning my theological studies. I found it necessary, therefore, to make choices based, not on intellect alone but, quite honestly, on a "gut reaction" to what felt right, intellectually, emotionally, and spiritually. I had to learn to trust my instincts rather than depend on the assertions of others. As I studied the seminal writings of womanists such as Katie Cannon, Jacquelyn Grant, and Delores Williams and met other womanists at the American Academy of Religion, I began to participate with them in the development and refining of womanism from a theological perspective.

Each of us who claims "womanist" as a critical aspect of our self-understanding does so from within the context of our own lives. But, at the same time, it is important that we recognize the many shared experiences that have shaped us as Black women as well. This is a critical part of defining the term "womanist" for ourselves. Thus, in order to understand my rendering of womanist, you also must know me. That was and is the purpose of the autobiographical bits interspersed throughout this piece. It is also important that you are aware of the context in which I now live and which continues to shape my theologizing, the Roman Catholic Church, a historically predominantly white church that is slowly and rather unwillingly being transformed, in this century, into a church of persons of color, African/African American, Caribbean, Asian, and Latino/a.

As a Roman Catholic womanist theologian, I seek to explore the intersection of race, class, gender, sexuality, and religion in an effort to reveal the role which the Christian religion, especially my own faith, has played in affirming, exploiting, perpetuating, and upholding understandings of the above social constructs in ways that have served to provide not only a language but also a pervasive, hegemonic, ethos of subordination and oppression of women and persons of color. Grounded in the Neoplatonic dualistic separation of the sacred and secular worlds, such an understanding has enabled the spread of a race-based hierarchical/patriarchal system which supported the enslavement not just of other human beings but of other Christians, the dehumanization of women and persons of color, and a stance which supports rather than challenges the oppression of far too many.[18]

The challenge for me today is to look at these social constructs, including religion itself as it has come to be constituted in the United States, through eyes which have been opened by the recognition of the "other-createdness" from which they emerged. Dualistic systems allow for the emergence of an "either/or" understanding of life, knowledge, morality, and society. It enables the differentiation of human beings into "us and them," into "human and non-human," into those we recognize as friend and "others" by whom we feel threatened. It speaks a coldly sterile language of negativity, dualism, separation, subordination, and alienation. New words must be spoken that promote life, love, healing, holism, grace, community, relationship, and hope.

## The Wisdom and Strength of Black Catholic Women

An important and as yet mostly untapped resource for Catholic womanist theologians to explore in their efforts to craft a more human-oriented way of being and speaking is to be found in the history of Black Catholics in the United States, especially Black Catholic women, lay and religious. Religious women laid the foundations of the Black Catholic community, establishing schools, orphanages, and old-age homes in the midst of the slave-holding South. Mother Elizabeth Lange, founder of the oldest Black religious order, the Oblates of Providence (Baltimore, 1829) and Mother Henriette de Lille, founder of the Sisters of the Holy Family (New Orleans, 1851) refused to allow others, especially white men, to define or constrict their womanhood.[19] Denied entry into white religious orders, they founded their own in the face of severe opposition by those of their faith who could not imagine a Black woman moral enough to be a religious sister. Unable to wear their habits in public for fear of being spit upon and stoned, these Black women, few in number but strong in faith, established institutions that persist to this day.

In a time when black people were accorded little or no respect or esteem, in a time when black women were degraded by slave holders or abused by white employers, in a society where black women were considered to be weak in morality, black sisters were a counter sign and a proof that the Black Catholic community was rooted in faith and devotion, for vocations arise from a faith-filled people. Lest it be forgotten, the two black sisterhoods were not European transplants, they were very much American in origin.[20]

Faith in God and in their community of shared faith and oppression gave Black Catholics, both free and slave, hope and enabled them to persevere against daunting obstacles which threatened not simply their identity but also their very lives. African American Catholic women's wisdom emerges from an experience of triple (and more) oppression. Denied the dignity of womanhood, condemned for their skin color, whether too dark or too light, and often imprisoned by miseducation, demeaning and meaningless work, and a denial of their very humanity, they yet managed to forge a spirituality of hope and survival that has sustained them for centuries. They dreamed dreams and had visions; imagining a time and place when the pain and indignity of their lives would be transcended not in some far off heaven but right here in the future of their children and their children's children. Somehow our foremothers persisted in their faith. They made rosaries out of beads and knotted string and learned Scripture by rote memory. They resisted as best they could anything and anyone who attempted to keep them from living their faith on a daily basis.

Once freedom, so-called, came, they struggled, despite the callous disregard of their fellow Catholics, to remain faithful. When their children were forbidden entry into diocesan schools, when they were required to sit in upper galleries and back pews, and to wait until last to partake of the sacraments, they did not suffer these indignities quietly but often walked out and with their meager resources built their own schools, holding church suppers and other events to raise the funds.[21] Somehow, somehow they wove a tapestry of love, faith, and hope, which they wrapped around any and all who came into their lives.

African American Catholic women, my sisters, as the bearers of many burdens, chosen and unchosen, have also been the bearers of culture as well. It is as the givers of life and the teachers of the future that they have suckled their children with a passionate anger and courage, which sustained the hope that always dwelled within them, "despite" and "through" it all.

It is the women who, a part of this church since its earliest beginnings, have influenced it as much as they were influenced. Although the first acknowledged convert to Christianity outside the Jewish sect, the Ethiopian eunuch, was male, he was joined by countless numbers of women in Africa and the Middle East, some of whom had followed Jesus and supported his ministry, others of whom followed him, like Saints Perpetua and Felicity, to their own deaths as martyrs for the faith. In the Americas, women of African descent arrived along with the Spanish and French explorers and the English Jesuits. They were an integral part of establishing the Catholic Church in what is now the United States for, as I said earlier, they were the bearers of culture. It was, and has always been, the women who passed down the songs, stories, and prayers of their people to the children and their children's children, preparing them for the future.

Black Catholic women continue to do this today in the face of many obstacles. Today we see communities and families that are crumbling due to the assaults made on them by an increasingly secular and individualistic society. We are in danger of losing the future because too many have either forgotten or never knew the past. The links in the chain of memory have become worn and some have even snapped apart, endangering the lives of our children and our children's children. We who are Black Catholic women, triply if not quadruply oppressed by reason of race, gender, class, and religious faith, know that many of our Black Protestant brothers and sisters do not understand, due to their own lack of historical memory, or respect, because of their ignorance of our faith, our persistence in "defending the faith that is ours" (1 Peter 1). They see the Catholic Church as a white institution that is racist, sexist, and classist, which too often sadly it is, but they fail to see the shortcomings of their own churches, which often mirror ours in many ways, especially with regard to the treatment of women.

Many of us have been called traitors to the Black community as well as to Black Christianity, by colleagues and friends because we either chose to become Roman Catholic or were born Catholic and have no desire to leave because of our foundation in the Catholic Church going back countless generations. This ignorance can only be addressed by acknowledging our own lack of knowledge of the 2,000-plus-year history of African people in Christianity and therefore in the Roman Catholic Church and then passing it on. Ignorance is unacceptable for any of us. We must together reclaim the rich history of Black Christianity in all of its diversity, Catholic, Orthodox, and Protestant, refusing to accept excuses just as we refuse to accept ignorance of Black history in any form as an excuse for those of other races and/or ethnicities to ignore our presence and contributions. This means we must also address the profound ignorance within our own churches regarding this history, which has been, consciously or not, overlooked, dismissed as of no consequence, or somehow whitewashed.

Black Catholic women, as all Black women, are still stereotyped in many ways, both in our church and in dominant society. Seen as sexually promiscuous and poor or as dominating male castrators, their issues and concerns are often overlooked or lumped together as social justice issues which do not affect the Church as a whole. This is not only a lie but an insult to our very humanity as creations of a loving God. If the words of Genesis are true, then all of humanity reflects God in God's great diversity. Added to that is the growing awareness, through DNA and other genetic studies, that the first woman from whom all of humanity descended was a Black woman, the true first Eve.[22] Black Catholic women can bring to the forefront of womanist dialogue images of Black women that contradict the dominant perspective, women such as Hagar, abused and misused by both her master and her mistress, yet taught by God how to survive in the wilderness as African American women had to do for centuries in this land. Hagar models strength, endurance, and the passionate love of our foremothers for those entrusted to their care. They did what they had to do not simply to survive but to ensure that their communities would also survive and be prepared for whatever future might come. And let us not forget the two Marys, one the mother of God who had the courage and audacity to say yes to God, an action that shattered all of human history, proclaiming in her magnificent song her awareness of her cooperation with God in an act that would change us all,[23] and Mary Magdalene, the Apostle to the Apostles, as she was honored in the early church as the first to see the risen Lord rather than the fallen and lowly woman whom Jesus had to save from stoning as she has been incorrectly described for far too long.

As a Catholic womanist, I insist that our voices never again be silenced or marginalized. We must continue to speak out about the declining numbers of women seeking vocations to the religious life while those in religious communities are growing older. We must question why the tipping number for Black women in predominately white orders is still in the twenty-first century usually one or two, and that only after great sacrifice on the part of those women of color. We must insist that the Church and its agencies and institutions open themselves to different ways of being a church, of being religious, of being Catholic. No longer can we affirm a uniform model, which is not universal, but Eurocentric, which strips us of our culture and traditions leaving us exposed and violated. We must return to our roots, following in the footsteps of Mother Henriette and Mother Elizabeth who did not allow anyone to define or limit them.

Those women who seek to be leaders in the Church but who follow a different vocational path from the religious life must also be encouraged and supported by the Church and all of its people, especially those within the Black community. For if we are to remain sane in our years of study and work within an institution still predominantly white in its leadership, even though increasingly unrepresentative of the people within it, we need the love and support of all our Black sisters and brothers. There is too much that still needs to be done for us to divide along religious and lay, degree and nondegree, Protestant and Catholic lines. Womanism gave me my voice and has done so for many Black women, who found themselves enmeshed in the trials and tribulations of professional careers whether religious or secular.

## The Struggle Is Ongoing

Patricia Hill Collins speaks of Black women, especially those now in professional fields, as "outsiders-within."[24] Our positions as women with degrees at the master's or doctoral level, especially in institutions of higher learning, provide us with an "insider's" status, enabling us to participate in academic discourse and have an impact on others in those institutions. At the same time, however, because of our personal situations as Black women, we are also "outsiders" whose views are not always welcomed and whose input is often trivialized. We find ourselves straddling two worlds, that of academia or other professions, and that of the Black community with its often very different perspective. In order to truly belong to one or the other, it is assumed that we must give up our existence in the other as they are not complementary. These assumptions, however, are cynically grounded too often in issues of power, control, and manipulation, yet again, of Black women's reality.

The exclusion of Black women's ideas from mainstream academic discourse and the curious placement of African-American women intellectuals in both feminist and Black social and political thought has meant that Black women intellectuals have remained outsiders within in all three communities. The assumptions on which full group membership is based—whiteness for feminist thought, maleness for Black social and political thought, and the combination for mainstream scholarship—all negate a Black female reality. Prevented from becoming full insiders in any of these areas of inquiry, Black women remain outsiders within, individuals whose marginality provides a distinctive angle of vision on the theories put forth by such intellectual communities.[25]

Hill Collins's words describe my experiences as a Catholic womanist theologian. I find myself straddling several often competitive worlds, attempting to juggle time, participation, input, and presence among them. The Black community is one of these worlds, one that is, as noted above, still heavily and often restrictively Protestant in its religious outlook and male in its leadership. In this community, my status as a Roman Catholic and as well as my gender often make me suspect, with my motives and concerns questioned. Issues that I and other Black Catholics find significant are often derided or disparaged as being irrelevant either to the academic world because they concern the Black community or to the larger Black community because they emerge from a perspective outside of Protestant Christianity. Thus, my participation in either community is denied and/or restricted.[26] The fact that I am also single and celibate is often a point of contention as well, strangely enough, for both men and women.

Another world is that of the university and its various scholarly organizations. Here the courses that I teach and the areas in which I do research, the communities of the poor and marginalized persons of color in the United States, are often looked down upon as not truly scholarly topics or worthy of academic discussion, perhaps because they deal with issues that are threatening to the status quo. At the same time the work that I do in the community is often rejected as "pastoral" rather than scholarly and a waste of time regardless of what benefit they may bring to others. Articles and scholarly texts that dwell in lofty climes are seen as having greater weight than efforts to heal the spirit of an abused woman or to help a parish tearing itself apart because of racial strife. Yet, here again, I have found that being a Black Catholic also makes me suspect as many seem incapable of conceiving of Blacks in any capacity except Protestant.

Finally, as a lay Black woman, I am suspect in the Roman Catholic Church, where women who speak out and challenge the Church and its teachings are condemned as radical and often as heretics, and where persons of color have been and continue to be marginalized, never fully accepted as truly and authentically Catholic.

Attempting to survive in these often contradictory worlds is a constant and often enervating challenge. I often feel as if I'm being torn in several directions, required to make choices that have severe consequences for my self-identity and for the work that I am trying to do. Throughout my experience as an "outsider-within," whether in the fields of law or theology or in nonacademic settings, I have come to realize once again the critical significance of language. It can be used both to include and to exclude, to invite and to bar, to uplift and to put down, to develop positive and negative understandings of humanity in its diversity.

In my work as a Catholic womanist theologian, I seek to remove the masks, which cover up the inherent illegitimacy of the existing forms of society and their use of language to exclude and restrict.[27] I do this by revealing other, more holistic, worldviews, which serve to bring about unity rather than division, harmony rather than discord. I have come to realize that in order to authenticate myself and legitimate the work that I do, I must also remove the masks which have covered the many worlds in which I find myself in order to present them to public view and develop a unified challenge to them and to those worlds with which they appear to conflict. The words "appear to conflict" are used deliberately for the reality is that they do not necessarily conflict but are made to appear so by those who are, in some way, threatened by them.

This means claiming the legitimacy of my being as a Black female professional and working to develop a critical understanding of both past and present in order to participate in building a more holistic future, one in which persons like myself will no longer be required to deny the totality of their being in order to "belong" but can embrace and be embraced for what they bring to intellectual and personal discourse in both the public and private arenas. In so doing, I, in company with other womanists, seek to speak in ways that are understandable to these communities but with a preference toward Black and other marginalized communities, recognizing that we may, as a result, be accused of being too "popular," a term often used to denigrate the language of persons of color, women, and those lacking a string of letters after their names.

[M]y choice of language—typifies my efforts to theorize differently. A choice of language is inherently a political choice. Writing—in a language that appears too "simple" might give grounds for criticism to those individuals who think that the complex ideas of social theory (and theology-DLH) must be abstract, difficult, and inaccessible. Populist ideas become devalued exactly because they are popular. This position reflects a growing disdain for anything deemed "public" and for the general public itself.[28]

The Black presence in Christianity, especially in the Catholic Church, serves as a subversive memory, one that contradicts the assumed reality and presents a paradoxical perspective. Black women are a critical part of that memory for without us, there would be no Black Christian or other communities today. We bring forth life, not solely from our wombs; we nurture it; we prepare it; we teach that life what it needs to know in order to survive and thrive, and then we set it free.

## A Womanist Challenge

As women of faith and courage, we must live our lives, both publicly and privately, in the same subversive manner that Jesus Christ led his. For our God is a God who takes sides, on the side of those most in need, to bring "the mighty from their thrones and exalt those of low degree" (Luke 2:52–53), as Mary proclaims in her song. Our God is a God who "preached good news to the poor" and release to those in chains, whether physical or those of the mind and spirit. To subvert means to turn reality upside down, to look at it in another light, to confound those who believe they are the only source of truth by presenting another, more far-reaching and earth-shattering truth. Sojourner Truth knew well the meaning of a subversive faith, noting that, "If the first woman God ever made was strong enough to turn the world upside down all alone; together women ought to be able to turn it right side up again."[29]

As women of faith, we must become "extremists in love," as Martin Luther King, Jr. urged, following in the footsteps of Jesus and the long line of saints and martyrs who followed after him; following also that long line of strong, proud, and loving Black women who were able to "run on for a long time." Only in so doing will we recapture the spirit of the early church which was "not merely a thermometer that recorded the ideas and principles of popular opinion; it was a thermostat that transformed the mores of society."[30]

We must do likewise; drink deeply of the word of God and set out to right the wrongs that have been inflicted upon so many in our nation and in our church for all the wrong reasons. This is the stance taken by strong, courageous, angry, hope-filled African American women down through the ages, who allowed no one to tell them who they were capable of being or becoming.

We must continue to be the "voices that speak when others fear to." As a people, as a nation within a nation, African Americans were never truly meant "to survive."[31] But that has never stopped us before and we cannot allow it to now. Black women's existence is "a continuum, an invisible thread drawn through the women's stories to women readers and the men who will listen."[32]

It is long past time for Black women to reclaim their voices, voices somehow silenced in a "culture that depended on her heroism for its survival."[33] That voice has been silenced because historically women lacked the power, as the "disinherited," to recognize and claim their own power. Womanists, in and out of the church, are making the claim that we have the right and the responsibility in today's world to name our own experience, and the experiences of our people, whatever they may be.

We have been nurtured and sustained by a spirituality which paved our way and softened the rough places just enough for us to continue. For, as an African people, we recognized the importance of and maintained our ties with the spiritual. We must return to the strengths, which reside deep within us and use them to challenge the status quo. It is time for us to walk out yet again on faith and proclaim our hope by having the courage to release a cleansing anger, which transforms not only ourselves but also our communities, our society, and even our world. Black women remain the "heartbeat" of our African American communities, a status for which we are both exalted and maligned. We must use the strength of that status to be, once again, the bearers of culture and the birthers of the future to confound the minds of those who look down upon us and to "critique all human domination in light of Black women's experience"[34] wherever that domination exists, in our homes, in our workplaces, in our communities, in our places of worship, and in our society as a whole.

Black women, in company with their Black men and their Black children, as family, have reason to hope. Ours is a hope firmly grounded in an incandescent love of self and community, a love threatened by today's "fatal attractions" but which persists regardless. We must pass on that love to those around us, teaching them how to love as well, across racial, sexual, ethnic, and class lines. We must love ourselves into life once again, thereby defeating the miasma of defeat and self-hate, which pervades our once-thriving communities. "We must love one another or die."[35] We must be servants not leaders; seeking justice not personal fame or fortune.

In spiritual solidarity, womanists have the potential to create a community of faith that acts collectively to transform our world. When we heal the woundedness inside us, we make ourselves ready to enter more fully into community. We can experience the totality of life because we have become fully life-affirming. Like our ancestors, using our powers to the fullest, we share the secrets of healing and come to know sustained joy. We must take a stand—a stand against the principalities and powers of our day. It must be revolutionary—that is, going against the grain, against the complacency, against the status quo that fosters injustice; it must be non-violent; and it must embody love.

Black women, as their people's bearers of culture, have, historically, been the forgers of new ways of being and speaking in the world. They recognize with Hill Collins that "(p)rivatizing and hoarding ideas upholds inequality. Sharing ideas through translation and teaching supports democracy."[36] It is our task today to speak life into the future, a future inclusive and representative of all. We do so by working to redefine what it means to be male and female in language that complements the actual experiences of those engaged in living out maleness and femaleness, in ways inclusive of both heterosexual and homosexual understandings. In our stories (history), songs (culture), prayers (spirituality), and God-talk (theologizing), Black women speak life into being, not a stunted growth unable to flourish and condemned to premature death, nor one confined to dry, dusty tomes read and understood by only a privileged few, but a life that is fruitful and representative of a diversity created, not by human hands, but by divine ones.

Today we who name ourselves womanists do so, not in opposition to others, for they must define themselves, but in creation seeking to "make community" wherever we find ourselves. We define ourselves not over against but in solidarity with, affirming that new ways of self-definition must emerge, not as hand-me downs or cast offs of others self-understanding but created out of the fabric of our own lives. In so doing, we are creating a new language of liberation that is open to any and all that are willing to speak plainly without assuming their language will give them power and/or authority over another. As womanists, our challenge is to gather the myriad threads of the richly diverse Black community and breath into it renewed life, which can serve as a model of life for our world. That model is centered on the cocreatedness by God of all, and thus the human dignity of all, regardless of efforts to separate. All who are oppressed share in solidarity with each other, a solidarity which should not be laid aside for individual desires or "battles." The struggle is communal, not individual, and can be won only if experiences are shared, stories are told, songs are sung, histories are reclaimed and restored, a new language emerges, which speaks words of peace and unity, which unites, which recalls both the pain and the joy of our different heritages and leads us into a brand new day.

## NOTES

1. I want to thank the young male student at Morehouse College who first used these words to speak of and describe his relationship with his own mother.

2. I do recognize that other women of color may also use the term "womanist," but I am deliberately excluding the use of the term by Euro-American (white) women as I believe Walker's description has been critically employed and developed by women of color (especially African American women). I do this in order to be clear especially to my white female students and others with whom I interact in the Roman Catholic Church who have a tendency to immediately appropriate the term for their own use. We who are of African descent must be able to define ourselves exclusively in ways that speak to our historical experience and contemporary situation. I realize there are womanists who disagree with my restriction of the term, at this time, to women of color and specifically women of African descent. However, my particular circumstances as an African American Catholic woman lead me to do so. I would hope that, in time, womanist would be adopted by all women as, unlike feminism, from its beginnings it has been a theology that attempts to deal holistically with issues of race, class, and gender (including sexual orientation).

3. Cyprian Davis, O.S.B., "Black Spirituality: A Catholic Perspective," in *One Faith, One Lord, One Baptism: The Hopes and Experiences of the Black Community in the Archdiocese of New York,* vol. 2 (New York: Archdiocese of New York, Office of Pastoral Research, 1988) 45. Davis speaks of Ethiopia, a Catholic nation that traces its Catholic identity back to the first century of Christianity.

4. Song of Solomon 1:5

5. Katie Cannon, *Black Womanist Ethics,* American Academy of Religion Series #60 (Atlanta: Scholars Press, 1988), 7.

6. Diana Hayes, "And When We Speak: To Be Black, Catholic and Womanist," in *Taking Down Our Harps: Black Catholics in the United States,* ed. Diana Hayes and Cyprian Davis (Maryknoll, NY: Orbis Books, 1999), 106.

7. Zora Neale Hurston, *Their Eyes Were Watching God* (New York: Harper-Perennial, 1998).

8. I believe it was either Katie Cannon or Delores Williams who related this experience but am not sure.

9. I recognize that the charge against feminists as "man-haters" is and has always been illegitimate. However, the movement, socially, politically, and theologically, still too often presents the issue of gender and sexuality in an "either/or," dichotomous way as if sexism is the only issue and the experiences of women are all the same because of it. As a womanist, I prefer to see and live holistically, seeing the possibilities of "both/and" thinking and acting while recognizing that historically my oppression has been based on skin color much more than on gender. Ironically, in many instances, being a Black woman has had advantages that Black men do not have.

10. Delores Williams, "Womanist Theology: Black Women's Voices," in *Black Theology: A Documentary History,* Vol. 2: *1980–1992,* ed. James H. Cone and Gayraud S. Wilmore (Maryknoll, NY: Orbis Books, 1993), 269.

11. Ibid., 270.

12. Ibid. In a recent work, Cheryl Kirk-Duggan builds on Williams's discussion of a womanist theological discourse, see *Refiner's Fire: A Religious Engagement with Violence* (Minneapolis: Fortress Press, 2001).

13. Delores Williams, *Sisters in the Wilderness* (Maryknoll, NY: Orbis Books, 1993), 60.

14. Ibid., 164.

15. Ibid., 167.

16. Ibid.

17. Walker, *In Search of Our Mothers' Gardens: Womanist Prose* (San Diego: Harcourt Brace Jovanovich, 1983).

18. See Kelly Brown Douglas, *Sexuality and the Black Church* (Maryknoll, NY: Orbis Books, 1999), 25–29, and Diana Hayes, "And When We Speak," in Hayes and Davis, eds., *Taking Down Our Harps,* 102–119.

19. Dianne Batts Morrow, *Persons of Color and Religious at the Same Time: The Oblate Sisters of Providence, 1828–1860* (Chapel Hill: University of North Carolina Press, 2002); Cyprian Davis, *Stamped with the Image of God: African Americans as God's Image in Black* (Maryknoll, NY: Orbis Books, 2003).

20. Hayes and Davis, eds., *Taking Down Our Harps,* 30.

21. Cyprian Davis, *The History of Black Catholics in the United States* (New York: Crossroad, 1990).

22. Stephen Oppenheimer, *The Real Eve* (New York: Carroll and Graf, 2003).

23. See Elizabeth Johnson, *Truly Our Sister* (New York: Continuum, 2003).

24. Hill Collins, *Black Feminist Thought: Knowledge, Consciousness and the Politics of Empowerment,* Vol. 2: *Perspectives on Gender* (New York: Routledge, 1990), 11–13.

25. Ibid., 12.

26. This is partly due, of course, to our small numbers. There are only seven Black Catholic systematic theologians in the United States today, of which three are women.

27. Today, for example, we are confronted by an administration that claims to be acting on behalf of peace by instigating war, to be helping the poor and unemployed by providing tax cuts and write-offs for the rich, and to be helping students by requiring standardized tests for children as young as three while cutting back on loans and grants for higher education. The language is cast in words familiar and soothing, but the effect of the actions behind them is oppressive and life-threatening to many.

28. Patricia Hill Collins, *Fighting Words: Black Women and the Search for Justice* (Minneapolis: University of Minnesota Press, 1998), xxi.

29. Sojourner Truth, "Ain't I a Woman?" A speech delivered at the Women's Convention in 1851.

30. Martin Luther King, Jr., "Letter from Birmingham City Jail," in *A Testament of Hope: The Essential Writings of Martin Luther King, Jr.,* ed. James Melvin Washington (San Francisco: Harper and Row, 1986), 300.

31. Audre Lorde, "A Litany for Survival," in *The Black Unicorn: Poems* (New York: W. W. Norton and Company, 1978), 31.

32. Gay Willentz, *Binding Cultures: Black Women Writers in Africa and the Diaspora* (Bloomington: Indiana University Press, 1992), xii.

33. Mary Helen Washington in Henry Louis Gates, ed., *Reading Black, Reading Feminist* (New York: Penguin, 1990), 5.

34. Katie Cannon in "Roundtable Discussion: Christian Ethics and Theology in Womanist Perspective," *Journal of Feminist Studies in Religion* 9, 2 (Fall 1989): 93.

35. King, "Letter from Birmingham City Jail," 298.

36. Hill Collins, *Fighting Words,* xxiii.

# Part II

# Traditional Communalism

TRADITIONAL COMMUNALISM—[the second tenet of womanism] 1. the affirmation of the loving connections and relational bonds formed by Black women—including familial, maternal, platonic, religious, sexual, and spiritual ties. Black women's ability to create, re-member, nurture, protect, sustain, and liberate communities which are marked and measured not by those outside of one's own community but by the acts of inclusivity, mutuality, reciprocity, and self-care practiced within it (opposite of the biological deterministic assumption that a woman's role is to serve as nurturer and protector)

"claiming space among enemies [and] making culture out of contradiction"   —Stewart

"Hospitality . . . to be neighborly, welcoming and to reserve judgment against those the society viewed as outcasts"   —Harding and Harding

2. the moral principles and practices of Black women living in solidarity with and in support of those with whom they share a common heritage and contextual language; having a preferential option for Black women's culture, esp. their constructive criticism, "tragicomic hope" (Cornel West), "in/visible dignity" and "un/shouted courage" [adapted from Cannon] which furthers the survival and liberation of *all* Black women and their communities

"uncovering and explicating life-giving norms embedded in black women's moral practices"   —Ross

3. the synthesis of double consciousness (DuBois) which occurs via the mastery of striking a balance between diametric opposites and the ability to address and readdress, deconstruct and reconstruct while simultaneously subverting the forces that destroy Black communities and devastate the lives within them

"to unearth a trajectory of hybrid experiences that in some senses attach [Black women] to the roots of their healthful traditional communal values and in other senses alienate us from the wealth of that communalistic heritage."   —Stewart

4. the ability of Black women to wrest younger Black women from the strongholds of internalized oppression (i.e., colorism) and self-delusion (i.e., exceptionalism) and restore them with self-awareness, collective memory, and communal pride

"moments of insight which has healed individuals and villages . . . mak[ing] the arcane available to the unlikely seeker"   —Westfield

5. The inherited and shared legacy of Black women who have "made a way out of no way" [Colloq.] from generation to generation.

"the women who kept their creativity alive 'year after year and century after century' even when such acts are considered as 'punishable crimes.'"
—Harding and Harding

# Reflecting\Black

## *Dianne M. Stewart*

sometimes i feel myself
liking black people
my people

the way they smooth things up
with spirit leaking from their bodies
making laughter with their feet
and flooding it with sea-water tears

sometimes i feel myself
liking black people
my people

for making love out of agony
for daring to feel pleasure
inside aching black skins
for bending low
with joy erupting in their bellies
performing miracles with Trickster Rituals

sometimes i feel myself
liking black people
my people

for knowing when to hit the right
key
string

speed of wind
for knowing when to pause
so that beats echo
with the pulses of black bodies
with the rhythms of black memory
so that beats
laugh
linger
with emotional clarity

for making scat-sounds talk
with good feeling
like silky~jazz~tones
rolling off
strings
keys
sun-dried goatskins

sometimes i feel myself
liking black people
my people

for wailing while they sing
for trapping ecstasy
with whispers of pain and hope
for claiming space among enemies
with collective rhythm
free unfettered rhythm

Yes
i like my people
making culture out of contradiction
descending into the habits of blue-nights
burying sorrow
resurrecting shadows of chaos
reflecting hope
remembering souls

lingering souls

# Chapter 5

# Dancing Limbo
## Black Passages through the Boundaries of Place, Race, Class, and Religion

*Dianne M. Stewart*

Exchange

my father takes crumpled dollar bills from his pocket
at my request
he gives saying

nothing

never asking why
never pausing to stare into my eyes
to trace his own frac-tured steps
through island groves
and city factories
his hand touches mine
and I take
It
barely whispering "thanks daddy"
and then sometimes saying

nothing

In considering Alice Walker's contribution to what might be called a womanist notion of traditional communalism, I find myself reflecting on how Walker's womanist definition calls Black women Home. It is impossible for me to read Walker's definition and much of her prose without being transported back to my roots—my childhood, community, and culture, and to the many exchanges that brought me to where I currently find myself as a Caribbean American womanist theologian. Although I grew up in America, I believe my womanist understanding of communalism is deeply inspired by Caribbean traditions of solidarity, honor, and character. Walker acknowledges these values and other practices such as loving, crying, and fleeing as essential to the maintenance of healthy communal relationships. She also suggests that these practices provide opportunities to experience and redefine multiple dimensions of Black identity, including hybridity, as symbolized through a litany of hues ("brown, pink, and yellow, white, beige and black"), both identifiable with and foreign to the racial classifications that define and often confine us.

Although Walker's womanist definition can be tapped from many different angles, this essay attempts to unearth a trajectory of hybrid experiences that in some senses attach Caribbean Americans to the roots of our healthful traditional communal values and in other senses alienate us from the wealth of that communalistic heritage. Through a conversation with womanists and other critical Black thinkers, it considers the experience of hybridity and the process that many Caribbean immigrants of African descent face in negotiating boundaries of place, race, class, and religion in a culture that despises blackness, demeans Black humanity, and portrays the Caribbean as a hot and exotic place where unbridled passions run rampant. The limbo dance, which engages participants in a constant process of negotiating space and boundaries, is a helpful image to explore these associations and experiences on personal and communal levels.

Dance, even the limbo, is the kind of intimate activity that frees and releases. Whether religious or secular, dance is a sensual practice of embodied therapy that disorients and reorients the dancer. The meaning I attribute to sensuality is best encapsulated by James Baldwin when he says "[t]he word 'sensual' is not intended to bring to mind quivering dusky maidens or priapic black studs. . . . [It is] something much simpler and much less fanciful. To be sensual . . . is to respect and rejoice in the force of life, of life itself, and to be *present* in all that one does, from the effort of loving to the breaking of bread."[1]

The story of the African diaspora illuminates all too well how significations of blackness, especially within the shadow of Western Christian cultures, chronically deprive us of the capacity to be sensual and to use sensual power as a liberation practice. Much of this is the result of prevailing conceptions in the West that collapse sexually loaded terms like libido and promiscuity with notions of sensuality. When I was growing up, I became ever aware of this tension in Caribbean culture as I observed how my father loved to dance and my mother, who vehemently resisted every invitation to dance publicly, was painfully shy about embodied performance. The polarity so evident in their attitudes toward dance speaks volumes about their divergent experiences of growing up in Jamaica. My father was less plagued than my mother by the colonial model of Success: to admire, imitate, and profit from all things European. For females, Success entailed complying with a "politics of respectability"[2] where approved standards of feminine grace and decency rendered African aesthetics and the African-based performance traditions of the popular Black communities primitive and pornographic.

Emilie Townes underscores this problem in her analysis of the representation and commodification of Black identity in mainstream American culture. In "Vanishing into Limbo: The Peculiar Career of Aunt Jemima," she examines how the ideology of Black inferiority is commercialized for an insatiable consumer audience; hence, the impervious presence of Aunt Jemima, Uncle Tom, Topsy, Rastus, Uncle Ben, and Sambo in American culture. Real Black people have been the casualties of these ubiquitous caricatures, especially, as Townes warns, because we do not know ourselves apart from these images. Not really.

Barred from controlling the most powerful public mechanisms for popularizing self and communal definitions and representations, White supremacist manufactured icons are the "controlling images"[3] that confirm and make truthful the most fictitious and absurd ideas about Black people's nature and abilities. Our dissonance of internal unrest with Black identities—manufactured and authentic—is our tragic dance, our limbo of sorts, in this diasporic experience of five centuries and more, narrating our abysmal alienation and dehumanization in the Caribbean and the Americas.

Thus, Townes employs the term "limbo" to underscore the perilous and vulnerable predicament in which Black persons and communities find themselves on the question of Black identity. She describes "limbo" as a tragic state of amnesia where memories can "vanish (into absolute neglect, into oblivion) only to filter back into our lives as shame or anger or pride or righteousness."[4] In other words, as Blacks are compelled to come to terms with the persuasive power of the reigning mythologies about Blackness and Black identity, we are often conquered by these mythologies, as evidenced in the "shame or anger" we feel toward ourselves and our race. In our attempts to conquer the same mythologies we might cultivate a prideful, righteous, or even celebratory self-consciousness about our Blackness. Both of these responses appear not only as personal self-defense strategies but also as wider sociocultural ideologies and practices evident in fashion, grooming, and other aesthetic trends that have waxed and waned in Black popular cultures over the centuries.

The motifs of self-repossession and self-definition in the womanist tradition inevitably challenge each womanist scholar to wrestle with her fractured identity and occasion the reprieve of going home by way of a distinct passage—what Patricia Hill Collins describes as a type of migration,[5] which allows for fresh even liberating insights into the Black experience of boundary crossing.[6] For me, going home means revisiting the contours of my First Arrival and entails crossing boundaries of academia and American immigrant Success to retrieve the resources of an indigenous intellectual and spiritual reservoir—my father's cultural knowledge —reflecting Africa in my history, repairing alienation, and empowering my reconstruction of a familiar yet unfamiliar past.

Linda Thomas maintains that getting in touch with our familial narratives is essential to the formation of womanist epistemology and the recovery of traditional communal practices. She encourages womanist projects that "unearth the ethnographic sources within [Black communities] in order to reconstruct knowledge . . . overcome subordination . . . decolonize the African mind and affirm our African heritage."[7] In my case, I continually discover that the African heritage is at the root of so many Jamaican traditions that affirm Black humanity and personhood—and I mean affirm in the way that Baby Suggs calls Black people to love ourselves, all of ourselves, from our skins to our internal organs.[8] Inspired by Walker and the womanist tradition, I accessed my father's cultural knowledge in an attempt to recover traditional communal practices that might inspire Black communities to tackle with enduring force the kind of distortions of Black identity and Black personhood Baldwin, Townes, and others contest in their works.

I especially interpret Townes's critical commentary as a charge to wrest Black identity from the property negotiations of macrobusiness capitalist industries and cultural institutions that recycle at will icons and stereotypes of Aunt Jemima, Uncle Tom, Topsy and "any of their kin."[9] Her use of the term "limbo" is most appropriate to signify the state of Black impotence with regard to operative self-definitions and self-representations and calls to mind standard definitions of limbo as "a state in which somebody or something is neglected or is simply left in oblivion" and "a place for the confinement of prisoners."

The term "limbo" is embedded with yet another layer of meanings for African Caribbeans in North America; for the limbo is also a Caribbean dance and a game of challenge and competition requiring great skill and ingenuity to contort and maneuver one's body into dimensions that allow passage from one side of a divided space to another. When I asked my father, who was born in Cotterwood, Saint Elizabeth, in 1937, to tell me about the limbo in Jamaica he described it as follows:

> The limbo is done in the countryside. Well I don't know if it is still done today, but when I was a boy it was done when they had dances and fairs during holiday seasons. We used to sing a special song to accompany the dance. . . . "limbo, limbo, limbo like me!" . . . You have to be very flexible to do the limbo. They would hold a broomstick or any stick at a reasonable height and people would pass under it as it was lowered each time. The challenge came when the stick was so low that only the very limber could pass under it without touching it. It was a contest. It's of African origin, I think, because they used to play the rhumba box, a little wooden box with a hole with three pieces of metal in front of the hole, and it would produce different sounds depending on how they played it. They used homemade banjos and guitars and drums with goatskin. If someone killed a goat they would dry the skin and use it to make drums. Plus, it was not something that White folks indulged in. Only Africans would do it and perform it— girls and boys, men and women, everybody, except the old people. Now it's part of the tourist industry and they have highly skilled people performing it today.[10]

My father's characterization of the limbo as an African-based tradition indigenous to the villages and rural populations of Jamaica, subsequently appropriated by tourist sectors of Jamaica's north coast, compels me to ask with Townes: What careers have been made of our heritages and identities? How expensive is our commodification to us and how cheaply is it bartered to foreigners? It is painful to admit that my most immediate thoughts of the limbo dance are saturated with commercial images of Black bodies negotiating boundaries and space on the sandy beaches of the Caribbean islands while White faces observe with amazement and pleasure their gymnastic feats. Do they ever pause to wonder where these dancers live, what salaries they earn, which roads they walk, which markets they frequent, and what they would really be doing with their minds and bodies if they had the entitlements of privilege and opportunity, the inheritance of a supremacy that eluded modern racial slavery[11] and colonialism, and the psychological affirmation that Blackness and the cultures of Africa are indispensable to the preservation of human civilization?

I also see Black hands holding two ends of a bamboo stalk while White tourists with bright floral colored shirts and Bermuda shorts attempt the limbo. Of course, as the bamboo stalk is lowered the participants are not able to cross under successfully. Could this limbo game be a metonym for the multiple passages characterizing the African diasporic struggle for what Delores Williams has called our "survival and quality of life?"[12] These passages are a distinctive mark on our Race, as W. E. B. DuBois noted over a century ago in *The Souls of Black Folk*. They converge in our psyche like DuBois's veil separating us from those who design the rules of the competitions that truly matter. But such passages also equip us with a "second sight"[13] that forever demands our deliberate fine-tuning. Behind the veil of colonialism, in the tiny villages and untamed bushes of Jamaica my father's generation was partially free to play its own games and to dance its own dances. His recollection of this custom is an example of the type of "'natural' memories" that Townes recognizes as having the potential to supplant alien constructs of Black identity that deform and disfigure the Black persona.[14]

Going home to the "'natural' memories" of my father positions me to revisit two of the major passage experiences that many Caribbean immigrants of African descent have in common: transitions in geographic location and socioeconomic context. Thus, our "vanishing into limbo" has a twofold meaning. To vanish into limbo can be both liberating and oppressive experiences of memory preservation and loss. The lessons learned from the loss of memory, however, encourage a reckoning with the boundaries surrounding us. For those of us in academia, this reckoning has personal and intellectual consequences for the quality of life we want to create for ourselves and for the kind of scholarly work we strive to produce.

The limbo is just the metaphor to signify the types of passages I endeavor to traverse in my struggle to create a meaningful life as a Black woman of Caribbean descent. The liberating meaning of my "vanishing into limbo" emerged as I conferred with my father. To hear my father speak with unsolicited ownership about limbo as his people's African-based custom was liberating not because I was unaware of limbo as a traditional Jamaican custom but because, when I attempted to recall the limbo practice, the salient images that crowded my mind with competitive dancing were commercialized ones and not the ones that appeared when my father began to describe the limbo of his childhood behind the veil. These images appeared as fragments of memory when compared with the commercialized images that dominated my consciousness. Because I felt insecure about my conflicting and imbalanced images of limbo dancing, I made the decision to call my father in order to judge the accuracy of my perceptions against his authoritative record of the custom. I simply asked him: "Daddy, what is limbo?" As noted in his response above, he only made a tangential reference to the type of limbo performed for tourists today in Jamaica as his closing remark.

In this exchange across the boundaries of generation, geography, education, class, and, to some degree, culture, my father's specific cultural knowledge displaced the images of my manufactured knowledge of the limbo. My father's memories enabled the vanishing of neocolonial commercialized limbo dancing, replacing its dominance in my memory bank with images of Africans in Jamaica, tucked away from the European gaze, reinforcing their cultural heritage and thereby solidifying their collective spiritual and mental well-being. As a consequence of listening to my father teach, I could see the limbo as a dance of resistance, as a ritual of boundary crossing, and a dramatic encoding of an exilic people's desire to go Home, that is to Africa, under seemingly impossible and treacherous circumstances.

Studies of Jamaican folk culture show that rural Jamaicans of my father's generation constantly journeyed Home in their daily habits and customs, keeping what Charles Long calls "the image of Africa"[15] at the center of their lives. For these reasons the limbo will always signify to me something emancipatory about African Caribbean self-determination and self-definition. Through their own ingenuity, enslaved Africans established Caribbean cultural conventions like the limbo that actually detached them from the opprobrium of the Middle Passage while inventing new passageways Home. As noted by the distinguished Guyanese writer, Wilson Harris, the limbo dance "emerged as a novel re-assembly out of the stigmata of the Middle Passage" and is "a gateway between Africa and the Caribbean . . . a human gateway which dislocates (and therefore begins to free itself from) a uniform chain of miles across the Atlantic."[16]

From another standpoint, the oppressive meaning of my "vanishing into limbo" pertains to the migration Home. In traversing the boundaries of generation, geography, education, class, and culture, I became keenly aware of my alienation from the breadth and depth of my father's cultural knowledge, which I struggle to claim as my inheritance. This led me to ponder the multiple reasons for this state of alienation. Again I was compelled to acknowledge the significance of the dance, the competitive game limbo, as well as one of its literal definitions as "a place for the confinement of prisoners."

Like most immigrants my family's passage from Jamaica to America was undertaken to pursue opportunity, primarily for socioeconomic upward mobility. As the orchestrators of our crossing, my parents sacrificed everything they had and wanted to prepare their five children for Success. As with many African Caribbean immigrant children and African American children, my journey toward Success in the United States has been one limbo dance after another. It is a journey that requires the vanishing of our Africanness, as reflected in our diasporic cultures. Thus, we struggle to modify, transform, upgrade, negate, alienate, forget, and even punish those parts of ourselves that connect us to our African heritage. Many of us never make it across the boundary from indigenous ways, African ways, Black ways to the ways of White folk.

Others of us make it across barely escaping contact with the limbo stick. I like to think of myself as someone who has crossed the boundary, yes, but who is forever conscious of the manufactured shame associated with the other side—the site of my birth, upbringing, and the communities of African descent that nurtured me for Success. My entry into the professional world of academia has made me painstakingly aware of the tremendous and deliberate effort required of all Black "achievers" if we are to traverse the boundary without fear, shame, or uncertainty about the parts of us that have been cultivated and sustained by the other side.

Although I understand the "why" behind Caribbean immigrant parents' limited sharing of their cultural knowledge with their children, the displacing and degrading of that knowledge, which occurs in exilic contexts of middle-class Anglo America, is proving to be far too pervasive and disruptive for their children's fragile psyches. The Success that our parents strive to see us achieve is indeed antagonistic to Africanness and is premised upon our vanishing into a limbo of ambivalence and tokenism, amounting to a tragic state of alienation from the very heritage that has allowed our parents to make meaning out of being human in multiple states of bondage. The greatest tragedy is that, for poor and working-class Caribbean immigrants, the Success our parents suffered to bring to our lives is the deep cleavage separating us not only from their sources of cultural knowledge but from them as well. There is an expectation that the old customs and traditions of our African Caribbean heritage are supposed to vanish into limbo. And for many Caribbean Success stories in the United States, they do.

Katie Cannon's insights on this issue are instructive for us all. As she discusses boundary crossing and going home, in her work with Sara Lawrence-Lightfoot, she captures the nuances of her passages through place, race, and class. In the foreword to *Katie's Canon,* Lightfoot describes a mature and profoundly reflective Cannon as follows:

> By the time Katie Cannon agreed to take the journey through [*I've Known*] *Rivers,* she was "ready to return home." She was ready to admit that identity and wholeness come with reconnection as well as retreat. She was ready to celebrate the richness of her impoverished past. At forty-one, she was ready to face what she enthusiastically refers to as "my middle-aged crisis." She now thinks of mid-life as a time of reckoning with loss, reconnecting with ancestors, "scraping the whites off of her eyeballs," honoring the goodness in her imperfect family, getting in touch with feelings, slowing down. It is also a time of making "the translation" from her childhood home (poor, Black, rural, chaotic) to her adult nest (abundant, predominantly White, urban, serene). "I come from a place," explains Katie, "where when people talk about *field work* they literally mean field work—work in the fields— not ethnographic research. I come from a place where there isn't but one kind of doctor, the person who takes care of you when you are sick."[17]

Cannon's coming to terms with all of who she is—who she has been and who she is becoming—adds texture and dimension to the truthfulness of her womanist scholarship. Townes also advocates self-reflection and self-discovery of this quality while cautioning all Black people, and womanist scholars in particular, against another type of dance with death—what she calls "our postmodern black slow drag of annihilation." Womanist thinkers like Cannon, Thomas, and Townes have actually created a space for me to process my own history of migration and boundary crossing as they pertain to two phases of transition marking deep episodes of cultural alienation in my life. The passage from Jamaica to North America and the passage from working-class African American and Caribbean immigrant communities to social environments dictated by established norms of White, middle-class academic culture have placed me in closer proximity, for the bulk of my time, to people who are most likely to be represented among the limbo-watching tourist crowds on the beaches of Jamaica than to people like my father. The formal education curricula to which our Success is attributed indeed require that "we act as if we do not know [people like my father] because this is what we have been trained to do as 'natural' memories can disrupt our status quo; because they do not rest solely or wholly on objectivity or facts; they materialize from emotions and sight and sounds and touch and smell; they come from the deepest part of who we are."[18] This turning away from our African origins is the slow drag we must refuse.

James Baldwin's *The Fire Next Time* takes up this issue from a slightly different limbo position of being trapped between the saved and the damned (in Paris, Baldwin literally escaping within a limbo of Otherness and exile to avoid the double negation of salvation and damnation). But Baldwin does suggest a way out of the "dungeon," indeed, a way Home, which hints at treasured resources preserved within our African religious heritage. The answer is not to invent another past. Such an endeavor is doomed to fail. The answer begins with facing the terrible circumstances of our life together in the societies we create and the beautiful life-sustaining promise of the anticipation of death.[19] Here Baldwin actually transits a Christian frame (something he constantly struggled with throughout his career as a literary and cultural critic) and enters an African religious frame, although I am almost sure Baldwin did not recognize these resources within him nor his penchant for this dimension of his uninvented past.[20] Baldwin poignantly discerns a spiritual deficiency in the human condition, especially in the White American posture toward death. Although human beings often fail to live in accordance with their most cherished principles, communal societies in Africa and other parts of the world were and still are very much aware of the value in dying and the tragedy in living. African religious traditions ideally orient humans toward modes of apprehending the profundity of this paradox, toward "earning death" in the way Baldwin speaks of it.

I think Baldwin (an honest, gay Black man) suspected that, as real and sensual (and African) as his threshing-floor experience was,[21] the Christian ethos that guided his feet to that spiritual dance floor on that night was grossly contaminated by a false theological consciousness that had misperceived the meaning of life and death and the passage in between. Baldwin's contemplation of these grave philosophical themes inadvertently engages the spiritual intelligence of African religious cultures, which are not anxious about death and are equally aware that "life is tragic." "Life is tragic," says Baldwin,

> simply because the earth turns and the sun inexorably rises and sets, and one day, for each of us, the sun will go down for the last time. Perhaps the whole root of our trouble, the human trouble, is that we will sacrifice all the beauty of our lives, will imprison ourselves in totems, taboos, crosses, blood sacrifices, steeples, mosques, races, armies, flags, nations, in order to deny the fact of death, which is the only fact we have. It seems to me that one ought to rejoice in the *fact* of death—ought to decide, indeed, to *earn* one's death by confronting with passion the conundrum of life. One is responsible to life: It is the small beacon in that terrifying darkness from which we come and to which we shall return. One must negotiate this passage as nobly as possible, for the sake of those who are coming after us. But white Americans do not believe in death, and this is why the darkness of my skin so intimidates them. . . . It is the responsibility of free [people] to trust and to celebrate what is constant—birth, struggle, and death are constant, and so is love, though we may not always think so—and to apprehend the nature of change, to be able and willing to change.[22]

Baldwin's insight about earning death and African orientations toward human life and destiny are analogous. The assumption in African religious cultures that humans come into the world with a "balance" due (preferably before death), with a debt each must pay to posterity, is essentially no different than Baldwin's position on death. In African communal societies, paying this debt (of transmitting humanity) is meritorious and positions one to anticipate death, in essence ancestorhood, with supreme satisfaction. One "earns" death, by paying one's debt to humanity, which is exactly what African religious cultures ideally educate humans to do.[23]

Baldwin does not directly address the source of the human subject's inclination to deny death. He does suggest, though, that for racialized human beings, we must attribute this denial to multiple sources, a principal source being mythologies of race consciousness. Indeed, when it comes to Black people's distortion of death,[24] I think Walker is correct in identifying the source of our distortion as our devotion to a God who does not adore Black people's or women's freedom.[25]

Embracing Walker's womanist insight means wrestling with her claim that "[w]e have been beggars at the table of a religion that sanctioned our destruction."[26] Baldwin's ambivalent struggle with that same religion, Western Christianity, was so genuine that he could actually see with Walker what many of us, even theologically trained thinkers, have yet to confront. In the same essay Baldwin declares:

> I am far from convinced that being released from the African witch doctor was worthwhile if I am now—in order to support the moral contradictions and the spiritual aridity of my life—expected to become dependent on the American psychiatrist. It is a bargain I refuse. The only thing white people have that black people need, or should want, is power.[27]

In other words, Black people never needed White people's religion or way of life. Thus, writes Walker, we "have been so successfully brainwashed to believe that white orthodox Christianity has given us something we didn't already have that we rarely think of what it has taken away."[28] Womanist theologians and scholars of religion must continually revisit this conversation for we are in the best position to think about not only what White orthodox Christianity has done to Black people and Black religion but also what it has taken away from Black people and Black religion.[29]

Walker is clear that American culture is not equipped with the spiritual apparatus to cultivate in its citizenry a healthful posture toward life and death. This is also why Baldwin queries: "How can one respect, let alone, adopt, the values of a people who do not, on any level whatever, live the way they say they do, or the way they say they should?"[30] Although policed by colonial structures, my mother and father were socialized within a culture that was still influenced by the traditional communalism Walker celebrates and by an African religious heritage that taught them how to be "responsible to life," how to "trust and to celebrate what is constant," including "birth," "struggle," "death," and "love."[31] We should not romanticize our parents' way of life, for they are far from any idyllic fantasy of cultural purity we may secretly long for in our hybrid souls. And, in any event, they were not unscathed by slavery, colonialism, and Western Christian orthodoxy (remember my mother's discomfort with dance).[32] However, they still possess some resources that can help us reclaim and redefine ourselves, even though the American experience often deprives us of remembering the value of those resources.

I now see that elevating my parents' narratives, something my father certainly neglected to do while raising his five children for American Success, is the most difficult intellectual task I currently confront as a womanist theologian. There is little encouragement for research of this kind in theological studies. Although theology emerges from suffering and struggle, womanist theology is only beginning to tackle issues of interior suffering that have formidable impact upon Black people's inability to enhance our quality of life in the many contexts that house our demons and eclipse our attempts at positive self-definition and self-representation. Yet in this one simple exercise of a ten-minute exchange with my father I experienced a healing of some of the most gaping wounds scarring my spirit. Perhaps this is the exchange augured in my opening poem. While growing up, I never took for granted the sacrifices my parents made to earn salaries that could support the material needs of their five children. I was affected though by how readily and unconditionally my father provided for my material needs, supplying me with money as requested, but never with stories—stories I yearned for and needed just as much to fill an indescribable internal void.

Privileging my father's voice and experience in this work also reinforces for me the significance of crafting a womanist method that will enable us to accomplish the task of recovering and preserving ancestral narratives. Our cultural flexibility and dexterity, which comes as a result of crossing boundaries and straddling various worlds, will no doubt aid us in this task. In her discussion of Sojourner Truth's ability to negotiate "multiple outsider-within locations,"[33] Patricia Hill Collins submits encouraging proposals regarding the various outsider-within posts still occupied by Black people in America today and the passages we often take to navigate the currents with those spaces. Hill Collins argues that outsider-within positions offer diverse resources for "epistemologies of empowerment" and "new angles of vision" that enhance Black feminist or womanist theorizing. Her analysis is an essential contribution to womanist thought, for she argues that our time spent in elite locations typically reserved for the White middle and upper classes is anything but wasted time. Indeed, the wide-ranging dynamics of Black female scholars' intellectual production, which includes migration and boundary crossing, "offers the possibility of creating new ways of theorizing and new types of critical social theory."[34]

If womanist scholars were to collaborate on a substantial project requiring the collection of personal, familial, and communal narratives as authoritative indigenous resources for a multidisciplinary womanist text on Black identity, we could take an essential step toward resisting alienation and the vanishing that takes place when we lose our connections to "the folks who are really just 'round the corner" whose "memories [actually do] disrupt our status quo."[35] As we compare the ways in which our parents' and grandparents' knowledges are both coherent with and oppositional to the knowledges we acquire in our intellectual disciplines, we can advance our own liberationist aims as a community of scholars with organic ties to alternative spaces of knowledge production that keep us connected to our African heritage.[36] For example, in the limbo, Wilson Harris finds a clearing space for Caribbean people to dance themselves free (like Baby Suggs's Clearing).[37] He assesses the limbo performance as a "gateway" introducing a certain disjuncture between the Caribbean future and the tragedy of the Middle Passage and contends that this dislocation "serves . . . as a corrective to a uniform cloak or documentary stasis of imperialism. . . . Once we perceive this inner corrective to historical documentary and protest literature which sees the West Indies as utterly deprived, or gutted by exploitation, we begin to participate in the genuine possibilities of original change available to a people severely disadvantaged at a certain point in time."[38]

The dislocation Harris sees the limbo providing indicates that enslaved Africans were more than their enslaved condition socialized them to be. The limbo and other African Caribbean customs reveal more subtle dimensions of the intense connections between Africa and the diaspora; and these connections are inevitable, with or without the Middle Passage. The very people who retain natural memories of limbo dances and other traditional communal practices can help us recover ourselves in healthful and promising ways. For the most part, they remain outside the halls of academia and will not enhance our work if we neglect their voices. As my exchange with my father signaled to me, womanist scholars need our foremothers' *and* forefathers' natural memories to provide texture and detail to those parts of our historical memories and cultural knowledges that are fading with time and with one-way passages to the exilic spaces that keep us in bondage. They can dance us free!

### NOTES

1. James Baldwin, *The Fire Next Time*, in *The Price of the Ticket: Collected Non-Fiction, 1948–1985* (New York: St. Martins, 1985), 350.

2. Evelyn Brooks Higginbotham, *Righteous Discontent: The Women's Movement in the Black Baptist Church, 1880–1920* (Cambridge, MA: Harvard University Press, 1993). See especially pp. 185–229.

3. Patricia Hill Collins, *Black Feminist Thought: Knowledge, Consciousness, and the Politics of Empowerment* (New York: Routledge, 1990), 67–90.

4. Emilie Townes, "Vanishing into Limbo: The Peculiar Career of Aunt Jemima," *Union Seminary Quarterly Review* 54, 3–4 (2000): 21.

5. Patricia Hill Collins, *Fighting Words: Black Women and the Search for Justice* (Minneapolis: University of Minnesota Press, 1998), 3–5, 231–234.

6. Gloria Anzaldúa, *Borderlands/La Frontera* (San Francisco: Spinsters/Aunt Lute, 1987).

7. Linda Thomas, "Womanist Theology, Epistemology, and a New Anthropological Paradigm," *Cross Currents* 48, 4 (1998–1999): 2.

8. See Toni Morrison, *Beloved* (New York: Alfred A. Knopf, 1997), 88–89.

9. Emilie Townes, "Vanishing into Limbo," 8.

10. Roydel Stewart, personal communication, October 28, 2001.

11. See Katie Cannon's discussion of racial slavery in chapter 1 of her *Katie's Canon: Womanism and the Soul of the Black Community* (New York: Continuum, 1996), 27–37.

12. Delores Williams, *Sisters in the Wilderness: The Challenge of Womanist God-Talk* (Maryknoll, NY: Orbis Books, 1993).

13. W. E. B. DuBois, *The Souls of Black Folk* (New York: Penguin, 1903). See especially pp. 43–45.

14. Emilie Townes, "Vanishing into Limbo."

15. Charles Long, *Significations: Signs, Symbols, and Images in the Interpretation of Religion* (Aurora, CO: The Davies Group, 1995), 187–198.

16. Wilson Harris, "History, Fable, and Myth in the Caribbean and the Guianas," in *Selected Essays of Wilson Harris: The Unfinished Genesis of the Imagination*, ed. A. J. M. Bundy (New York: Routledge, 1999), 157–159.

17. Katie Cannon, *Katie's Canon*, 13.

18. Emilie Townes, "Vanishing into Limbo," 21.

19. James Baldwin, *The Fire Next Time*, 368–375.

20. Baldwin wrote these reflections after visiting Africa in 1962. Though he does not attribute his ideas on life and death to his experience in Africa, I do not think it is mere coincidence that Baldwin engages in such profound reflection, which parallels so well African-centered approaches to life and death, after having returned from Africa. Also see Femi Ojo-Ade, "Africa and America: A Question of Continuities, Cleavage, and Dreams Deferred," in *Of Dreams Deferred, Dead or Alive: African Perspectives on African American Writers*, ed. Femi Ojo-Ade (Westport, CT: Greenwood Press, 1996), 16; Marion Berghahn, *Images of Africa in Black American Literature* (Totowa, NJ: Rowman and Littlefield, 1977); and Ezenwa-Ohaeto, "Notions and Nuances: Africa in the Works of James Baldwin," in *Of Dreams Deferred*, ed. Femi Ojo-Ade, 107–114.

21. James Baldwin, *Go Tell It on the Mountain* (New York: Dell, 1981), 193–226.

22. James Baldwin, *The Fire Next Time*, 373.

23. There are numerous sources on African religions that document the saliency of this principle in African cultures. I came to this awareness most keenly through the scholarship of Eboussi Boulaga. See his *Christianity without Fetishes: An African Critique and Recapture of Christianity* (Maryknoll, NY: Orbis Books, 1981).

24. For example, we might consider the kind of distortion about death—Paul Tillich might have called it an anxiety about death—Baldwin once embraced as a victim of White supremacy and Western Christian salvation history. The distortion I speak of has convinced so many Black people that their pre-Christian African ancestors are primitive and lost souls confined to perdition and that the same fate was/is theirs but for the beneficence of chattel slavery, which rescued Africans from the dark continent and provided them and their descendants exposure to White civilizing Christian culture.

25. Alice Walker, *Anything We Love Can Be Saved* (New York: Ballantine, 1998), 25–26.

26. Ibid., 25.

27. James Baldwin, *The Fire Next Time*, 375.

28. Alice Walker, *Anything We Love Can Be Saved*, 21.

29. We have been prolific as black and womanist theologians in identifying what Christianity has done to us and our ancestors in Western contexts of bondage and oppression. I do not think we have spent enough time identifying what Christianity has taken from us. This pursuit would require us to consider beyond cursory reflection the value of our African religious heritage.

30. James Baldwin, *The Fire Next Time*, 375. Though written in 1962, Baldwin's question is ever so timely for our current post-9/11 geopolitical climate. Do most White Americans understand that if one of America's native sons can ask this question, entire populations in the Muslim world and elsewhere must be asking the same thing of the so-called free world?

31. Ibid.

32. This is why, in this instance, I went to my father's feet for answers to my queries about limbo dancing in Jamaica. My mother's inhibitions about embodied expression and her phobia of dancing persuaded me to turn to him for a definition of limbo.

33. Patricia Hill Collins, *Fighting Words*, 231.

34. Ibid., 235.

35. Emilie Townes, "Vanishing into Limbo," 21.

36. Linda Thomas offers important methodological suggestions for approaching this type of womanist theological project. See her article "Womanist Theology, Epistemology, and a New Anthropological Paradigm."

37. Toni Morrison, *Beloved*, 86.

38. Wilson Harris, "History, Fable, and Myth in the Caribbean and the Guianas," 159.

# Chapter 6

# Hospitality, Haints, and Healing
## A Southern African American Meaning of Religion

### Rosemarie Freeney Harding with
### Rachel Elizabeth Harding

### A Daughter's Preface

In 1997, my mother was awarded a fellowship to the Mary I. Bunting Institute at Radcliffe College. At the time she was very sick. She had recently been diagnosed with diabetic neuropathic cachexia (a rare and debilitating neurological complication of diabetes) and was struggling to find a treatment that her very sensitive body could tolerate. She wanted very badly to accept the fellowship and do a research project on connections between spirituality and social justice activism among veterans of the southern Freedom Movement. I had just finished graduate school and was taking care of her as her condition became more acute, so I accompanied my mother to Cambridge, Massachusetts where we shared a one-bedroom apartment for almost a year. We began work on a collection of essays and stories, poems and recipes, play fragments and autobiographical remembrances that connected my mother's history with those of her mother and grandmothers, and with the stories of many of the extraordinary women and men she knew from the movement days. My mother called the collection *Remnants: A Spiritual Autobiography.*

From September to June we visited medical specialists, experimented with various treatments for the wracking pain and extreme weight loss she was experiencing, and in the moments when she was strong enough to sit with a tape recorder, we talked—about family history; about activism; the joys and lessons of her childhood; the strangeness and meaning of her current illness; the plays and performance pieces she envisioned as healing ceremonies for our fractured nation; the ancestors, the orixás, and God; and the black southern mysticism that informed so much of her mother's and grandmothers' wisdom.

This essay is drawn from a lecture my mother gave at the Bunting Institute in the spring of her fellowship year. It examines elements of an indigenous, southern, African American religious orientation. Essentially a personal reflection on the cultural/spiritual experience of a single Georgia family, the text also explores the significance of specific traditions in the shaping of a generalized worldview. Ghost stories, death rituals, communions of food and conversation, midwifery, and herbal medicine are among the components of that worldview discussed here. Not by chance, the stories my mother tells resonate strongly with the ethics and spirituality of Alice Walker's Womanism. The lives of black folks in rural Georgia in the early to mid-twentieth century shared a great deal in common, and it was this rural southern experience that informed the religious and cultural orientation of my mother's family, as well as the grounding out of which Walker's life and writings emerged. Examining the rituals, stories, healing practices, and welcoming ways of five generations of a family (especially its women), "Hospitality, Haints, and Healing" identifies the foundations of a meaning of religion in the black southern context that includes, but is by no means limited to, the institutional church. In fact, this particular analysis employs a much wider understanding of religion as *that which keeps us human in the world.*

In March 2004, my mother passed on. I thank her for everything she left me.

## Introduction

My family is a southern family. Though we have lived in Chicago for five generations now, we are, in many respects, still deeply influenced by the rituals and traditions that traveled with us on the Seminole Limited from Macon, Georgia. My parents, grandparents, aunts, uncles, and most of my brothers and sisters were born in small southwest Georgia towns—Leesburg, Poulan, Albany, Macon. In the nineteen-teens and twenties, they began to move north. First my mother's sisters, their husbands, my father, and his brother. Then other relatives—wives, children, and parents. They were drawn to jobs in steel mills and railroad yards and escaping nightmares of lynching and the stinging, arbitrary humiliations of daily life in the South between the wars. In some ways they were pulling up roots, moving to Detroit, New York, Philadelphia, and Chicago. In other ways, they were simply stretching the roots, changing the contours a bit, but holding fast to the deep nourishment that rose there.

Recently, I have been reflecting on what religion may have meant for my great grandmother, Mariah Grant, who is the oldest remembered ancestor on my mother's side of the family. Not only am I working to understand the meaning of religion for Mama Rye, as we called her, but I am also trying to trace the religious and spiritual values that have come down to the family through her and through her daughter, Liza, who was my grandmother.

Some who remember the stories say that Mama Rye was born in Africa. If she was, she was probably born around 1824 and must have come to the United States as a young girl in one of the last shipments of the (then illegal) slave trade. She died in 1930 or 1931 in Macon at the age of 107. She had worked in Virginia and along the eastern seaboard on a ship where she cooked for the captain and crew. By the time my grandmother, Mama Liza, was born, freedom was three years old and Mariah and her children were living in Georgia.

In my attempts to examine and understand the religious and spiritual values that have come down to my family from Mama Rye, I am deeply influenced by the work of historian of religions Charles Long and playwright-philosopher George Bass.[1] The meaning of religion for black folks, they insist, is in the heart of our history, our trauma, and our hope. It is in the way we have oriented ourselves—over the long centuries in these Americas and extending back before our arrival on these shores—to "mash out a meaning" of life in the midst of tremendous suffering and pain. Religion, in this sense, is not simply a doctrine of faith or the methods and practices of church, rather it is all the ways we remind ourselves of who we really are, in spite of who the temporal powers may say we are. Religion is how we situate ourselves, how we understand ourselves, in a particular place and time vis-à-vis ultimate reality, vis-à-vis God. It seems to me that this too is the meaning of religion for the women Walker recalls and honors in the essay "In Search of Our Mothers' Gardens,"—the women who kept their creativity alive "year after year and century after century, when for most of the years black people have been in America it was a punishable crime for a black person to read or write."[2] It was these women, Walker's mother, my mother, our grandmothers, and aunts and the "crazy" ladies down the street, who "order[ed] the universe" in the image of their own conception of Beauty, their own understanding of who and how they were in relationship to God.[3]

Black religion, then, is not only in the music, the drama, the communion, and the interpretation of text within the walls of the physical church, but it is also in the orientation of black people to so-called secular culture. Black religion is Otis Redding and D'Angelo as much as Mahalia Jackson and Mary Mary; it is as much hip hop as holy dance; and root work as much as the laying on of hands. It is how we make meaning and joy out of our human experience. With this understanding in mind, I am looking within the myriad cultural and spiritual traditions of my family for the meanings and manifestations of a distinct, southern, African American orientation to being. I am looking at how we have come this far and how we continue on.

This orientation is not unique to my folks. Having grown up with many extended families of black Mississippians, Alabamans, and Georgians (and having lived for many years in Georgia as an adult), I am keenly aware of the pervasiveness of the orientation that I describe. However, because the experience of my family is the one that is closest to me, most of the examples I use in illustration come from stories and traditions I witnessed, heard, and participated in as a member of the Freeney-Harris clan in Southside Chicago.

### Hospitality

My mother and aunts always kept a ready pitcher of iced tea or lemonade in the refrigerator and a plate of cookies, a fresh-baked cake, or rolls with homemade preserves on the counter. Anyone who came by to visit was offered something cool to drink (unless it was winter, of course, when they'd be offered coffee or tea) and something tasty to eat. In the years when I was growing up, people visited back and forth at each other's homes more regularly than folks do now and our house seemed to be an especially popular destination for neighbors and relatives. This was partly due to the fact that we had a large family and my older brothers and sisters were all outgoing with lots of friends. And it was partly because my mother and father made the house so welcoming. Sometimes, it seemed almost "too" welcoming—all kinds of people would come through, not just relatives and neighborhood friends but peddlers and preachers, professional gamblers, and union organizers, petty thieves, street walkers, and people we would probably refer to today as homeless. Mom loved "bad" people—that is, people other folks thought were "bad." She didn't judge and she taught us how to respect, how to listen, how to learn from everyone. Mom would set out beautiful china dishes and slices of her homemade pound cake for all of them—especially for the most transient-looking people it seemed sometimes. As if she knew they needed the extra attention and acknowledgment. But then too, Mom genuinely enjoyed their conversation and wisdom.

I remember there was an itinerant bookseller, an immigrant from Europe, who would come to visit Mom now and then. The two of them would sit down in the dining room with Mom's best dishes and talk for hours about the events of the world and the world of books. The man was not always very clean and sometimes, especially in the winter when the heat was on full blast in our house, we could smell the mustiness of his old and ragged clothes, the heavy acrid sweat of his body. He talked funny too, and as children, we were occasionally tempted to laugh—as much from awkwardness as anything else. But if we let loose the tiniest snicker, Mom would cut her eyes at us deftly, and we would abandon the temptation and keep our faces straight.

As I said, I have a large family. My mother birthed sixteen children, although only nine lived to adulthood. We nine were just one contingent of a large coterie of cousins, uncles, and aunts, some of whom I didn't know were *not* blood kin until I was grown with children of my own. Until 1976, when my father died and my mother sold the house, there was always someone living with my parents at the family home at 4160 South Wentworth—a child, a niece, or nephew, then later grandchildren, grand-nieces, and grandnephews. Mama and Daddy Freeney always made room and any of us could always come home. Hospitality was a foundation of my family's spirituality, as it had been for so many southern blacks. The efforts my parents made to be neighborly, welcoming, and to reserve judgment against those the society viewed as outcasts, served as important examples for their children and grandchildren as we grew into adulthood.

## Ghost Stories and Boundaries

My mom used to love to tell ghost stories. They were a tradition of the Georgia woods that she brought to Chicago, and Mama Freeney was an expert ghost story-teller. She could scare you so bad you'd be afraid to go to the bathroom by yourself to pee. Some of the stories she told were regional favorites that she most likely inherited from older family members like Mama Rye. But many of my mother's ghost stories were from her own experience. As my sister Mildred says, she wasn't telling "stories" she was telling "what happened"—meaning, it was true. She would tell us about the ghost-lady who tried to push her creaking, transparent babyless buggy alongside anyone who passed through a certain stand of pines at a certain hour of the evening. She reminisced with my father about a beloved and well-trained horse who reared up on his hind legs and stubbornly refused to cross a particular bridge one moonless night. The fact that Mama Freeney often had corroborating witnesses only made her stories more terrifying and delightful. But I have remembered very few of the tales on my own and had to ask my sisters and other relatives to help me piece the stories together again. I seldom heard the full versions as a child. (And when I did remember, I tried to forget.) Whenever Mom started to tell about the headless man she met on the road from Leesburg to Albany, or the time the door to her house was locked and there was no one at home but all the lights were on and she could hear voices inside—whenever she started to tell one of *these*, I would get up and go into another room. I didn't take well to being terrified.

My own sensibilities aside, these stories were a great entertainment for the family, but they were not just entertainment. My mother told these stories and others as a way to pass on lessons. One of the most important lessons was that of acknowledging the reality and presence of spirit. Whether one called them ghosts, haints, angels, spirits, presences, or winds, the beings that inhabited Mom's stories were recognized, on some level, as real. Through her stories we learned a respect for the unseen/the unknown and an appreciation for the transmutability of reality and form.

Most of the ghosts and haints of my mother's repertoire were essentially harmless even if frightening. But there were other stories that emphasized protective relationships between humans and the spirit world. For example, my mother and other members of my family have had experiences of being helped by people who show up out of nowhere and disappear the moment danger is no longer present. My sister Alma had this experience years ago in a long pedestrian tunnel in a Chicago subway. It was late one evening and Alma was alone, except for a tall, white policeman who stayed a few dozen feet ahead of her as she walked. The tunnel was quiet in the resonant way of tunnels and Alma was intensely aware of her surroundings. Once she got to an open gate near an exit, she looked around, and the policeman (who had never turned toward her and never acknowledged her calls out to him, even though he was clearly in hearing range) was suddenly no where to be found.

Mama Freeney's transformative energies were sometimes unnerving— to both family and strangers. My sister Mildred recalls with humor that some people thought Mama was a conjure woman because of the way she engaged and inhabited the world of the spirits. Our mother could so convincingly evoke the presence of an unseen person in the room that her listeners would swear they felt the breeze in the wake of the invisible woman's skirt as she walked past them. "There she go!" Mama Freeney would whisper with urgency and certainty, pointing a finger to the space just in front of her grandchildren, indicating the path of the unwitnessed visitor. Conjure indeed. Although the term was probably not meant as a compliment by those who used it, I think that in its broader signification it is true. Conjure and healing are both forms of transformation. And Mama Freeney was capable of shifting herself and the atmosphere around her in myriad ways, especially for the benefit and protection (and even amusement) of others.

Carrie Lewis was a childhood friend of my mother who was as close to her as a sister. They played together as girls, went to school together, got married around the same time, and had their first children within months of each other; both babies were boys. When Carrie's son, Everett,[4] was very young, he sometimes suffered from the presence of an unwelcome spirit that would appear and hover over him. Carrie would bring the baby to my mother's house anxious and frightened for her child. I am told that Mama Freeney would call the spirit by its name and say "Get away from that child." Although Carrie couldn't see the spirit the way Mom could, she could feel its presence, heavy and threatening around her baby, and she would instinctively shield Everett with her body and call out to my mother, "Ella, tell it to go away." Mama and Carrie would cover the child with their arms, talking to the entity and praying to God to keep the spirit away from Everett, and eventually there would be a respite. When Carrie got ready to leave, Mama Freeney bundled up her own baby, my oldest sibling whom everybody called Brother, and the two women and their children would walk down the road to the fork where Carrie and Everett would turn off to go home, finally undeterred.

This kind of encounter reinforces the idea that while a connection or affiliation exists between humans and other, less readily visible entities, there is also a boundary—and the need to recognize and at times insist upon that boundary. This has been one of the most valuable lessons of African American mysticism for my life and work. As my mother emphasized in her stories and as the family experienced in other ways as well, a healthy respect for the unseen is essential to understanding the nature of human life and the web of connection that binds all beings to each other. As in many other places of the Afro-Atlantic diaspora, the Black South, through stories, ritual, and family traditions, cultivated an appreciation for both interdependence and restraint. The world is full of all kinds of living beings—humans, animals, spirits, plants, earth, waters, and winds—and we are all related to each other, but there are both appropriate and inappropriate ways for each to interact. It was important for us to know this and one of the ways we learned it was through the stories my mother told.

Fluidity and constraint, connection and boundary, were also present in interpersonal and familial relationships. In most southern black families I knew growing up, children and adults of various ages spent a great deal of time together. There were often three generations living in our household. The young people benefited from the loving presence and guidance of grandparents and older relatives. Conversely, the older members of our family could always count on the energetic companionship of younger ones and did not have to worry about being alone or abandoned in the final years of their lives. In these multigenerational households, children were taught to respect their elders and to recognize that there were spaces and times when they could not enter "grown folks' business."

There was also a certain formality of relations, rooted in southern and African traditions, in which respect was shown through the courteous use of titles when talking to strangers, persons of authority, and anyone in an age-group higher than one's own. Women were always "Miss" or "Mrs." So-and-So and men were called "Mr." (unless they were relatives, and then they were called Auntie, Uncle, or Cousin). As children our responses of "ma'am" and "sir" indicated the good "home-training" we had received from the adults who raised us. Even among adults of comparable age and status, who had known each other for many years, there was often a kind of quasi-ceremonial care in the way they interacted with each other. In some respects, this must have been an antidote to the indignities these men and women regularly suffered from a discriminatory white society. But, from all I can tell, this practice of almost exaggerated mutual-deference and politeness was an important element of interpersonal relations in many of the West and Central African communities from which most

North American blacks originated, and it was a common feature in slave communities throughout the Americas.

The recognition of boundaries is, I think, also related to an acknowledgment of and respect for others and the limits of intrusion into another person's space. This kind of respect is actually a foundation for compassion, and I used it as the basis of my social work practice in Chicago and later in Denver. In spite of policies that encouraged imposing questions and miserly reckonings of financial need, I tried to interact with my clients in a way that emphasized their intrinsic value as human beings and their integrity.

## Dreams and Sight

Closely related to the experience of ghosts and spirits in the African American mystic tradition are dreams, visions, and sight. Anyone familiar with southern folk traditions—black and white—has probably heard of the "caul." Some people are believed to have the gift of divination or foresight because they were "born with a caul" or a "veil," which means that the amniotic sac was on their head and face when they came through the birth canal. My mother and great-grandmother were recognized as having this kind of sight. But Mom used to say that she could "see," not because of being born with a caul, but because she came from a "clean womb." When my grandmother, Eliza Harris, affectionately called Mama Liza, was pregnant with my mother and very close to her delivery date, she tripped on a railroad tie and fell in a truss. It was a hard fall and she feared for the well-being of her unborn baby. Mama Liza's water broke, but the baby wasn't delivered for a few more days. When my mother finally came into the world there was hardly any water or blood—because Mama Liza had lost it all in the accident. But the child, Ella Lee Harris, was born healthy and lived to be 103 with a number of abilities, the greatest omen of which she attributed to coming from a "clean womb." Interestingly enough, I discovered later that there is a tradition among Tibetans that their diviners and seers are born from "clean wombs."

"Sight" and "seeing" is not simply a matter of the ability to foretell future events. It is part of a larger orientation which recognizes the existence of a variety of means of access to information, help, wisdom, and warning. Here, too, as with the ghost and spirit stories, is a vigorous connection between the seen and unseen worlds. Dreams, visions, and signs are other axial elements of this orientation. There is a vast tradition among African Americans of dreaming and paying close attention to dreams. Dreams can be auguries of coming good or ill. Dreams of deceased relatives and friends are often interpreted as forms of communication with them, and the sharing of dreams within a household or among friends is a way to connect with a collective wisdom regarding the meaning of a particular feeling or event. (Furthermore, there is a whole industry of books and pamphlets for playing *policy* and lottery numbers based on dreams.)

## Death and Dying

My mother often "saw" the impending deaths of family members in dreams and signs. She recalled, for example, that a rainbow she saw in her sleep, days before her husband died, was an omen that his time was not long. (I don't know if my mother was conscious that the rainbow is a symbol of the continuity of life and death among the Yoruba and Ewe peoples of West Africa.)

Death and dying were surrounded by signs in my family. Omens and forewarnings: My grandmother, Mama Liza, standing before my mother and rising from the floor in a whirlwind. My brother's gift of red roses falling over new in a vase. Aunt Mary fighting with her arms and fists as if death were a man, "Ella do you see him. Do you see him Ella?" And her sister, Ella, my mother, helping her to hold off death's hunger for a little while. The three days of snow when Aunt Mary finally went on. And the rainbow sign of my father's time coming.

The time of dying is an important moment, an important process, in many cultures around the world. This was certainly the case in my community as I was growing up, and to a large extent, it remains so. I learned from my parents and other relatives how to accompany people in death, through death. The dying were never left alone and children were included in the process of comforting and encouraging them. My mother used to take me with her whenever she visited people who were dying. I grew up with a great respect for death, but no fear of it. It was a very sacred time. And even though I didn't always understand what was going on, I was aware of the special nature of the moment, its mystical quality. There was a reverence for the dead and we were taught never to speak ill of them.

Most of the people we visited died at home—some were family members, some friends. In the 1930s and 40s, the practice of dying in the hospital was not common among African Americans. Often we carried food, but sometimes we would just go and visit and sit. Sometimes talking, sometimes not. Many of the people we visited had come up to Chicago in the same era as my parents, and they would reminisce with my mother about old times, good times, in the South. I enjoyed listening to the adults talk. I was aware that their remembrances were always positive, joyful ones —how they joked and laughed. But I also saw the sadness in my mother's face as she acknowledged to herself that a good friend, a cousin, or a sister was leaving. It gave me a sense of how one balances one's own grief with the need to encourage a dying person to leave amid as much happiness as possible. The need for joy around death, happiness amid mourning, seems to me now a central element in my family's cultural traditions. We learned to laugh and joke and have a good time in life, and simultaneously to understand that life means mourning too.

My mother was a consummate teacher. She could use any opportunity to pass on a lesson—and half the time she did it so well you didn't even know you were learning anything until you thought about it later. When I was about ten, my Uncle Clarence died of a cancerous tumor in his face. My mother visited him in the days and weeks before he passed and took me along. It was a difficult thing to see—his entire right jaw was a gaping hole and he was in almost unbearable pain. He turned his head toward us when we walked in, but he couldn't speak.

On the way home from the visit my mother said to me, "Do you know where he got that cancer from? From working with all that bad meat." We could smell the stockyard from where we lived. Sometimes it reeked so overpoweringly we ourselves felt sick. "How many men work at that stockyard do you think are sick like your uncle?" I didn't know the answer, but the question got me to thinking. "Rose," my mother said, "all races of men work there. And it's dangerous for all of them." Soon my mother and I were having a conversation about the extremely unhealthy conditions of the Chicago stockyards, a filthy, disease-producing environment, where many men labored under insufferable conditions with little concern from their bosses for protecting their health.

From experiences like this, I learned very early about injustice. My mother was using an African American cultural tradition—that is, not shielding children from the reality of pain and death—as a bridge to help me understand some broader truths about exploitation and serious social inequity. In the midst of it all, was the caring and concern for Uncle Clarence and for many others like him. And so, even with our anger, our pain, our profound sense of the wrong we had been done, we talked to Uncle Clarence, tried to make him laugh a little, and remembered together the stories that made us all feel more human.

Death is also an important time for gathering. The wake and the dinner after the funeral are unique moments of fellowship and abundance. There is a plenteousness of everything: food, people, laughter, liquor, music, and memory. At funerals, family who have not seen each other for years will come back to celebrate and remember the life of the loved one they have lost. Old ties are renewed and new relatives are introduced to each other— the children and grandchildren of cousins, the new spouses, and the new babies. It is as if in compensation for the loss, we use the time of death as an opportunity to assert the continuity of life, the line going on.

Fortunately, we didn't wait for death to create occasions for gathering and joyousness. We are a family that likes to laugh. We have been blessed with singers, musicians, and a wide strain of humor in the family genes. Whenever more than two or three of us are together, we make each other happy. African American humor has long been recognized for its emotional flexibility—the ability to speak to the absurdities and humiliations of racial discrimination and to reveal those abasements as essentially ludicrous (albeit often painful). In my experience, laughing and joking give black people more room to "be" in the world. Dance and music do this too. They all expand the space that we live in—stretch it beyond the limits of our assigned "places" in society. Transform the air we walk in so that we can breathe.

### Healing and Transformation

The work of transformation, changing the insides and outsides of a situation, is a long and venerable tradition in the southern African American experience. Looking back on our history, one sees a tremendous flexibility among people who had to navigate the vicissitudes of life under a violent and arbitrary Jim Crow segregationist system and yet continually cultivate a sense of their own personal and collective dignity. My parents, grandparents, aunts, and uncles were among the southern blacks who decided that the best way to respond to the terror they were experiencing was to leave it, but I have other relatives and friends who searched for alternative ways to address the madness and remain in what had become our homeland. In both cases, the internal work, the work of physical and psychic healing, was an important tool in the creation of individuals, families, and communities who could continue reaching for the best in themselves and the best in the society in which they lived, people who could "keep on keeping on."

This work of inner transformation, calling on the deep mystic resources, was aided by our churches, our singers, our dancers, our artists, our musicians, our teachers, our poets, and our healers. My great-grandmother, Mariah, was in this mystic line. So were the "sainted" women Alice Walker recalls, the ones Jean Toomer had seen as he walked across the early twentieth century south. Walker writes in "In Search of Our Mothers' Gardens," these women were not merely the possessors of an intense and deep spirituality, but, living with the grave limitations of the place and time, they sometimes appeared strange, crazy, or "sainted."[5] These were the women who "went off" into the edges of the vast pains, the afflictions both personal and transatlantic. Sometimes they could heal themselves and others with what they found there and sometimes they were overwhelmed.

Most of the people in the family who remember Mama Rye are gone now. But the stories that remain of her include recollections of her healing work and her African ways of perceiving and inhering in the world. Mama Rye was a root doctor. She collected plants and flowers, roots and leaves in the fields and forests around her Leesburg and Macon, Georgia homes and made these into medicines to treat family members and others who came to her for advice and counsel. When she was in her nineties, she was still fishing in the Kinchafoonee Creek every day and her grandchildren would take turns accompanying here to and from this meditative recreation. Mama Rye tried to teach various ones of them what she knew. Some showed more interest than others. But even those who thought they were leaving "the old ways" behind would call on the collective wisdom of the family to remember at least a few of Mama Rye's herbs and recipes when they needed them.

Mama Liza, one of Mariah's daughters, carried on her mother's healing tradition in another way. In Lee County, Georgia, Eliza Harris was known to be an excellent midwife, assisting the deliveries of both black and white women. My cousin Pansy tells me that Mama Liza brought hundreds of babies into the world. Even white doctors in the area called on her to help them with difficult pregnancies because of her successful reputation. Following Mama Liza, there is a tradition of nursing among women in my family. My Aunt Mary and my sister Mildred were nurses and I too studied for a time to practice nursing. I like to think that my continuing interest in natural healing and counseling are part of my inheritance from the medicine women in my family.

My mother, Mama Freeney, shared many of the healing qualities of her mother and grandmother. When I was a child, she used to keep herbs in the kitchen pantry to make teas for us when we were sick. Her pantry was something akin to a local herbal pharmacy, serving friends and neighbors as well as family. She also used home remedies like placing socks with thin slices of onion on the feet of a person with fever to draw the heat out. My mother and her sisters firmly believed in the power of spirit to heal, to transform. When my sister Alma was a little girl, she was struck with tuberculosis of the bone and doctors told the family that her leg would have to be amputated. Instead of yielding to the doctor's orders, mom and Aunt Mary took Alma home and through a combination of poultices and prayers Alma kept her leg.

In my own life, I am drawn to traditional, natural healing modalities, remembering the tea recipes and home remedies of my mother and great-grandmother and learning as much as I can about laying on of hands —massage therapies, acupuncture, Therapeutic Touch, Feldenkrais, and other techniques of alternative care. But even beyond issues of personal health and well-being, I try to follow the examples of my mother and aunts in recognizing the need to create a larger atmosphere of healing and wellness at the level of human relations and societal structures.

Throughout the 1980s, my husband and I cotaught a course at the Iliff School of Theology called, "Healing of Persons and Healing of Society." We introduced students to the concept that the body politic is, in many ways, analogous to the body human—intensely interdependent in all its parts and very responsive to both negative and positive stimuli. Texts from folks as varied as Buckminster Fuller, Hannah Arendt, Howard Thurman, and Thich Nhat Han were central readings, emphasizing that the Spirit, the Universe, does indeed provide abundantly for all living beings on earth. There is truly enough for everyone. The offense is greed. And it is just as destructive to societies as it is to the organisms of individual people. Guests came to the course to share their perspectives and stories— community activists, philosophers, physicians, scientists, religious leaders, writers. Our students were always deeply encouraged by the connections the guests made between caring for the well-being of individuals and creating more humane and compassionate societies.

In fact, our present work, The Veterans of Hope Project, arises directly from this experience and others of sharing the "testimonies" and encouragement of social change activists with a younger generation of people concerned for justice, healing, and nonviolent social transformation. It is fundamentally to my mother's credit that I am able to recognize and appreciate the links between personal health, generosity, and social transformation—for Mama Freeney's hospitality and welcome were as healing as her teas and touch.

## Secrecy and Discretion

The final aspect in this brief discussion of a black southern religious ethic is secrecy. There were certain things in my experience as a child, certain events, which were never discussed. Some stories, some customs, were shared only as knowledge was necessary and then with an attitude of hesitation, reticence. My sense is that the reasons for concealment centered around two issues. Sometimes, the information revealed was too painful —so tremendously and profoundly painful that the act of recognition risked the release of a haphazard power, an energy whose discharge required a careful, almost ritual attention. This, I believe, was the case in the almost complete lack of conversation about the horrors that sent my family fleeing to the North in the late twenties. It was not until 1960, when I was preparing to return to Georgia to work full-time in the Freedom Movement, and when white vigilante terrorism—and the economic and political system that supported it—was being confronted with a mass movement, that my father and mother began to open up about some of the barbarities they had experienced. Events like the hanging of a pregnant woman, upside down, with her womb split open and her body dragged then through the black neighborhoods of Macon were a large part of the reason my family left their farms and moved away. I didn't hear those stories until decades later. It was as if there had to have been a way out of (or the urgent concern for a daughter who was going into) the madness before it was safe to talk about it.

In other cases, secrecy is a sign of intimate connection to the life-force. There are certain practices around birth and death that my relatives refuse to register on audiotape. Certain spirit stories which are told only in hushes when told at all. As with the ghost stories, where we began, there is, here in the matter of secrecy, a strong element of propriety at work. Some things are kept protected—either so that their strength will not do harm to the unwary or so that their energy and efficacy will not be diluted by misuse and misinterpretation.

## Mariah's Legacy

Mariah Grant's children and grandchildren manifested a remarkable diversity of approaches to organized religion. Many were regular churchgoers, and while the family lived in southwest Georgia, they mostly attended Baptist churches. In fact, my grandfather, Papa Jim, was a deacon at Shady Grove Baptist in Leesburg. When the family moved to Chicago, some of Mama Rye's granddaughters joined the Congregational Church, others remained Baptist, and some, like my mother, went to church only occasionally.

Among the next generation, my siblings and cousins—Mariah's great grandchildren—there has been even more variety in the church traditions we have chosen. One of my sisters married into the Roman Catholic faith, another is a matron in a Presbyterian church. I have a cousin who is Soka Gakkai Buddhist and another of my sisters was a founding member of a Mennonite mission church in Chicago. This sister, Alma, was my inspiration for joining the Mennonite church. I used to watch the way she cared for her children, the compassion and sense of security she gave them, as well as the way she took care of other people in the neighborhood where she lived. Alma's house was a lot like Mama Freeney's in that sense, everyone was welcome, and Alma always had an open heart, a good word and good food to share. My sister's example and the nonviolent, reconciliatory witness of the Anabaptist tradition in the Mennonite church were strong attractors for me. And though I have since embraced other religious traditions as well—Sufi Islam, Gnostic and Contemplative Christianity, Tibetan Buddhism and Vipassana meditation, Jewish mysticism and early-Christian Celtic traditions—the foundations of my spiritual values rest in the southern, African American orientation to being that I learned from my family.

I am convinced that this openness, this acceptance of the diversity of God's witness in the world, is a legacy of the wisdom Mama Rye brought with her from Africa. Indigenous African religions are known for the inclusivity of their worldview—most tend to find ways to absorb and adapt new traditions (even those of conquered and conquering peoples) into a fundamentally accepting and essentially flexible whole.[6] The meanings of religion we learned from Mariah, her ancestors and contemporaries, are one of the great resources African American culture offers to those who seek its discernments. In the insights of womanism, Alice Walker traces this path and leaves her own indelible marks: an ethic of joy and inclusion; a tenacious creativity that is both gentle and fierce; and a love and honoring of all our mothers and all the beauty and nourishment they carve from unsteady ground for us to feed on and grow strong.

NOTES

1. See Charles H. Long, "Perspectives for the Study of African American Religion in the United States," in *African American Religion: Interpretive Essays in History and Culture,* ed. Fulop and Raboteau (New York: Routledge, 1997), and Charles H. Long, *Significations: Signs, Symbols and Images in the Interpretation of Religion* (Philadelphia: Fortress, 1986). Also, conversations with and lectures by George H. Bass, African American Studies courses, Brown University, 1983–1990.

2. Alice Walker, "In Search of Our Mothers' Gardens," in *In Search of Our Mothers' Gardens* (San Diego: Harcourt Brace Jovanovich, 1983), p. 234.

3. Ibid., p. 241.

4. I have changed the names of the friend and her son to protect their family's privacy.

5. Walker, "In Search of Our Mothers' Gardens," pp. 232–234.

6. On the inclusivity of African Traditional Religions, see John Mbiti, *African Religions and Philosophy,* 2nd ed. (Oxford: Heinemann International, 1990).

# Chapter 7

# Lessons and Treasures in Our Mothers' Witness

## *Why I Write about Black Women's Activism*

### *Rosetta E. Ross*

Building on the opening provided by Alice Walker's *In Search of Our Mothers' Gardens,* womanist religious thought is providing intellectual space to unearth many treasures[1] long that come from black women's lives. In my own work, this involves uncovering and explicating life-giving norms embedded in black women's moral practices, especially by exploring black women's activism and attending to the pragmatic way many black women activists engage religion. When I look closely at religion in some of these women's lives, I see a complex working out of what it means to be black and Christian, a working out that involves not only engaging the meaning-making power of religion, but also interrogating religious traditions and practices while assessing functional uses of religion for shaping social action. The complexity of these women's religiosity both challenges traditional conceptions about black Christians and black churches and pushes toward transforming traditional practices in black churches and black Christianity.

In this essay, I use black women's activist religiosity to show examples of persons who break rank with the tradition in many black churches of separating reason and spirit. Among black women religious activists are examples of persons who, in the midst of their ordinary lives, use critical analytical and reasoning skills to assess the usefulness of traditional religious conceptions and to construct new ways of making religion functional. My primary argument in this essay is that in the United States, the predominant failure in much "customary black Christianity" to unite critical-analytical and spiritual capacities throughout routine religious practices leaves a gaping void in the black religious psyche that is both waiting to be and being filled by content that helps persons make sense of and assign significance to their ordinary and extraordinary experiences. By "customary black Christianity," I am referring to the thought and action of persons who regularly populate black churches, from denominational presidents, bishops, presiding elders, and district superintendents to local church pastors, church school teachers, youth and youth leaders, mothers, deaconesses, deacons and missionaries, choir members, ushers as well as less other active but steady church attendees.

Two presuppositions inform my argument. First, if black religious institutions do not critically evaluate the meaning of practices of religion, black religious institutions cannot respond meaningfully to challenges facing black peoples. Second, since practices of religious traditions and religious traditions themselves evolve over time, it is important to consciously and critically engage this process of evolution. This discussion begins by exploring the emergence of evangelicalism in the United States during the eighteenth and nineteenth centuries as related directly to anti-intellectual impulses among black Christians. I then suggest that an overemphasis on piety, deriving from a narrow evangelicalism, contributes to deemphasizing critical thought about religious practice and that overemphasizing piety and deemphasizing reason is far too prevalent in African American Christianity. Noting the long, though less popular, tradition of African American critical religious thought, I conclude the essay by exploring the critical religious thought and practice of two twentieth-century black women activists—Pernessa Seele and Ella Baker—as models of persons who both practice and critically engage religion.

Many contemporary black Christians in the United States have adopted a strong evangelicalism and contend that it is the only authentic means of practicing Christianity. Deriving directly from revivalism of the "Great Awakenings" during the eighteenth and nineteenth centuries, evangelicalism is deeply embedded in African American Christianity and African American culture. Emphasizing the significance of human action and choice in following God (as contrasted with the Calvinistic idea of predestined salvation or damnation), evangelicalism proceeded from the Great Awakenings as an emphasis on conversion, affect in piety, orthodoxy of belief, suspicion of worldliness, and general practice of good works. Interestingly, the evangelical focus on human action engendered Christian social activism such as Abolitionism, temperance, benevolence societies, and prison and other social reforms.

Since independent black churches in the United States emerged in the middle of the Great Awakenings, evangelicalism influenced the identity of the first self-governing black denominations and congregations. The existence of these bodies also informed some emphases on evangelical social activism. Yet, even as they separated themselves from parent bodies, black churches maintained theological and doctrinal consistency with white predecessor institutions. The determination of black churches to maintain theological and doctrinal continuity with white Christianity stagnated development of critical theological thinking within much black Christianity, eclipsing responses to questions such as: What was or may have been the systematic theological contribution to black Christianity that derived from continuity of religions of enslaved peoples and African religions? What rituals and creedal affirmations might be developed to address the enormous need for healing the wounded black consciousness? Peter Paris argues that for black churches, this "has constituted an ecclesiastical dilemma involving no small amount of moral and political *ambiguity.*"[2] On issues of racism and racial justice, activities of many black churches contrasted with the practices of most white Christianity. However, the antiracist practice of black churches generally was viewed by black Christians as arising from implications of the then current evangelical theology, without evaluation of the way that same theology supported slavery and sustained segregation. To be sure, there also were separate, indigenous moral and theological perspectives informing black Christian social action. For example, use of the term "heaven" by enslaved persons usually expressed pragmatism about an earthly value, although the orthodox understanding of heaven separated it from earth.[3] Another indigenous moral perspective is evident in the black church independence movement itself which complicates the notion of the Church Universal by its assertion through action that separation within the Church was necessary to the well-being of African American Christians. In addition to these general oppositional theological ideas, there also was a nascent black intellectual tradition that challenged evangelical Christian orthodoxy. In spite of these other streams of thought, most independent black denominations and independent black congregations of white denominations generally adopted theological frameworks of their parent bodies.

One legacy of this failure by the earliest independent black churches to work through and institutionalize theologies, doctrines, and creeds opposing the reigning evangelical theology is that many African American Christians find it threatening and sacrilegious to question any aspect of the received religious tradition. Not surprising then is the tendency throughout black Christianity in the United States to treat as separate, distinct, and mutually exclusive, the human capacity to engage in critical-analytical reasoning and the human capacity to have religious experiences and engage in religious practice. As a consequence, many black Christians are left without (and actually antagonistic toward) use of critical reasoning capacities to provide religious interpretations of social and political life. In such instances, many African American Christians are vulnerable to and rely on contemporary evangelicalism as articulated by white Christians to determine their own political perspectives and personal moral practices.

While adoption of eighteenth- and nineteenth-century white theology and the attendant evangelical emphasis on orthodoxy stagnated creative black Christian theological thinking at the birth of black church independence, black Christianity's adoption of another evangelical emphasis, "affect in piety," helps maintain the division between critical thought and religious experience. Initially, revivalistic evangelical piety embraced reference to outward acts reflecting the inner change of conversion and included acts of social reform. However, as the evangelical emphasis on conversion evolved, attention to internal aspects of individual devotion increased, making less important the practice of social reform as a reflection of religious piety. Since the narrowed understanding of piety primarily focused on individual morality, this evolution in evangelicalism that eventually dichotomized outward action and inner disposition concurred with the predominant antebellum Christian theology in the United States that allowed and even affirmed enslavement. In the mid- to late nineteenth and early twentieth centuries, the emphasis on moral piety had a special significance for African American religiosity. Both whites who blamed black immorality—especially sexual immorality and indolence—for the plight of African Americans and black elites concerned with racial uplift saw practice of moral piety as a means of changing African American circumstances. In view of the significant desire of black Americans for acceptance and integration into the larger society, moral uprightness became comingled with industriousness as a means of expressing Christian piety and realizing racial uplift. This was especially evident during the era immediately succeeding emancipation, when personal morality and industry *for the sake of acceptance by white persons* came to dominate the meaning of being Christian and to shape the thinking and practices of African Americans. Writing about this phenomenon, Latta Thomas says:

> Whatever favored White advantage became "good," and whatever tended toward Black advantage, Black freedom, and rebellion became a "sin." . . . In the days after Emancipation the catalog of sins dictated by the White power structure and many Black churches consisted of a ban against alcohol, sexual activity, frolics, gambling, and riling the tempers of Whites. . . . The whole point of the matter is that the string of petty sins formed another mental chain around the minds of Blacks.[4]

At the present time in the United States, the authenticity and legitimacy of much institutional black Christianity is severely threatened by the legacy of overemphasizing piety and deemphasizing independent critical reasoning. This threat is intensified when the piety/reason dichotomy is connected to increasing separation of the black poor from the black middle classes, increasing emphasis on individual success, and increasing emphasis on religious entrepreneurialism.

In spite of much customary black Christianity to accommodating white theology, there has long existed a strand of resistance to the predominant tendency of wholesale adoption of a narrow evangelical piety. Frederick Douglass and Harriet Jacobs, for example, criticized the Christianity that allowed white church leaders and members to practice a form of religious piety and enjoy moral esteem while enslaving and brutalizing black persons.[5] Other persons such as Alexander Crummel challenged the traditional view of agape and lamented a one-sided piety, and Anna Julia Cooper, writing in 1892, berated a religion that allows one to draw "circlets," limiting "'universal brotherhood' by shapes of noses and texture of hair."[6] In the mid- to late twentieth century, there has developed a vibrant and growing tradition of black male and womanist theology and black male and womanist biblical interpretation among a group of black religious intellectuals. There also has existed alongside these articulations of indigenous theological perspectives, religious movements (such as Garveyism) and individual congregations (such as those intentionally identifying themselves as afrocentric) seeking to work out and express an African American theological perspective and practice. Hip Hop culture also contributes to this tradition through the work of persons such as Lauryn Hill and Kanye West, who use imagery and themes from Christian tradition to present their messages. In the acceptance of predetermined theologies, what resources for an authentic black religious identity were overlooked? In what remains of this essay, I want to examine the practices of two black women religious activists—Pernessa C. Seele and Ella Baker—whose thought and action present models of persons using critical reasoning capacities to work out their theological perspectives as they engage religion for identity integration and social practice.

Fifty-year-old Pernessa Seele, is founder and CEO of The Balm in Gilead, Incorporated, a fifteen-year-old nonprofit, nongovernmental organization that seeks to decrease the spread and effects of HIV/AIDS among black people internationally by "building the capacity of faith communities [to provide] HIV/AIDS education" and services. This organization coordinates work through partners in faith communities in every U.S. state as well as in twelve geographically diverse locations in Canada, the Caribbean, and five countries in Africa. Balm in Gilead programs help thousands of local faith communities engage in work that seeks to lessen effects of HIV/AIDS by providing "comprehensive educational programs and offering" guidance encouraging "those infected to seek and maintain treatment."[7] The Balm in Gilead's work includes four program initiatives: The Black Church Week of Prayer for the Healing of AIDS, Our Church Lights the Way: [An] HIV Testing Campaign, [a] Faith-Based HIV/AIDS National Technical Assistance Center, and the Africa HIV/AIDS Faith Initiative.

Seele spent her childhood and adolescence in Lincolnville, South Carolina, a relatively rural black community near Charleston. When telling her story, Seele emphasizes as significant the influence of growing "up in an all Black community where the people in charge were Black people."[8] She describes this as a context in which she came to know herself among continual conversations about "saving the race" and among family and extended family who were deeply involved in black churches. Seele says her family understood church as inclusive community, access to which she experienced as unlimited even by practices her community discouraged such as smoking and homosexuality. The result is her view that "People are just people and everybody is in church on Sunday trying to get some grace and mercy, and understanding of what they believe Jesus or God to be."[9] Seele encourages moving beyond centralizing piety as the means of expressing religiosity. Instead, she recommends relating to persons by

"Deal[ing] with them as they are in there trying to get some grace and mercy just like me."[10]

In the mid-1970s, Seele completed a B.S. in biology at historically black Clark College, an institution affiliated with the Methodist Episcopal Church, the denominational tradition in which she primarily had been reared (although on Sunday afternoons she attended the "AME church, the Church of God in Christ, and everybody else's church"). Seele also includes in telling her story her participation "in college . . . with the group that went to church on Sunday,"[11] in spite of the fact that she eventually became an outsider to this group when she engaged in critical study of religion and began to explore less mainstream Christianity by attending a congregation in the Unity church tradition. After completing an M.S. in immunology at nearby Atlanta University, Seele worked as an immunologist at the Centers for Disease Control in Atlanta. In 1979, she moved to New York where she continued work in immunology, first at Rockefeller University completing malaria research, then at Sloan-Kettering Hospital. Eventually, Seele took employment with health programs of the city of New York, including work at the now-defunct Interfaith Medical Center in Brooklyn, where she helped develop an AIDS project for a methadone clinic.

Seele's early AIDS-work put her in proximity of but not in persistent, prolonged contact with persons who had contracted and were dying from complications related to AIDS. This early work led to employment as an AIDS educator with the AIDS Initiative Program at Harlem Hospital in the late 1980s. In that position Seele says she "had to actually go up on the ward and actually see people in the hospital dying of AIDS." This was an experience she did not have at the methadone clinic. Because she was so disturbed by interacting constantly with people dying from AIDS, Seele says she struggled with the reality of death and began to pray both for herself in her work and about the circumstances of the many who were dying. She identifies this praying as the seed that became the Balm in Gilead, Inc., and as the place where she began consciously to connect her life's work to her early moral formation.

Seele identifies herself as standing in the religious tradition of her forebears. Her formative context, Seele says, colors her work at the Balm in Gilead. She says she sees herself as involved in what it means to save the race in this present time which requires, as it did for leaders in her childhood community, engaging religious institutions as central to black community survival. "I am," Seele says, "that child that they prepared, and I am that child who they gave that mantle to [saying] that you had to work hard to save the race. And who knew that HIV would be the work that I would be in?" In spite of situating herself within her forebears' tradition, Seele clearly rejects uncritical acceptance of traditional religious conceptions. Of her own continuing engagement with Christian tradition, Seele emphatically declares, "I choose, I choose, keyword on choose, I choose to be a Christian."

Seele's emphasis on "choosing" Christianity reflects her understanding of being "religious" as not limited to being Christian. Though she draws meaning from her primary engagement with Christian tradition, in her own religious practice and beliefs Seele ventures well beyond the bounds of Christianity. "I love . . . being at Grace Baptist Church on Sunday morning," she says of her current primary worship context. "[T]he first Sunday . . . morning is still my high holy day . . . because it connects me to my folks in Lincolnville. . . . It is . . . communion Sunday that connects me to growing up in Lincolnville, . . . back to how my folk back home, how they drew strength every day from their beliefs in Jesus and all that other stuff that they did." However, Seele also passionately states that her religious practice includes engaging other traditions: "I love going to the [ashram] and meditating. . . . I love going up to . . . chant with a Buddhist group. I love African traditions. I would say that I am a universal spirit who loves the intersection of Black people and their faith and I am rooted in Jesus Christ."[12]

Seele's "universal spirit" was, perhaps, quite influential in jump-starting the Balm in Gilead. Along with her own prayers about her work at Harlem Hospital, Seele organized a day for joint Prayers for Healing by black religious communities in Harlem. Seele's invited participants came from five religious traditions: Yoruba practitioners, Ethiopian Hebrews, Native American spiritualists, Muslims, and Christians. The event occurred first in 1989 as the Harlem Day of Prayer for the Healing of AIDS and then annually in 1990, 1991, and 1992, as the Harlem Week of Prayer. Rapid increases in AIDS challenges meant the project became popular quickly as word spread. It soon evolved into a national week-long program in primarily, though not exclusively, black churches. The name Balm in Gilead emerged as Seele developed the project into an organization.

Seele articulates clearly the usefulness of religious communities and the significance of the role of the pastor or other religious leader for engaging black faith communities in HIV/AIDS work. Seele considers the spiritual dimension as central in the lives of African peoples. "I love Black people and their religion," she says. "I am fascinated on how Black folks all over the world find their center in whatever their belief is, they find their center in it." As a consequence, she identifies faith communities as the essential context for beginning to make changes in black communities. This is why, she says, the mission at the Balm in Gilead is "to build the capacity of faith communities to address HIV and AIDS." But in seeking to build capacity within faith communities, Seele says, she has had to continually "build relationships with the pastor" or other religious leader, who, in most cases, "ultimately . . . makes [the] decision whether that church is going to address HIV, AIDS or not." Understanding the role of the religious communities and religious leaders also is knowledge Seele says she brings forward from her youth, having seen through her family's interactions "firsthand how Black folks revered, respected and took care of the pastor and how important the pastor was in this community the Black community."[13]

Seele's work at the Balm in Gilead may be seen as religious practice. At the same time, through the lens of her practical recognition of religious contexts as the space for engaging HIV/AIDS work, Seele's religious practice also reflects her rational consideration of the usefulness of religion for forming and initiating social action. Moreover, by scrutinizing and evaluating religious practices, Seele both carries on and alters the tradition of Christianity in which she stands. Five perspectives mark Seele's critical-analytical religiosity. First, Seele critically understands the practice of religion as essential to the sense of spiritual well-being for black peoples including herself. Second, Seele is pragmatic about her own engagement with religion. She affirms its meaning-making role but does not let go of her reasoning capacities in making choices about religious engagement. Third, Seele holds that subscribing only to a narrow piety restricts the ability of persons to relate meaningfully to others. She prioritizes (or collapses) relating to and addressing the needs of persons over practicing moral piety. Fourth, Seele is not restricted by "orthodoxy" and the fear of "losing her religion." She is open to learning and engaging new religious ideas and practices and expresses confidence in her ability to critically evaluate what she encounters. Finally, Seele recognizes religion as useful for shaping social action and engages religious persons and religious traditions for that purpose.

Seele is not unlike other persons whose "pragmatic spirituality"[14] allows them to fashion a religiosity that carries on while expanding the tradition from which they emerged. Another example is evident in the life and work of Ella Baker: focused social activism. Born in 1903 in Norfolk,

Virginia, Ella Baker has become known as one of the persons who helped conceptualize, shape, and carry on the Civil Rights movement. Baker attended and graduated from Shaw University in Raleigh, North Carolina, in the 1920s. After graduation, Baker decided against the anticipated profession of schoolteacher, and instead moved to New York where she took odd jobs while developing a career for herself in community work. During the 1930s, Baker was an active officer of the Young Negroes' Cooperative League which sought to improve the lives of Depression era black persons through co-op buying. From around 1940 to 1946, she served as a field secretary and later as director of branches for the national NAACP. After leaving NAACP employment, she worked with the Urban League and a local New York NAACP branch. Because Baker began her lifelong vocation of community organizing as early as the late 1920s, she was not only deeply familiar with evolving social and political developments in the country, but she also was insightful enough to recognize and to take full advantage of the potential of the time during which she lived. This is how she came to help shape the Civil Rights movement.

From New York, Ella Baker supported the Montgomery Bus Boycott through fundraising efforts. Later she helped initiate organization of the Southern Christian Leadership Conference (SCLC) to capitalize on the boycott's social gains after it ended. In 1957, Baker moved south to Atlanta and developed the administrative and programmatic infrastructure of the newly formed SCLC, becoming its de facto first executive director, though her gender and her status as a lay person prevented Baker's ever formally holding the title. As her work with the SCLC was ending, Baker helped organize student leaders of sit-ins and, seeing great potential in the young people's energy and enthusiasm, Baker encouraged students to form their own organization. This resulted in emergence of the Student Non-Violent Coordinating Committee (SNCC). Over the course of her career Baker emphasized empowering people. She once said, "Give people the light and they will find a way."[15] This central value evolved from, but was not limited by, Baker's early religious formation.

Ella Baker's perspectives on empowering people to care for themselves originated during her childhood and young adult years. Baker grew up in a household that included a Baptist minister grandfather and Baptist missionary mother, both of whom shared their resources to help others survive, paying special attention to the indigent and infirm. As a girl Baker participated in this work. She helped take care of children of a neighbor who had lost his wife and affirmed her own understanding of the value of individual persons when, in one instance, she reported to her mother that a mentally impaired neighbor needed medical attention. Describing her action later Baker said, it was required because "'she was a *person*. You couldn't just pass her by and say, 'Oh, that's Mandy Bunk, you see, who also raised a pig in one room and herself in the other room.' You don't do that."[16] Alongside community ministry and missionary activity, Ella Baker grew up participating in various traditional religious rituals. She regularly attended worship at her grandfather's church and read scripture as a child and young adult. Following the lead of her cousins, at age nine she decided to participate in her denominational practice of confession and baptism by immersion. After Baker left home to attend Shaw University (a Baptist-affiliated institution) for high school and college, she continued regular scripture reading and attended worship daily.

When Baker moved to New York, during the height of the Harlem Renaissance, she encountered New York as "a hotbed of . . . radical thinking." Baker fully engaged in Harlem's renaissance, and intrigued by new ideas throughout New York, she "went everywhere there was a discussion" to take advantage of the "opportunity to hear and evaluate whether or not this was the kind of thing [she] wanted to get into."[17] Baker integrated the new ideas into her expanding worldview, even as she maintained ties with Friendship Baptist Church in Harlem for regular Sunday worship while in New York and to which she sent back contributions when she missed Sundays while working in Atlanta.[18] Still, as her worldview evolved, Baker moved away from some traditional black Christian ideas about God. For example, Baker was pragmatic about the idea of divine intervention in human affairs to provide relief. Instead, she stressed what may be called a positive theological humanism that emphasized what people can achieve cooperatively by their own organized initiatives on the basis of longings and capacities given by God. "I always like to think," Baker once said, "that the very god who gave us life, gave us liberty. And if we don't have liberty, it is because somebody else stood between us and that which god granted us."[19] Baker believed deeply and frequently emphasized the potential and responsibility of organized groups, especially local communities, to change their own lives. In one instance, Baker described her NAACP work as uplifting the people, "'getting people to understand that they had something within their power that they could use, and it could only be used if they understood what was happening and how group action could counter violence."[20] Her work also included overcoming some issues of intrarace social class divisions rooted primarily in observations about moral piety. She sought to determine ways to help less economically vulnerable African Americans recognize their commonality with drunks or streetwalkers who were brutalized in jail. Baker's goal was pointing out that "as long as . . . violation of the rights of Tom Jones can take place with impunity, you are not secure."[21] Baker's concern to empower people persisted in her work with the SCLC, where she criticized the focus on charismatic leadership and mobilization and instead argued in favor of organizing and developing local leaders. Her emphasis on organizations empowering people to take charge of their own lives was particularly significant to the structure and work of SNCC, since she influenced SNCC students to "adopt a group-centered style of operation and to focus on empowering and training leaders indigenous to local communities."[22]

As compared with Pernessa Seele, Ella Baker's religious perspective is less marked by understanding of the practice of religion as essential to the sense of spiritual well-being for black peoples. Baker places more emphasis on recognizing one's own sense of dignity and its commonality with the dignity of others. Similar to Seele, Baker was pragmatic about her own engagement with religion. She affirms its meaning-making role through her persistence in engaging some of its practices, but she maintained and accented practical reasoning capacities in making choices about religious interpretations of social and political life. Very much like Seele, Baker felt that subscribing to a narrow piety restricts the ability of persons to relate meaningfully to others. Baker is similar to Seele in her willingness to move beyond "orthodoxy" and engage new religious ideas and practices and even to interpret and use "secular" ideas religiously. Finally, Baker recognized the usefulness of religion for shaping social action and engaged religious persons and religious traditions for that purpose.

Seele and Baker are models of religious practitioners, who are both carriers of the tradition of religious meaning as well as innovators who alter the meaning conveyed in religious tradition by expanding practices and engaging religion pragmatically. Many other persons like Seele and Baker exist who demonstrate intentionality in shaping and reshaping their understanding of Christianity. Identifying and systematically examining similar examples may be one way for black denominations and congregations to begin the work of articulating and developing authentic and relevant womanist theologies, creeds, doctrines, and study materials. Widespread lay examination of such models might also provide space for using one's own reasoning capacities to critically evaluate the meaning of practices of religion.

NOTES

1. See Katie G. Cannon, "Unearthing Ethical Treasures: The Intrusive Markers of Social Class," *Union Seminary Quarterly Review* 53, 3–4 (1999): 53–64.

2. Peter Paris, *The Social Teaching of the Black Churches* (Minneapolis: Fortress, 1985), 43, italics added.

3. Gayraud Wilmore, *Pragmatic Spirituality: The Christian Faith through an Africentric Lens* (New York: NYU Press, 2004), 7.

4. Latta R. Thomas, *Biblical Faith and the Black American* (Valley Forge, PA: Judson, 1976), 118.

5. See Frederick Douglass, *Narrative of Frederick Douglass, a Slave: Written by Himself* (New Haven: Yale University Press, 2001), and Harriet Jacobs, *Incidents in the Life of a Slave Girl* (New York: Dover Publications, 2001).

6. Gayraud Wilmore, *Black Religion and Black Radicalism: An Interpretation of the Religious History of Afro-American People* (New York: Orbis Books, 1986), especially 114–115; Anna Julia Cooper, *A Voice from the South: The Schomburg Library of Nineteenth-Century Black Women Writers* (New York: Oxford University Press, 1988), 300.

7. Balm in Gilead, "Our Mission," http://www.balmingilead.org/about/mission.asp, p. 1.

8. Pernessa Seele, interview by author, October 8, 2004.

9. Seele interview.

10. Seele interview.

11. Seele interview.

12. Seele interview.

13. Seele interview.

14. I borrow this phrase from the title of Gayraud Wilmore's recent volume, cited in n. 3.

15. Barbara Ransby, *Ella Baker and the Black Freedom Movement: A Radical Democratic Vision* (Chapel Hill: University of North Carolina Press, 2003), 105.

16. Rosetta E. Ross, *Witnessing and Testifying: Black Women, Religion, and Civil Rights* (Minneapolis: Fortress, 2003), 34.

17. Ellen Cantarow and Susan O'Malley, *Moving the Mountain: Women Working for Social Change* (Old Westbury, NY: Feminist Press, 1980), 64.

18. Joanne Grant, *Ella Baker: Freedom Bound* (New York: Wiley, 1998), 114.

19. Ella Baker, "Address to Mass Meeting in Hattiesburg, Mississippi," January 21, 1964, quoted in appendix of Catherine M. Orr, "'The Struggle Is Eternal': A Rhetorical Biography of Ella Baker" (Master's thesis, University of North Carolina at Chapel Hill, 1991), 78.

20. Ross, *Witnessing and Testifying,* 42.

21. Cantarow and O'Malley, *Moving the Mountain,* 70, 71.

22. Ross, *Witnessing and Testifying,* 45.

# Chapter 8

# "Mama Why . . . ?"
## A Womanist Epistemology of Hope

### Nancy Lynne Westfield

### Introduction: Definition or Prophecy

The four-part definition, though deceptively Webster-ian[1] in form, function, and format, is a masterful definition by a Black woman who knows Black women intimately and loves us fiercely. It feels like a love poem as much as it is a definition. It is equally a word sculpture filled with passion and delight as it is a scholarly work giving credence to the Black women's essence and experience. On the other hand, perhaps being deceptively Webster-ian implies that it is not, at its core, a definition at all. Perhaps, upon close scrutiny, we discover that *Mother* Alice has written for us more a prophecy than a definition. As I understand it, prophecy takes our past to herald our future while at the same time locating the activity of love in our present. Prophecy connects the past with the future by naming the present as belonging to God. Walker's description of a womanist maps the terrain of knowing who we have been and who we are to become while signifying who we are here and now. *Professor* Walker's definition-turned-epistemology is as much concerned with revealing the future as she is in describing the past and defining the present. This way of knowing and being known, as revealed by Walker, has been with us in the past, is with us now, and promises to sustain us into a hopeful future. There is, I would argue, shamanic activity in her audacity to write this work in this way. It is a literary work that has demonstrated the power to open spiritual doors and bind up undesirable forces. It has brought moments of insight which has healed individuals and villages. It makes the arcane available to the unlikely seeker. So I say, for those who do not know and do not have the eyes to see, sometimes revelations look like definitions.

The purpose of this essay is to consider Walker's definition/prophecy in terms of epistemology, pedagogy, and didactics. I will argue, in this essay, that (1) daring to write a definition is an act of audacity; (2) the womanist epistemology is an epistemology of hope. I will mention as the third major point of my argument; and (3) my personal attempt to embody the womanist epistemology in my classroom assignment. This last part is a brief conversation concerning the womanist pedagogy that might be informed by this epistemology of hope through the specific assignment of questioning.

Lastly, I need to remark about my writing and my writing style. I move, in this essay, between past tense, present tense, and future tense. I jump from first person to third person, sometimes in the same paragraph. *Dr.* Walker's definition/prophecy lives, I believe, personally as well as corporately—in the "I" and the "We." It is a literary work that spans the generations and speaks us into the future—in then, now, and yet to be. So, when I wrote this essay, it seemed fitting, even necessary, for verb disagreement. Also, in my essay, I mix poetic-prose with scholarly-speak. I even occasionally make up a word or two. *Teacher* Alice, poet and scholar, would understand.

## The Audacity to Define

Anyone who coins a term and creates a definition has seized power and is exercising great authority. A Black woman who would have the audacity to define *anything,* but most especially her own kind and her own thinking, is a Black woman deeply in touch with the necessity for resistance and hope. It seems only right that a poet, scholar, novelist, activist, former Christian, pagan, African-American, woman should set a Black woman's definition to paper. Dr. Walker's act of determining and settling by way of coining and defining the term "womanist" was an embodiment and an example of the very nature she defined. It is exquisite artistry coupled with profound integrity to exemplify the very concept of womanism by a womanist. The coining and defining of the notion of womanist was born into the world as an act of resistance due to *Dr.* Walker's own "outrageous, audacious, courageous, and willful behavior." When she wrote this definition she was acting "womanish" and trying to be grown. The act of composing a definition is tantamount to setting new orbits, creating new fusions, conjuring new possibilities. It was a characteristic act of daring and risk that has honky-tonk swagger and panache. In short, the coining and defining of this term is an act of purple.

There is power in naming, renaming, defining, and redefining the worlds we inhabit. I would liken *Dr.* Walker's act of "defining" with many of the acts of naming, name changing, and renaming in the Bible. Adam used his God-appointed power to name the beasts and birds. Saul picked himself up off the ground, cleared his sight, and thereafter answered to the name of Paul. Abram and Sarai, as a symbol of covenant with God, were called Abraham and Sarah. Our sister Hagar whispered the name Elroi as the first person in biblical history to name God.

New names mark new beginnings, events which commence new phases, new seasons of life. Perhaps, *Dr.* Walker was like the Egyptian princess who renamed the Hebrew baby, changing his slave name to the name he would use as the prince of Egypt. The Egyptian princess looked at the slave child and saw potential, saw life, saw love. The baby's new "definition" given by his Egyptian mother would become synonymous with the act of liberation and freedom for generations. The newly named, thus defined or redefined Moses, would be the symbol of transgression and freedom fighting even until today. By this name change, his destiny was set. Perhaps, Alice Walker, like the Egyptian princess, changed our slave names from "Nigra," "Jezebel," "Sapphire," "Aunt Jemima," to a name that was to be known as the symbol of transgression and freedom fighting as we settled in our days of living in Pharaoh's palace or what we now call the "academy." Maybe, like the new definition/distinction of "Moses," our naming as "womanist" gave us a new destiny or at least heralded the destiny of freedom and freedom fighting that was in store for us. Perhaps, womanists will dwell in the academy only until we see with new eyes the brutality plaguing our sisters and brothers and act in radical ways of justice—it will be then that we will become such a threat to Pharaoh that he will drive us out—out toward our destiny of liberation for all.

In this salvific text of Exodus, the name of the Pharaoh's daughter is never called. What we know about her is the way she acted—the way she treated other people. We know that she was willing to look into the face of a doomed infant, hear his cries, and take him into her own house. The Pharaoh's daughter was willing to let the gaze of the baby's Hebrew sister and mother fall upon her without retreating or flinching. A womanist perspective allows us, like Pharaoh's daughter, to define the world not by preconceived labels or status of persons but by their action. The Pharaoh's daughter did what Black women have done for centuries, that is to say, heard the cries of other people's children, took in the children, and raised them as our own. The unnamed daughter's love for the child allowed her to claim her father's enemy as her own family. Pharaoh's daughter asked herself a version of the question, "Mama, why are we brown, pink, and yellow, and our cousins are white, beige, and black?" The "Mama-consciousness" of the Pharaoh's daughter answered, "Well, you know the (human) race is just like a flower garden, with every color flower represented." I conjecture that Alice Walker was like the Pharaoh's daughter, not because of her status or affiliation with established power, but I label her as such because she acted like a woman who heard the cries of babies who, without her intervention and care, would have died alone in the water. The Pharaoh's daughter heard the baby's cry, plucked him up out of the water, and renamed him. *Rev.* Walker heard the cry of African-American women and in renaming us, nurtured us. Naming was an audacious act in the Ancient Near East and it is an audacious act in twentieth-century North America. Additionally, we have contemporary exemplars like Sojourner Truth who were equally audacious.

Sojourner Truth harnessed the power of naming and defining when she asked the now infamous question, "Ain't I a Woman?" In the speaking of and speaking on this question, the definition of womanhood was exploded. No longer was woman relegated to the likes of Princess Di, or Marilyn Monroe, or Lucille Ball. Sojourner's question expanded the category of woman to include Zora Neale Hurston, Jacquelyn Grant, bell hooks, and Lil' Kim. The daunting question stretched the category of woman to also include our Latina sisters, our Asian sisters, our Native American sisters, our Muslim sisters, our Buddhist sisters, our pagan sisters. The audacity to name and to define our world and how we think it ought to be is, by the telling of Alice Walker, simply, a womanist way of being in the world.

### Wanting to Know: An Epistemology of Explosive Proportion

Walker's four-part definition of womanist suggests in part 1 that a constitutive element of womanist includes, "Wanting to know more and in greater depth than is considered 'good' for one." The radicality of this statement as it relates to and portrays Black women could easily be overlooked or dismissed. For African-American women to still "want to know more and in greater depth" after hundreds of years of the most heinous version of slavery known to humanity, then the brutality of segregation and Jim Crow, and now the insidiousness of invisible racism/sexism in this post-modern era, is, for me, astonishing—is remarkable. I want to say two things about womanist epistemology. First, African-American women survived systems that were intentionally designed to silence and render us docile and obedient, in every sense of the word. These systems were designed to strip us of our humanity, to strip us of our capacity to love and be loved, to strip us of our will to know and be known.[2]

Scholars have debated if the article entitled "Let's Make a Slave"[3] attributed to Willie Lynch is fiction or nonfiction. Womanist theologian, Dr. Delores Williams, suggested in a lecture at New Brunswick Seminary (2001) that regardless of the genesis of this text, there is truth to be mined from its gruesome disclosure of the treatment of African slaves by White slave owners. Dr. Williams argued, and I concur, that some sources used by scholars can be sources whose origins are questionable, but whose content is irrefutable.

The Lynch article demonstrates the formulaic approach suggested for "breaking" African and African-American slaves into subservience. Specifically about African-American women the article states:

Take the female and run a series of test on her to see if she will submit to your desires willingly. Test her in every way, because she is the most important factor for good economics. If she shows any sign of resistance in submitting completely to your will, do not hesitate to use the bull whip on her to extract that last bit of bitch out of her. Take care not to kill her, for in doing so, you spoil good economics. When in complete submission, she will train her offspring in the early years to submit to labor when they become of age. Understanding is the best thing.[4]

African-American women survived[5] a holocaust that intended, not our death, but intended to rob us of our ability to determine and choose. The systems of oppression have attempted to force us to believe that other people, specifically White folks and Black men, better determine what knowledge is, what we are to know, what we need, what we think, and how we are to be and become in the world. These systems of domination told Black women that we will not and cannot determine what is "good" for our selves. "Breaking" us meant that African-American women should only want to know what the "master" wants us to know. We are intended, as oppressed people, to distrust our own judgment, our own processes of knowledge. What is "good" for us is told to us by the oppressor—all we need to do is comply.

Walker is suggesting that after surviving the well-documented history of forced labor, beatings, bombings, lynching, rape—terrorism of unfathomable proportion—Black women wanting to know more and in greater depth is a testament to the indomitable spirit of Black women and our seemly limitless quest for and ability to create hope. Walker's epistemology of hope is born in the moments between "Nobody Knows the Trouble I Seen" and "Glory Hallelujah."[6] It is between "Oh My God!" and "Oh Thank God!" that hope has her agency. Hope bridges the paradox between the downtrodden reality described by Lynch and our wanting to know more and in greater depth than is considered "good" for one. This knowing the world through the lens of hope is, for African-American women, a knowing that believes and stands in solidarity with the notion that "earth has no sorrow that heaven cannot heal." Ironically, the buttress for the bridge of hope between our tortured reality and the sweet by and by is described in the words penned by a slave ship captain:

> Through many dangers, toils, and snares,
> I have already come;
> Tis grace has brought me safe thus far,
> And grace will lead me home.
> The Lord has promised good to me,
> His word my hope secures;
> He will my shield and portion be
> As long as life endures.[7]

African-American women, by *Dr.* Walker's telling, have fought and will continue to fight for our ability to choose and determine for ourselves. We still, after generations of cruelty, are unwavering in our belief that we have the right to exercise choice. We refuse anyone's will but our own.

Black women's refusal to let others determine for them includes our relationship with the Divine. God told Adam and Eve to leave the tree of knowledge alone. Eve, in the womanist spirit, said that she wanted to determine what to know and how to know it. Genesis 3:6 reads, "So when the woman saw that the tree was good for food, and that it was a delight to the eyes, and that the tree was to be desired to make one wise, she took of its fruit and ate; and she also gave some to her husband, who was with her, and he ate (New Revised Standard Version). For Eve, all knowledge should be made available to her, by her own choosing. The necessity for a woman to control her own determination and ability to choose is so critical that, for Eve, even God could not make the determination for her. Womanists, like Sister Eve, resist having others control our knowing with every fiber of our collective being. Dr. Williams said parenthetically at the New Brunswick lecture, "If you got any bitch left in ya' you better keep it." In typical womanist fashion, Dr. Williams demonstrates the Black woman's ability to take what is considered "bad"—in this case being a bitch—and turning it on its head to become not only good but also desirable. We audaciously take the theological, moral, and social boundaries placed on us by White society and by men and shatter those expectations and limitations. A womanist epistemology affirms what others condemn. It is an epistemology that explodes what others would say is uncouth, impolite, or sinful. Womanists take the story of Eve and turn it from a story of human condemnation to a story of self-determination. A womanist epistemology pushes preestablished boundaries—even boundaries as sacred as the role of Eve in the fall. This epistemology of hope is able to hear the essential gospel no matter where it comes from—even when it comes from the cracked and parched lips of a slave ship captain singing about "amazing grace."

When our Black, male counterparts were shaping Black theology in the templates of Barth, reinforcing a ransom theology whose salvation was dependent upon spilled blood and Patriarchy, womanist theologians looked past Abraham and saw Hagar. Womanist theologians speculated another way of conceiving the world and our place in it is as children of Hagar. Our epistemology of hope is grounded in the notion that change, reframing, re-thinking, re-imagining, re-naming, re-structuring, re-conceiving—birthing anew, is not only possible but also necessary.

And second concerning womanist epistemology, African-American women invested in controlling our own determination and purpose has an additional dimension of astonishing proportion. Consider that knowing, at its best, expands to include issues of ethical reflection. Ethical reflection moves beyond issues of self-care and self-worth into realms of care for others and care for the planet. When Black women say we want to "know more" we are including dimensions of ethical considerations. For Black women, knowing does not dismiss the oppressor nor overlook the oppressor. Instead, knowing includes care for those who seek to oppress us along with the oppressed. Knowing includes the creativity necessary to care for those who tortured us as well as care for the tortured. Knowing includes the experiences of the perpetrators of violence as well as the victims of violence. The pop-culture psychology being espoused through the media would argue that it is not "good" if knowing included care by the rape victim for the rapist; love by the tortured for the torturer; compassion by the lynched for the noose-man. Our society would ask that we see reality in a feeble dichotomy—care of self OR care for others. Black women have refused this false dichotomy. Black women know we must care for self AND others—it is a "both/and" reality. We earnestly cared for the children we mammied while at the same time fervently plotted to sabotage the plantation and gain our freedom. This "both/and" vantage point allows Black women to explode old paradigms of hopelessness and set about the creation of new worlds of liberation, forgiveness, and redemption. The epistemology that Walker describes in her definition/prophecy is a radical epistemology steeped in hope and framed in self-determination. This womanist epistemology breaks through and expands Christian paradigms and strains toward a new reality.

## Questioning for Investigation Rather Than Exhibition

I am concerned now in this final section with bringing *Dr.* Walker's definition of womanist and my reflection on epistemology into action in the theological school classroom. I want to briefly describe a dynamic of my classroom that helps me see the epistemology of hope taking shape for my students.

Classrooms can be places where learners attempt to reduce knowledge to that which can dazzle or deceive. Too often, learners are more concerned with the appearance of knowing than with the genuine investigation which will enable one to come to know, deeply, a subject and our world. In our antiquated educational system, teaching has been reduced to and cheapened into a privatized delivery of facts and data. Classrooms are too often places of violence where questioning has more to do with conquest than inquisition.

Teaching which emerges from a womanist epistemology is teaching that wants to know in greater depth than is considered good for all parties involved. A womanist pedagogy would invite teachers and learners alike to act grown up, responsible, serious. Love of self, others, subject, and the Spirit would be a hallmark. Parker Palmer writes, "Teaching, like any truly human activity, emerges from one's inwardness, for better or worse. As I teach, I project the condition of my soul onto my students, my subject, and our way of being together. The entanglements I experience in the classroom are often no more or less than the convolutions of my inner life."[8] For a womanist teacher, "projecting the condition of my soul" often means projecting my hunger and thirst to know the right way.[9]

All professors have taught classes with one or two students who, when a question is posed, raise their hands or blurt out an answer—a kind of "first strict" in the classroom dialogue. These students believe that it is more important to get the attention of the teacher by answering the question quickly than it is to have a good answer. This technique is often employed by the student who has not read the assigned readings nor has taken time to understand the assigned readings. The student believes that if he/she answers early and often this will give the teacher the impression that they have read and have something of value to add to the conversation, when, in fact, the student who speaks first often has the agenda, not of learning, but of giving the perception of learning. In these instances, answering is reduced to exhibitionism. The student assumes that the more they speak, the more favorably the teacher will look upon them. The trite contribution of these students often reduces class discussions to a pooling of ignorance. In a effort to squelch these kinds of power plays in my classrooms and in an effort to demand that my students prepare themselves for class by reading and discussing before class, I have assigned each student, as homework, to bring three questions to class based on the readings. Then, instead of me asking questions, they ask the questions. It is quite easy to judge, even by fellow students, those questions that reflect a measure of having read the assignments and possess a depth of understanding.

The assignment is very straightforward. Students are to write three questions which arose for them from the reading assignments. They are not to bring answers to class, only the questions. I tell my students that the questions are more important than the answers. I explain that whoever asks the questions has the power. I chide my students by telling them that the great task of faith is to ask questions.

I further explain that there are ways to strengthen questions. Some questions are stronger than others. Questions need to be clear, fairly succinct, and direct. If the question is convoluted, then for our purposes, it is a weak question that needs to be strengthened.

There are strong questions and weak questions. Weak questions merely require regurgitation of facts or data. Weak questions assume a basic lack of knowledge and ask only that the answerer demonstrate minimal comprehension. Weak questions ask "how" a concept is applied or "how" information is to be used—fishing for recipes or formulaic approaches. Weak questions are more concerned with eliciting information than promoting reflective analysis. Strong questions, I explain, encourage the answerer to seek analysis by seeing patterns, organizing, and recognizing hidden meanings. They encourage the answerer to use old ideas to create new ones. They assess, evaluate, or verify.[10] Once the majority of the students begin to consistently write strong questions (in two to four weeks), we move to the political nature of questions and questioning. I suggest to students that questions conjure dreams, dreams of how it could be or might be. Questions are tools of hope. I cite the following possible political agendas or politicized strategies of questioning. We ask questions to (1) promote awareness in another—questioning forces people to deal with the particular perspectives, worldviews, values, and attitudes. Sojourner Truth asked, "Ain't I a Woman?" The Egyptian princess, by bringing a Hebrew child into the palace, raised questions all over Pharaoh's court. We question to (2) protest—questioning puts people on notice of an intent not to comply or an intent to continue to think differently; refusal. Celie, of *The Color Purple*, asked, "What God done for me?" Willie Lynch and those like him needed such a systematic plan because African-American women had steely attitudes of refusal—they had unrelenting questions even while shackled. We question to (3) suppose—questioning is a gesture of hope and possibility. Song writers use questions to inspire and to encourage: "Why Should I Feel Discouraged?" "What Shall I Render?" "I Do, Don't You?" "Ain't Dat Good News?" "Didn't My Lord Deliver Daniel?" Alice Walker set out to describe and define a source of hope, a deep well which had sustained our people for generations. Her definition asks that we, this "here-and-now" generation, pay attention to that which has sustained us to this point. We question to (4) explore existential realities of identity and self-hood, "Mama, why are we brown, pink, and yellow, and our cousins are white, beige, and black?" Eve, like most of us, asked for that which would make her wise.

I remind my students that questions are never politically neutral. I recount *Dr.* Walker's caution concerning wanting to know more than is "good" as a caution for the necessity of keen political antenna. Knowledge is power. The yearning to know and the will to find out in depth puts womanists at danger with White folks, Black men, and at times, other women of color. By week five or six of the semester, composing questions has captured the imagination of most of my students. I witness their move from mechanically fulfilling a homework assignment to attempting the artistry of questioning in earnest. I remind them that the shape of their question is critical to their investigation because the question will dictate the journey. Students who take on the challenge of learning to shape strong, pithy, interesting questions become intolerant of students who only want to get the teacher's attention with trite answers.

Once my students know how to write strong questions and can see the inherent political nature of questioning, my final goal is for them to take on the task of writing interesting questions. I tell my students that questions which echo the norms of their local church and stay within the confines of established religiosity and political correctness are, by my standard, uninteresting. If in their questioning, I sense that they are simply trying to build a better mouse trap—I call those questions uninteresting. Uninteresting questions are the mundane, stale, rehearsed, misplaced questions that seem like they are out of sync for our complex reality. For example, my Black, women students might ask, "Isn't the man to be the head of the household and the church?" Or my White students will ask, "Wasn't the civil rights movement a 'Black' movement?" Or they will ask, "Why don't lay people in the church know more about the Bible and theology?"

I ignore their uninteresting questions and tell them that interesting questions are those questions that presuppose a pioneering mentality. I look for questions which reject, shatter, even, explode the rehearsed doctrinal answers of bygone church days. Interesting questions are those which invite the Holy Spirit to show herself in new ways, act in new ways, bless us in new ways. Interesting questions are open and honest—they demonstrate curiosity, empathy, and hope. They are questions, that when I hear them in class, make me shout "That's it—Bingo!" An African adage says that where you start will be where you end up. If you start your inquiry with a dull, unimaginative, prearranged question, your journey will be likewise. If you start with an imaginative, creative, life-giving question the possibilities are vast. It will be from interesting questions that we will create new metaphors for theology, theodicy, and the better practice of ministry. Like Nelle Morton, I am attempting to hear my students into speech.[11] I believe that teaching students to question is a liberative act—it is teaching as a practice of freedom.[12] Their questions allow them to explore and interrogate their own terrains and their own adventures. The course moves from an experience of the professor's thinking into an experience of our collective thinking.

We, as Christians, have never been faced with the challenge of being faithful in a technological age. Our ancestors faced the challenges of their eras and our presence attests to their faithfulness. We are now faced with the task of faithfulness now. That is to say, how will we be church, do church, in an era that is just being born, just being refined. We are enmeshed in a post-modern, technological era, dank with racism, classism, sexism, heterosexism, and imperialism, where domination is seen as the better way of being. Recognizing that we are pioneers in this era where faith has not been tested nor honed, we must pay close attention to the questions we ask if we are to attend in new ways to the cries for justice and liberation. When my students ask strong, interesting questions, with a political agenda in mind, is when I know my students are beginning to know more and in greater depth than is considered good for them or me.

NOTES

1. The author has coined a word here by adding—ian to the word Webster, which refers to the commonly used Webster's Dictionary, and using it as an adjective.

2. Patricia Hill Collins, *Black Feminist Thought* (New York: Routledge, 2000).

3. www.angelfire.com/ne/savedbygrace/lynch.html.

4. Ibid., 3.

5. Lyrics, in part, from the hymn "Come Ye Disconsolate."

6. A reference to the Negro spiritual "Nobody Knows the Trouble I Seen."

7. Lyrics from the popular hymn "Amazing Grace."

8. Palmer Parker, *The Courage to Teach* (San-Francisco: Jossey-Bass, 1998), 2.

9. Ibid.

10. A reference to Bloom's *Taxonomy*, http://www.coun.uvic.ca/learn/program/hndouts/bloom.html. Adapted from B. S. Bloom, ed., *Taxonomy of Educational Objectives: The Classification of Educational Goals: Handbook I, Cognitive Domain* (New York: Longmans, Green, 1956).

11. Nelle Morton, *The Journey Is Home* (Boston: Beacon Press, 1994), 55–56.

12. bell hooks, *Teaching to Transgress* (New York: Routledge, 1994).

# Part III

# Redemptive Self-Love

REDEMPTIVE SELF-LOVE—[the third tenet of womanism] 1. an assertion of the humanity, customs, and aesthetic value of Black women in contradistinction to the commonly held stereotypes characteristic of white solipsism. The admiration and celebration of the distinctive and identifiable beauty of Black women. "I am *black and beautiful* O ye daughters of Jerusalem." Song of Solomon 1:5, NRSV

"celebrating life in the midst of suffering and walking in love in the midst of hate. This power of wisdom, love, and creativity found in God and omnipresent in creation"   —Baker-Fletcher

The ability and permission to know "that it is all right to be black and female."   —Douglas

2. a re-affirmation of Black womanhood in all of its full creation. The essence and freedom of Black women's cultural, physical, spiritual expression

"the Spirit of life"   —Baker-Fletcher

3. Black women's unconditional and relentless resolve to enjoy the range of their common sense and the pleasures of their individual senses

"making the invisible visible in a movement to garner freedom in love . . . regardless."   —Kirk-Duggan

"to walk the path of light with enlightened ancestors and Spirit while fulfilling one's given destiny"   —Settles

# I've Been Mixed Like Cornbread

## *RevSisRaedorah*

I've been mixed like cornbread
And I'm not that instant brand
Measured out, not by metered cup
But with the skills of a knowing hand.

The flour of my soul
And the meal of my mind
Rises with the yeast
And the salts of time.

    I've been mixed like cornbread.

Two eggs for self identity
A dash of sugar to make me sweet
Add the day old fatback drippings
And this cornbread's complete.

    I've been mixed like cornbread.

I tickle your taste buds to a salivary greeting
After exactly 23 minutes at 375
Top me off with the real fresh butter
You welcome our meeting as I now arrive.

    I've been mixed like cornbread.

So, serve me up I'm a favorite dish
With the likes of collard greens, buttermilk, or fish.
I've been mixed like cornbread
And I'm here to compliment
Your first course in life.

# Chapter 9

# Twenty Years a Womanist
## *An Affirming Challenge*

### *Kelly Brown Douglas*

A womanist is "interested in grown up doings." "Serious." She "Loves herself. *Regardless.*"[1] I remember the struggle well. "Go out and play," my mother would say exasperated with the questions I asked. I asked about this man Martin Luther King, Jr., who was on the news all the time. I asked about those four little girls in Birmingham who adults whispered were killed at church. I asked about the riots that were going on all around. But, my mother said those were grown-up things and I needed to go play with the other children. I remember the struggle well. I was too "serious" because I liked to read. I was too much of a "tomboy," because I liked sports. I wasn't a "fly girl" because my hair was too coarse and my skin was too dark. I wasn't this; I wasn't that. I remember the struggle well. And so, many years later, when I first opened Alice Walker's book *In Search of Our Mothers' Gardens* and read her womanist definition, before I knew it—before I could do anything about it—tears were flowing from my eyes. The words on that page connected with me in a deep place; a place of pain, a place of struggle, a place of trying to fit in, a place of trying to be me and to love me, "regardless."

A womanist "is to feminist as purple is to lavender." She is "committed to survival and wholeness of entire people, male *and* female."[2] I remember well the pull and the push. I remember the not knowing where to be, not knowing how to claim my space. I remember the feminists on my college campus—Ann and Anne, Nancy and Joan. I remember them telling me that I belonged with them, that it was a new day—women could stand on their own. But I did not want to be with them. I did not want to be on my own. Didn't they get it? I was black, and my color made a difference to me.

I wanted to be with my brothers. I wanted to be in the Black Student Union. I remember well the pull. Yet, I also remember well the push. I remember the brothers in seminary telling me that women did not belong in the pulpit. I remember the "brother" priest trying to stop my ordination to the Episcopal priesthood because I was female. Didn't *they* get it? Instead of being against one another we needed to be with and for one another. I was committed to them, why were they not committed to me?

I remember well the profound sense of being torn. I did not know where I was going to fit in, with the feminist or with the brothers. And so, when I first read Alice Walker's words something swelled up inside me that I could not control; with tears in my eyes I jumped out of my chair and leaped into the air shouting, "This is it! This is it!"

Twenty years ago my first encounter with the idea of being a womanist was an affirming encounter. The womanist idea affirmed who I was as a black woman. It affirmed me in all of my uniqueness. It let me know that it was all right to be black, female, and me. "Womanist" allowed me to affirm myself. It, thus, gave me a place from which to speak. It gave me a voice. It gave me the voice to speak out of my own experience of pain and struggle. It gave me a place to stand. It allowed me to stand with my black female sisters as they also struggled to find their way, their voice, and their place. Essentially, Walker's notion of womanist lifted up the black female story. It verified the power of the black female voice to speak with authority about the complicated and wonderfully "adventurous" reality of being embodied black and woman. The womanist concept quickly moved from being words on a page to symbolizing a movement of black women claiming our voices, claiming our spaces to tell our own diverse stories of living.

As I have looked back over these twenty years, there is no doubt that for me the most significant part of my encounter with the womanist idea was that it provided me the space to be my black female self, and most important, to feel good about it. It was not until I was able to stand confidently and securely in my own experience that I was then able to enter into dialogue with the women of my past and my present, and to learn from and be challenged by them. It is for this reason that the aspect of the womanist idea that is most significant to me as I do womanist theological work today is its dialogical nature.

## The Significance of the Womanist Dialogue

### Epistemological Privilege

The womanist dialogue goes like this: "*Mama*, I'm walking to Canada and I'm taking you and a bunch of other slaves with me." Reply: "It wouldn't be the first time."[3] This dialogue, first and foremost, reminds me from whom I receive my wisdom: from my mama and all of those other black women not necessarily in the academy—those everyday women who sit in the pews of black churches on Sunday morning looking for the sustenance to carry on during the week. These are the women who supply womanist religious scholars with the substance of our work. They are the resources of our knowledge about God and the meaning of God for black women and men in struggle. It is their faith that provides the foundation of our womanist theological claims. It is from out of their experiences of crafting a life for themselves and their families that our theological questions and even answers come. Essentially, the womanist dialogue makes clear that it is these everyday women, the "mamas," within the black church community who have "*epistemological privilege*" in womanist work. Let us thus explore what it means that these women have epistemological privilege.

First, the epistemological privilege of everyday black women readily challenges notions of knowledge. It compels womanist scholars to recognize that knowledge is not simply that which has been legitimated by the standards of a white patriarchal academy, indeed, such legitimated knowledge may not be knowledge at all. Rather, knowledge is characterized by that "taken-for-granted wisdom," to which sociologist Patricia Hill Collins refers.[4] This is a wisdom that emerges from the lives of black women as they struggle for well-being and freedom for themselves and their families. For womanist theologians to take seriously the "taken-for-granted wisdom" of our mamas means that we must, as Hill Collins suggests, listen to this wisdom and then rearticulate it in such a way that it continues to sustain and empower black women in their daily struggles against oppressive realities. To privilege this "taken-for-granted" wisdom further means that womanist scholarship must steadfastly affirm that *authentic* knowledge is that knowledge which is intimately connected to life sustaining and liberating activity. It is that which contributes to "survival and wholeness of entire peoples," particularly black people. Womanist theology, therefore, must make clear that authentic knowledge is not that which fosters any form of oppressive power. On the contrary, it is that which challenges dominating power, including the complex discourses that help to maintain such power.

Michel Foucault reminds us that "power," especially inequitable power, projects a "will to knowledge." In other words, power enlists the "intellectual" community to provide the necessary knowledge base to legitimate and sustain it.[5] During the eighteenth century, for instance, white racist power called upon the scientific and religious communities to provide scholarly and theological justification for the inhumane enslavement and brutalization of black people. Both communities cooperated with white racist power, thereby generating the troubling discourses of scientific and religious racism. Womanist theology must consistently point out the specious reality of discourses of power. Specifically, it should clarify that discursive power is not knowledge at all, but only an insidious pretense to knowledge.

Essentially, the epistemological privilege of "everyday" black women means that womanist theology is constrained to contest what black mama's have regularly challenged in their daily realities through their taken-for-granted-wisdom: the validity of discursive power. Such contesting wisdom often questions the "truth" of this discourse, thus impugning its very validity. In so doing, black women's taken-for-granted wisdom provides a buffer of resistance to the influence of discursive power on the lives of their children, if not communities. Such contesting wisdom is exemplified by a dialogue I had with my grandmother one day: "What did you learn in school today, she asked?" I replied, "I learned that Thomas Jefferson was a great man. He was the father of democracy." And she retorted, "Yeah, did they also tell you that he owned slaves?" Such wisdom is also found in an observation made by my mother when she saw me rooting for the cowboys as I was watching TV. She said simply, "Be careful who you root for because they might not be rooting for you."

Again, it is the taken-for-granted wisdom of everyday black women, a wisdom that comes from out of their daily experiences of living, that suggests the meaning of authentic knowledge for womanist work. Authentic knowledge is that which challenges the discourses of oppressing power at the same time that it sustains and empowers black people, especially black women in their daily struggles against such power. This understanding leads us to a second implication of everyday black women's epistemological privilege.

That everyday black women have epistemological privilege obligates womanist theologians to maintain a meaningful dialogue with the black women in our black church communities. This is the important, privileged dialogue. It is not only from these women that we must learn, but it is also to these women that we are most accountable. What we as womanist religious scholars say must "ring true" to their struggles and dreams for a free, liberated, and whole life. Our work must speak to their complex life realities. The "truth" of our theological claims does not depend upon its conformity to certain "scholarly," that is, theoretical notions of "right thinking," especially as those notions are disinterested in the life and well-being of black women and men. Rather, womanist theological integrity is measured by its life-enhancing value in the lives of black women and those they love. Inasmuch as womanist theological claims foster the life and dignity of black women and men, then they have credibility. When they do not, they loose their credibility.

Hence, what we as womanist religious scholars do in the academy is at best a second step. The primary focus of our work is black church women. The integrity of womanist work depends on such a focus. In this regard, womanist religious scholars must resist the temptation to retreat behind the walls of seminaries and universities. We must continue to remain involved in the lives of ordinary black women in the church and in community organizations and groups. We must persist in doing the hard work of finding creative ways to make our work accessible to these women, so that again, it remains true to its central concern: to move black women and men forward in their struggles for life and wholeness. Recognition of this concern suggests another challenge implied by the womanist dialogue itself.

## Moral Agency

Again, the womanist dialogue goes like this, "I'm going to Canada, and *I'm taking a bunch of other slaves with me.*"[6] Not only does the womanist dialogue remind womanists from whom our knowledge comes—and hence the epistemological privilege of everyday black women—but it also clarifies the meaning of "true moral agency." Moral agency is not characterized by the systemic and institutional forces that undercut the well-being of black women. Instead, it is seen in the unfailing physical, emotional, and spiritual energy black women have historically marshaled to engage in acts of resistance to their oppression, be it spitting in a master's cup or leading hundreds of enslaved toward freedom. Moral agency is

thus defined by efforts to frustrate and dismantle any systems or structures based on unjust privilege, such as the privilege of being white, of
being male, and/or of being heterosexual. The moral agency suggested by
the struggles of black women means that womanist work must not be
concerned with securing privilege in places of power, even if that privilege
is for black women. Rather, womanist moral agency manifests itself as
womanists firmly attest that certain systems and structures, which serve to
exclude and penalize people for not being of the "privileged" race, gender,
or sexual orientation, are inherently evil and cannot be mended to be
more just. Consequently, compromises should not be made with insidious
systems. These systems must instead be dismantled.

Womanist moral agency further requires that we as womanist scholars
name our own relative points of privilege within our various institutions
and communities. Similar to Jesus asking the man with many demons to
name the demons that inhabited him before he could be healed, before
our community can be made "whole," womanists are required to name the
demons that are ours, that is, the ways in which we benefit from or even
wittingly or unwittingly participate in and/or sustain structures of dominating power.[7] For instance, many of us enjoy the privilege of education
and subsequently maintain a certain status within various institutions and
communities. Some of us may also benefit from heterosexual privilege,
thereby allowing us to enjoy certain rights not granted to nonheterosexual
persons in a heterosexist church and society. Yet, the moral agency of
womanist work is found not in securing or creating a place of privilege
for ourselves in society, the academy, or any other institution of power.
Rather, it is found in naming and disrupting systems of unjust privilege.
Regardless of the relative societal and institutional privilege that we may
have, womanist moral agency demands that we work against any sense of
privilege or comfort. If nothing else, we as womanist scholars must work
from our spaces of discomfort, not privilege, holding ourselves accountable not to those on the inside of various institutions or at the center of
particular communities, but to those who find themselves on the very underside of them. In short, the moral agency of womanist religious scholarship is found in doing the kind of work that responds to the voices from
the underside, thereby agitating for the radical and revolutionary change
required to ensure that all human beings have access to what is needed to
live and to fulfill their God-given potential. It is, in other words, characterized by agitating against systems and structures which confer unjust privilege, even when that privilege may be our own. Womanist moral agency is

about nothing less than "taking a bunch of other slaves with us," toward life and wholeness.

## Beyond Racialized and Genderized Paradigms

The nature of womanist moral agency also necessitates another dialogue: one with others who also find themselves marginalized and on the underside of white, patriarchal, heterosexual webs of privilege, whether or not those others are black. As true moral agents, womanists are compelled beyond simple racialized and even genderized paradigms of oppression. Womanist theology is in fact constrained by its own defining commitment to the "survival and wholeness of entire people" so that to clarify that womanist identity requires more than simply being born black and female. While the significance of black female identity should remain a primary marker of what it means to be a womanist, as womanist does point to the lived experience of being black and female, it cannot be the sole measure of what it means to be a womanist. Womanist identity also necessitates an existential moral commitment to advancing life, freedom, and dignity for all people, "regardless." In this respect, womanist moral agency means that womanist theology must always oppose, and certainly not collude with, human oppression, whether or not the oppression is racially coded or gender based. Such an understanding of womanist moral agency, and hence womanist identity, leads to another challenging aspect of Walker's womanist definition particularly as it involves womanist dialogue.

A womanist, Walker says, is "audacious" and "courageous." If womanists are to be guided by Walker's definition and live into the womanist identity, then to be womanist is not only to engage in the easy dialogues but also, most especially, to engage in the difficult ones. It means raising issues that maybe our mamas would not dare to raise or even know to raise.

It has perhaps become easy for us as womanists to engage in dialogues on race or gender oppression because, for the most part, we are really talking about a "them," not an "us." Womanists represent the oppressed race and/or the marginalized gender. Yet, we are obligated to move beyond the places of our displacement to the places of our discomfort and thus to enlist the difficult dialogues. To reiterate, we are to name the unjust privilege that even we/us may be wittingly and/or unwittingly complicit in maintaining. Womanist moral agency requires that "unctuousness" which Katie Cannon identifies—that boldness to expose the sin of our comfort zones.[8] And so, this means that we cannot ignore that part of Walker's womanist definition that says a womanist "loves other women sexually and or non-sexually." It cannot be said enough that womanist theology cannot refrain from addressing the difficult issues. It has to move beyond the boundaries of race and gender to confront issues that in any way involve the dignity and freedom of black women in particular and other persons in general. To do any less would be to betray the very meaning of womanist. Most urgently then, womanist theologians must address the challenges of sexuality.

## A Matter of Sexuality

The black community has suffered too long under the silence which it has typically maintained on matters of sexuality. Such silence has contributed to its slow response to the HIV/AIDS disease. Moreover, this silence has left unchallenged within the black church community heterosexist views and homophobic practices that generally negate the full humanity of non-heterosexual women and men. It is the task of womanist theology to forthrightly engage those beliefs and practices within the black faith community that indeed diminish and perhaps even terrorize the humanity and worth of particular human persons, namely, nonheterosexual women and men. Womanist theologians are compelled by our very womanist identity, and by the lives of those to whom we are accountable, to critically address the complex heterosexist socio/political/ecclesiastical realities and the homophobic theo-ideology that sanctions these realities. We, therefore, must do the hard work of frustrating and "debunking" heterosexist structuring and delegitimating homophobic rhetoric so that women and men can love as they choose to love—a love that begins with the ability to "love themselves, regardless." Let us briefly examine how womanist theologians might go about this task.

Womanist theologians must begin by challenging the view of sexuality that permeates black churches, that is, the view that affirms only "reproductive" sexual expression and condemns all other forms. Such a view is reflective of a *platonized* Christian tradition that has suborned the oppression of black people and women in general. This tradition has permeated the black faith tradition. In order to appreciate the influence of this view and the necessity for a womanist critique of it, let us look a little more closely at that which I am identifying as *platonized* Christianity.[9]

## Platonized Christianity

One of Christianity's greatest paradoxes is its attitude toward the human body. Since its origins in a first-century Hellenistic world, Christianity's regard for the body has been enigmatic. Christianity's central confession, God's unique presence in the first-century Jew from Nazareth, basically esteems the body as a vessel of divine revelation. The divine incarnation ostensibly precluded as acceptable to Christianity any belief that reviled the human body/flesh. Yet, there has been a prominent Christian tradition, platonized Christianity, that has denigrated and demonized the human body and thus become problematic for various peoples.

In efforts to peaceably exist in the Greco-Roman world in which they were a part, as well as a reflection of the Hellenized Jewish tradition from which they emerged, early Christian thinkers and apologists integrated into their Christian theologies the most prominent Greek philosophies of their day. In so doing, they established within mainstream Christian thought a platonic- and stoic-influenced view toward the body and sexuality. The platonic belief in the perfect immaterial world (the world of reason/spirit/soul) and the imperfect material world (the world of passion/flesh/body) became a part of a significant strand of Christian thinking. The stoic regard for reason and disregard for passion was also integrated into Christianity. As this body-devaluing ideology was appropriated by influential Christian interpreters, platonized Christianity developed.

Platonized Christianity invariably places the body in an antagonistic relationship with the soul. The soul is divinized while the body is demonized. The soul is revered as the key to salvation. The body is condemned as a source of sin. The locus of bodily sin is human passion, that is, sexual pleasure. Hence, a "sacred" disdain for the sexual body pervades the Christian theological tradition.

In the American theological scene, platonized Christianity found perhaps its most comfortable home in Evangelical Protestantism. Within this tradition, the measure of one's salvation is notably marked by one's ability to be "converted" from the ways of the world. True piety is marked by "self-denial" and resistance to bodily temptations, such as sexual pleasure. Evangelical clergymen such as Cotton Mather prayed that God would not hold against their children the activity they engaged in to produce them.

Perhaps ironically, at the same time that religious racism began to flourish in America (owing in no small way to platonized Christianity), black people were most influenced by platonized Christianity. During

America's eighteenth-century religious revivals, a significant population of black women and men were converted to Evangelical Protestant thought. In large measure then, it was as a result of these eighteenth-century conversions that platonized views toward the human body and thus sexuality were integrated into black religious thinking, eventually becoming a substantial strand within the black faith tradition.

Clearly, one of the most problematic aspects of this platonized theological tradition, especially as the black faith community has appropriated it, is its view toward sexuality. Platonized Christian theology advocates a dualistic perspective on sexuality. This perspective suggests only two ways in which to engage in sexual activity, one tolerable, not inherently sinful, and the other intolerable, sinful. Procreative use is tolerably good; nonprocreative use is intolerably evil. Characteristic of platonized Christianity, a third possibility is not offered. A platonized perspective on sexuality does not allow for sexual activity to be an expression of an intimate, that is, loving relationship. For all intents and purposes, platonized Christianity severs intimate sexuality from loving relationality. This dualistic platonized perspective is what pulsates through the Apostle Paul's warning that it is "better to marry than to burn with passion."[10]

Womanist work must challenge this platonized view of sexuality. In so doing, it should make clear that it is this platonized view of sexuality that has suborned the sexualized terror of black people and the sexualized oppression of women. And, it is this view that secretes and maintains the socio/political/ecclesiastical tyranny of homophobia and heterosexism.

Characteristically socially oppressed and marginalized groups, such as black people and nonheterosexual men and women, are a sexualized people. They are routinely objectified according to their sexuality, which has already been essentialized in respect to genital activity. Therefore, they are defined according to their supposed sexual activity and prowess. For instance, a prominent justification for the exploitation of black bodies and general terrorizing of black people has been the notion that black people are a hypersexualized people. Hence, white racist power has characterized black men as rapacious predators—"mandingo bucks"—and black women as promiscuous seductresses—"Jezebels." Given the ideological notion that black people were naturally given to sinful sexual activity (that is, lustful not procreative sex), white society was able to cast black men and women as evil beings in need of control if not destruction. To be sure, such a sexualized view of black men and women has allowed for the consistent dehumanization of them and the denigration of their bodies with relative "theological" impunity.

Similar to black people, the oppression of nonheterosexual people has also been supported by an erroneous sexualization of them. They too are wrongly caricatured in relation to their presumed sexual practices. Consequent to being characterized as a people categorically engaged in non-procreative sexual activity, nonheterosexual persons are at best deemed sinners in need of redemption (i.e., conversion from a nonheterosexual lifestyle) or at worst incorrigibly depraved. The point of the matter is, a platonized view of sexuality readily lends itself to the sacrosanct derision and disparagement of certain peoples. For inasmuch as certain people are considered a "lustfully" sexualized people, and lustful sexuality is seen as sinful, then those people are likewise deemed sinful, if not evil. Moreover, their marginalization within church and society finds sacred, theological cover.

Once again, womanist identity, and thus moral agency, necessitates that womanist theology challenge this platonized view of sexuality in an effort to dislodge heterosexist and homophobic oppression within the black church and community. In so doing, womanist theology is compelled to put forth a new sexual ethic. Such an ethic should reflect the sacred regard for the body revealed by God's incarnate revelation in Jesus. At the same time, this ethic should restore the relationship between sexual intimacy and loving relationship, therefore disavowing a platonized, dualistic view of sexuality. To reiterate, a platonized view of sexuality views sexuality as either reproductively good or lustfully bad. There is no third sexual option. Sexuality is not granted the space to be relationally right. It is disconnected from intimate relationality and, thus, not seen as an expression of loving relationship. A womanist sexual ethic will restore the connection between sexual intimacy and loving relationship. This ethic will clarify that inasmuch as sexuality is expressed in such a way which fosters loving relationship, then it is sacred and not sinful. It is only when sexual expression is objectified and disconnected from loving relationship that it becomes sinful. Within womanist theology sexuality itself will not be portrayed or seen as sinful. The objectification of sexuality, however (be it procreative or lustful objectification), will be regarded as sinful. The implications for such a sexual ethic are clear.

A theological view of sexuality that does not deem sexual expression itself as sinful mitigates the possibility for Christian collusion in the sexualized oppression of various peoples. Moreover, to reclaim the sacred dimensions of sexuality beyond procreation permits sacred validation of same-sexed loving relationships. In the end, for womanist theology to advocate a sexual ethic that challenges a platonized view of sexuality allows for womanist theology to live into its womanist identity and thus promote commitment to "survival and wholeness for entire people."

### The Womanist Affirmation

Not too long ago I was on a college campus delivering a lecture on the justice politics of the Black Church, particularly as it involves nonheterosexual expressions of sexuality. During the question-and-answer session a young black man stood up, identified himself as "unapologetically Christian," and then went on to vociferously make his point. He said that he did not understand why homosexuals had to insist on being where they were not wanted. He offered that they were not wanted in the church so they ought to leave. But then he ended by saying, quite proudly, that because the people of his church were so Christian they did not make the homosexual people leave. "Regardless of their sin," he said, "we love them and we make a place for them." After he completed his statement, the significantly black audience, erupted into applause. What I attempted to do in response to this young man was explain how the attitudes that he held toward nonheterosexuals mirrored the attitudes of whites toward blacks. I further explained that the sacred canopy he placed over his homophobia was the same one placed over racism. Essentially, I tried to live into my womanist identity by making clear that there could be absolutely no compromise with any kind of theo-ideology that justified the oppressive treatment of any human being.

After this same lecture, another young black man came up to me afterward. He pulled me aside and literally with tears in his eyes, he said, "Thank you. If just for a night I felt affirmed." This takes me back to where I began this essay.

My first encounter with the womanist idea, as I stated above, was an affirming encounter. It affirmed my voice. It affirmed who I was as a black female. What I have discovered over these last twenty years is that as I have tried to live into the womanist idea, it is in fact about affirmation—the affirmation of the voices of the weak, the powerless. The Apostle Paul said that God sometimes uses the weak to confound the strong. To be womanist is to know that God *does* use the weak to confound the strong, even when the strong may be our very black female selves.[11]

NOTES

1. Excerpted from womanist definition, Alice Walker, *In Search of Our Mothers' Gardens* (San Diego: Harcourt Brace Jovanovich, 1983), xi.

2. Ibid.

3. Ibid., xi, emphasis mine.

4. Patricia Hill Collins, *Black Feminist Thought: Knowledge, Consciousness and the Politics of Empowerment* (New York: Routledge, 1991), 31–32.

5. See Michel Foucault, *History of Sexuality: An Introduction*, vol. 1, trans. Robert Hurley (New York: Vintage Books, 1990).

6. Walker, *In Search of Our Mothers' Gardens,* xi, emphasis mine.

7. See, for instance, the story of Jesus and the man with many demons in Mark 5:1–20.

8. Katie Geneva Cannon, "Unctuousness as Virtue: According to the Life of Zora Neale Hurston," in *Katie's Canon: Womanism and the Soul of the Black Community* (New York: Continuum, 1995), 91ff.

9. This discussion of platonized Christianity is adopted from various discussions of this tradition in my previous work.

10. See 1 Corinthians 7:9.

11. See 1 Corinthians 1:27.

# Chapter 10

# A Womanist Journey

## Karen Baker-Fletcher

### First Steps

I remember the first day I ran across the word "womanist" in Alice Walker's *In Search of Our Mothers' Gardens*. It was sometime during the academic year of 1983–84. I was a third-year Master of Divinity student at Harvard Divinity School. I had been reading Walker's work along with the work of other black women writers and black feminist activists since around 1979–80. I called myself a black feminist but was frustrated with the agendas of white feminists at that time. In those days when one asked, "What about black women" in predominantly white feminist meetings, several white feminists inevitably responded that it was *more important to talk about women, because we are all women, than about race*. It was also common to hear the following logic when noting the importance of black women's thought and contributions: "But what about *women*?" "Black women are women," we would respond. This left me and many other black feminists during those days frustrated with the feminist movement. I say "in those days," but this logic continues to erupt among students that I teach today.

Gloria Hull, Patricia Bell Scott, and Barbara Smith wrote a book in 1982 entitled *All the Women Are White, All the Men Are Black, but Some of Us Are Brave*,[1] to name this frustration with the white feminist movement. They were also naming frustration with black men, activist and non-activist, who insisted that "feminism is white women's thing." Both sides, white women and black men, were insisting: "Are you black first or a woman first? Which side are you on?" The feminists insisted sexism was a deeper problem, while black men insisted racism was a deeper problem. It was as if we were being asked to split ourselves in two in some cruel game of tug-of-war. The underlying assumption on both sides was that we had no authority, agency, or freedom to name our whole selves.

When I read Walker's poetic coining of the term "womanist," I had that feeling I so often experience in reading a text by a black woman writer. I saw myself and the black women who had raised me, my elders and ancestors, cousins and aunts, living and dead, in her definition. I felt like I could breathe again as I read her definition of "womanist." I felt the roots that are the veins of my body being watered with the Spirit of life as her words touched my heart. Many black women around the country had a similar experience upon encountering Walker's words.

In 1982–83, I was the student member of a committee reviewing applications for the Women's Studies Research Associate and Fellowship Program at Harvard Divinity School. Katie Cannon's application was in the mix. Cannon was proposing a course on "Black Women's Literature as a Resource for a Constructive Ethic" which was just what I had been looking for and argued we all needed. By then, the faculty knew my own commitments to using black women's literature as a resource for constructing theology. There were other students who would take such a course. In the past, the program had invited Delores Williams, Marilyn Richardson, and Jacquelyn Grant as fellows for similar curricular reasons. Very quickly it became clear to the committee and eventually the faculty, that it was important to bring Cannon to the Divinity school for a year of research, writing, and teaching.

Cannon became a womanist mentor for several of us. It was a joy to receive "The First Katie Geneva Cannon Award," a freshly bound copy of her dissertation which gave me hope for my own future as a womanist scholar. I had had a desire for some time to get a Ph.D. focusing on black women's literature and theology. Cannon brought focus to this desire. I would not be writing this essay without her influence and without the movement of the Spirit. Womanism did not begin merely as an academic decision in a classroom, or at a meeting, but as a movement of the Spirit. This movement of the Spirit began before there was a womanist group at the American Academy of Religion, before anyone published an article or a book. It began with a melting of the heart when so many of us read Walker's words, based in the folk-culture of black women, particularly in America, of the last several centuries to the present.

## *Walker's Definition*

The term "womanist" was coined by the black American writer and activist Alice Walker (1944–). When Walker introduced a poetic "definition" of "womanist" in 1983, she described a "womanist" as "a black feminist or feminist of color." The term "womanist" is derived from the black folk expression, "You're acting womanish," as in "grown up" and "in charge."[2] In black culture, "womanish" signifies acting like a wise woman with agency.[3] A womanist is audacious and courageous. She is aware that the colored race is like a flower garden.[4] Walker's 1983 description reminds readers that African Americans used to call ourselves "colored people" because of our mixed ancestry. We come in many colors from the dark brown of pure chocolate to the hues of red clay, golden sand, and ivory. Historically, much of this mixture was the result of white men raping slave women or of loving relationships between black women and Native Americans. Walker, like others increasingly since the mid- to late twentieth century, has a multiracial daughter, Rebecca Walker, from her early marriage to a white, Jewish man.[5] Whether our children have been borne of violence or love, black women, in wisdom, have loved them in the power of the Spirit.

While much of black women's experience has been oppressive and painful, the power of creativity and love has emerged in the midst of the complexities of evil and suffering. Wisdom has been gained from the spiritual power of creating beauty out of ugliness, celebrating life in the midst of suffering, and walking in love in the midst of hate. This power of wisdom, love, and creativity is found in God, the Spirit that is omnipresent in creation.[6] Walker writes that she grew up in a small shack in rural Georgia. Her parents were sharecroppers. The shack had holes in the walls. To make their home beautiful, Alice Walker's mother placed yellow sunflowers in the "holey" shack, if you will.[7] In the power of the Spirit, she transformed ugliness into beauty. Walker's mother also kept a flower garden with brightly colored petunias that people came from miles around to see. Like so many poor, hard-working black women, she took scraps of clothing to make beautiful quilts to keep her family warm in winter.[8] My own grandmother, Lizzie Mae Baker, also made quilts. She could take scraps of food to make feasts for her family. This is what womanists mean in saying "God makes something out of nothing," "God makes a way out of no way," or "make do with what you've got." Divine creativity, the Spirit which is Love, is embodied in black women. It is present in all of creation. Womanists pass on the wisdom that has emerged from relationship with divine creativity and love to the generations.

In Walker's definition, a womanist desires healing and wholeness for *entire* communities, male and female.[9] She is committed to participating in what Charles Hartshorne calls "unsurpassable," "cosmic love."[10] This love is God's action toward the world. God is love. Alfred North White-head places this love in the fourth creative phase "in which the universe accomplishes its actuality." In this final creative phase, "the love of God for the world," there is an integration of the Spirit and creation in which the initial aim of God is realized on earth as in heaven.[11]

For Walker, by entering creation and loving it, we love the Spirit. She calls all creatures, including herself, "earthlings." She believes that through love, the earth, who is our mother, and its earthlings can be saved.[12] Walker's term, "womanist," accurately represents the type of unconditional love that black women historically have passed on to the generations. The process metaphysician Charles Hartshorne refers to this type of love as "cosmic love" and "unsurpassable love"[13] Such love does not fear oppression but overcomes it. Womanists can agree with process metaphysicians that liberation movements require an understanding of God as loving, creative activity. Divine, loving, creative activity is the power of liberation movement in womanist theology. Without cosmic, creating love, womanists are bereft of power and hope.[14]

Perfect love, then, is courageous. It is the type of love that was embodied by Harriet Tubman, who freed more than 300 slaves and is known as "the Moses of her people." This is unsurpassable love. This unsurpassable, cosmic love which restores right relationship between God and creation is not limited to black women and women of color. Yet womanists, in their particular processes of becoming, articulate it in novel ways. Womanists love the Spirit, the folk, creation, and themselves, "regardless" or in spite of the racial-gender oppressions they survive daily.[15]

## Diversity of Womanists

The definition of "womanist" is broad and deep, intentionally left open for interpretation within certain limits.[16] For example, a womanist is never a white woman or a white feminist, because womanism emerges from what Cannon calls "the real-lived experiences"[17] of black women or women of color in response to experiences of modern slavery, racism, segregation, colonization, and globalization. Most simply, a womanist is a black woman or woman of color committed to freedom from gender, racial, economic, planetary, and sexual oppression. Predominantly Christian, womanists are also religiously diverse, including pagans, Muslims, Buddhists, and practitioners of Yoruba. Womanists are academic and nonacademic. They are diverse theologically, economically, in sexual orientation, and in livelihood. Womanist scholarship has developed in multiple directions and disciplines, particularly within the field of religious scholarship. "Womanist" denotes the communal, cultural, activist thought and practice of ordinary black women or women of color in response to social-historical experiences of slavery, colonization, genocide, apartheid, racism, sexism, classism, heterosexism, and globalization.

The understanding of "womanist" presented here emerges from my communal womanist experience, research, and writing for many years. It also emerges from conversation with the lively group that constitutes the womanist network. Womanist identity is not individualistic, but communal. The womanist network is made up of ordinary black women and scholars, all of whom are activists for communal survival, freedom, and wholeness. Womanists are global, working in the United States, the Caribbean, and various African countries, particularly South Africa. Womanist theologian Diana Hayes likes to emphasize that to-date womanists are *all* black and predominantly Christian.[18] It is important to note that in the early years, Rita Nakashima Brock, who is of Asian and Hispanic heritage, talked of being womanist. In a recent trip to Seoul, Korea, I noted that some Korean women identify with womanism more than feminism. It is striking that Walker was present in Seoul during the same week in May 2004 to present her work to Korean feminists at Ewha Women's University and at a global women's summit. Does this mean that global feminists of color may identify as womanists? There are some social-historical differences and tensions regarding our understanding of one another that need to be worked out, but the possibilities, given our common struggles with Western colonization and globalization as women of color, could make for strong relationships of solidarity.

On occasion, scholars fluent in Howard Thurman's work have commented that my thought reminds them of his. For many years, Thurman was the pastor of a church called The Fellowship of All Peoples, committed to opening its doors to people from all cultures and backgrounds globally, in San Francisco, California.[19] When it comes to relationship with women of color globally and even to white feminists who advocate womanist thought, my vision does share some similarities with his. In the range of womanist perspectives, I find myself echoing my grandmother Lizzie Mae Baker's sentiment, "I just want everybody to love everybody." My womanist sisters who want the same thing less idealistically than I remind me to "Keep it real." I am reminded to continue delving into the much neglected research area of black women's religious thought and practice. The world has cruelly placed black women at the bottom of the totem pole. This requires us to protect one of our few oases. There are people who, in spite of their expressed intentions, would destroy what we womanists, who have been all black, as Hayes observes, have developed for the last twenty years. Other women of color claiming the "womanist" nomenclature and identity *must be in authentic relationships of mutuality, equality, and respect with black women.* Womanists are open to such women of color identifying as womanist. This realistic assessment emerges from black women's experiences of liberating hope mixed with racial, gender, class, and sexual oppression in daily acts of survival.

Sexism, racism, classism, heterosexism, ableism, and ecological destruction are interrelated systems of oppression in womanist understanding. While not all these forms of oppression have received equal attention in womanist publications (particularly heterosexism, ableism, *global* economic oppression, and ecocide), within the wider, womanist network there are womanists working on all these issues. One area that requires more *internal* attention given the diversity of economic realities *among* womanists is class. The masses of black women in the United States work in the lowest paying jobs and struggle to feed their children. They have not benefited from higher education with its economic opportunities. Middle-class womanists in academia, like myself, experience less economic oppression than many poor black women in the United States and abroad. Statistically, the masses of black women and men in the United States die at younger ages than white Americans because of poor food and poor medical care. While those of us who are middle-class womanist scholars often write about these issues and participate in various forms of social-political and economic activism, we live in paradox. In spite of our activism, we benefit from global economic structures of oppression. Yet, we experience sexism and racism everyday even as we challenge oppressive, economic structures. This paradox merits further reflection.

## Transitions in Womanist Identity

Over the years, some would argue that Walker has moved so far from her rural Georgia, black roots that many ordinary, non-middle-class black people find it more and more difficult to identify with her and her work. Few ordinary black people have had the opportunities for travel, exploration, and diversity that she has had. This is the struggle of middle-to-upper-class, highly educated, and well-traveled womanists who write for popular culture or, in the case of many womanist scholars of religion, for academia. Generally, womanists in academia are engaged in some type of activism in black communities to keep us grounded. Walker is engaged in global activism, but her writings in recent years do not reflect the grounding in the local black community of earlier writings. See, for example, her most recent novel, *Now Is the Time to Open Your Heart,* about the famous black woman writer and shamanist-loving, yage-tripping[20] protagonist Kate Talkingtree, whose economic wealth takes her to spiritual journeys on the Colorado River and in South America, but whose connection to poor black communities is distant.[21] Must this be the plight of middle-to-upper-class womanists?

Some womanists argue for going beyond Walker's early definition. Womanist Bible scholar Renita Weems, who left a tenured position at an elite white academic institution to work more extensively with women in black communities, describes Walker's "definition," written in a synthesis of dictionary format and lyricism, as "a cultural image, not a hard and fast definition, that she has bequeathed to us."[22] She warns against a fundamentalist use of the definition. Yet, it is important not to move so far beyond Walker's definition that we do not recognize its historical significance, Weems observes. I am among those who are concerned that womanists give attention to the richness of Walker's original definition, as we continue to develop womanist thought and practice. While her lyrical[23] definition was never intended to be confining, it was created to suggest general cosmological and social principles. Joan Martin agrees with Weems's understanding, adding her own cultural, theoretical analysis to Weems's commentary:

> if [Weems] agrees to the use of her comment, then "cultural image" becomes a rich means of defining "womanist." As such, "womanist" is a generative dimension of spirituality and cosmology which surfaces in and acts as a signifier of black women's engagement in social movement and transfor-

mation at the foundational level of community. Womanist, in this sense, is a communal and transformative signifier rather than an individually and autonomously defined identity.[24]

In sum, "womanist" is a term that emerges from black culture, which is historically communal in nature. When defined autonomously, it lacks the depth and breadth of experiential wisdom that black women bring to womanist identity. Those who attempt to define the term "womanist" individually meet a plethora of voices who caution that the single-lensed perspective must be sharpened into a prism to cast the multicolored light of communal womanist wisdom.

## Womanist Limits and Struggles with White Feminists

The term "womanist" was coined to denote a particular kind of feminism, some would say, that emerges from novel, very distinctive social-historical experiences of slavery, dispossession, segregation, apartheid, racism, sexism, classism, and heterosexism. As noted above, Walker defines "womanist" as a *black feminist* or *feminist of color*. Rather than qualify the term "feminist," however," "womanist" is *one word* that describes black women or women of color who are committed to freedom and healing *in their wholeness*. The term "womanist" demands recognition of our *wholeness*.

Some womanists identify with feminists, particularly with Third World feminists, observes womanist ethicist Joan Martin. Others, womanist theologian Diana Hayes notes, reject the term "feminist" to emphasize independence from white feminism. During the spring of 2004, Joan Martin and other womanists lifted up the name of recently deceased Gloria Anzaldúa, the Chicana feminist theorist whose work womanists first read in *This Bridge Called My Back*.[25] Her work, too, is honored as part of the womanist canon along with that of Audre Lorde, Gloria Hull, Ntozake Shange, and others. While womanist relationship with white feminists is tenuous in its struggle for mutual respect, womanist relationship with global feminists of color is long-standing. Martin and Linda Thomas work with South African feminists. Emilie Townes has taught several summers in Brazil. Others, like Cannon, have shared womanist thought in West Africa. During discussions with the womanist network, the most compelling reason for defining "womanist" as "black feminist" on occasion is to signify connection with black feminists like Angela Davis, bell hooks, Audre Lorde, and Patricia Hill Collins.

Given Walker's use of the term "feminist" in her early definition of womanist, there are always white feminists who ask, "Can I be a womanist?" and "Why not?" This leads some to reject "feminist" identity in order to make a clear demarcation between the life-work of womanists and white feminists. Diana Hayes, for example, offers the following commentary to my occasional self-definition as an "Alice Walker womanist":

Sisters . . . I have enjoyed reading your discussion of how we do, can and should define womanism. I find myself, however, disagreeing with some of you in terms of how we speak of the meaning of womanist and womanism. Quite frankly, I do not see myself as an Alice Walker womanist but believe I and many others have moved beyond esp. the first line of her definition: "a womanist is a black feminist or feminist of color." I have dropped "feminist" completely from my self-definition of womanism because I believe that the word carries too much baggage and we, as women of color need to be about defining ourselves in a new unwritten page of history. Also perhaps because of my experience as a Black Catholic teaching in a predominantly white school and often addressing predominantly white audiences, I tend to be a bit more restrictive, defining at least the phase of womanism now in full bloom in the US as a theology of African American Christian women open, however, to the voices and contributions and experiences of other women of color, such as the Korean women mentioned and African, esp. South African women, who are also exploring the term. I do this not to be separatist but, as Walker notes, for reasons of health.[26]

Hayes, like all womanists, corrects white feminists who want to appropriate womanist identity, which would disassociate it from its social-historical and cultural contexts. Womanists as a whole observe that historically, white Americans have stolen the most creative, cultural productions of black people. Hayes comments:

I have been teaching womanist theology for over a dozen years now and the first thing that usually happens is that young white feminists begin to declare themselves as womanists. I have reached the point now that I simply tell them that is not possible. Too often movements have been started by persons of African descent and have been co-opted and eventually distorted into something we no longer recognize—not out of meanness, etc. but simply because our white feminist sisters seem too often to feel they have the right to participate in any and every movement regardless. I have been accused of being exclusive and separatist by white female students and I tell them they are correct but that everyone has to have the freedom and space to define themselves as beings in their own right rather than in response to others who have already been on the playing field for much too long.[27]

For womanists, the response to Hayes's words is a resounding, "AMEN." *White women can learn from womanists and advocate womanism without being womanists.* This is similar to others learning from the wisdom of Asian or Native American feminists *without claiming to be* Asian or Native American feminists. The goal is to develop relationships of mutuality while respecting boundaries. One of my responses to white women who want to *be* womanists, rather than advocate womanist thought, has been, "Are you willing to stop identifying as 'white' and live *every* moment of your life as a black woman?" In order to do this, one would have to *be* black *in community with black people,* with all that means: self-identity in the workplace, with friends, in the neighborhood, shopping, in worship, with family, etc. It entails giving up *every* vestige of white privilege, including skin color, when mistaken for white I have not met anyone who was willing to give up white racial privilege to this degree. Several have walked off offended by the suggestion that they should ever want to be black. Most, finally recognizing the differences in social-historical experience, culture, and identity, have realized the absurdity of the question. Can a white woman be a womanist? "NO."

I include Hayes's commentary here, because it is vital to understanding what it means to define oneself as womanist in community. Moreover, her commentary clearly highlights one of the most troubling struggles womanists have engaged in: respect for our self-definition as black women. Why, womanists often ask, is our very power, freedom, and authority to be self-naming quickly questioned and disrespected? White women must stop asking if they can be womanists. It is important to understand that this is not viewed as a compliment, but as disrespect for the freedom to be collectively self-naming as black women or women of color. White women who protest the boundaries of womanist identity are oppressive. Such response says that, once again, such white women want control. Why, womanists wonder, is it so difficult for so many white women to give up control of how others define themselves? Why is there this demand among so many white women to own black women's self identity? White women who "want to *be* womanists" talk about being "included." *Womanists, how-ever, are certain that the deeper, unexamined issue at stake is power and ownership. We will not be reenslaved.*

This does not mean that womanists and feminists are not to or ought not be in relationship with one another. *Womanism does not reject white feminists but rather invites dialogue, mutuality, and respect.* The exclusion-ary nature of "womanist" identity says to white women, "You cannot walk in my shoes. You cannot be me and you are forcing intimacy to a level you cannot reach." American Indians, as many prefer to name themselves, have made similar observations regarding white American desire to become "the other." *The only way to attain healing and freedom is not to become the other, which would be a form of self-hatred, but to love and respect the other as oneself.* The other side of the exclusionary nature of "womanist" is an affirmation for white women to be holistic *as feminists*. Hayes asks what the restrictions and exclusionary nature of the definition of "womanist" entails in making room for dialogue:

> How do we remain open to others while at the same time developing a safe and sacred space for our theologizing as African American women and women of color? To be a womanist is to be holistic, open to dialogue with women and men of every race, ethnicity, gender and sexuality but also free to seal oneself off from those who do not share the same experiences in order to listen and learn and regroup. Thus I always state clearly that I am not a feminist, Black or otherwise; I am a womanist, a term needing no qualifiers of color or race but it is sufficient unto itself.[28]

At this point, there are some distinctions between my thought and that of Hayes. We have in common a similar understanding of openness to dia-logue. I frequently define "womanist" as "a black feminist or feminist of color." In this particular area, I share more in common with womanists who still employ this part of Walker's definition. At the same time, wom-anism is open enough for womanists to reject the "feminist" nomenclature altogether. We do not *have* to define "womanist" as "a black feminist or feminist of color." It is reasonable to say that "womanist" *is sometimes defined as a black feminist or feminist of color.* After all, the term "woman-ist" was coined in order for black women to be able to use *one word* that describes our movement for survival, freedom, and wholeness. Hayes re-minds us that the term "womanist" points to the truth that we are not adequately described by "a color or a pre-defined term."[29] Womanism is holistic.

There is a good reason for sometimes recalling the first part of Walker's 1983 definition in certain contexts. In defining "womanist" as "a black feminist or feminist of color," it is clear that a womanist *is not a white feminist.* For this reason, I continue to define it in this way for predominantly white audiences unfamiliar with the term. Walker's 1983 definition clearly points to black women's social-historical and cultural experiences.

This allows me to encourage white feminists to delve into the most healing, neglected areas of their own histories rather than fruitlessly attempting to become the other—womanists. The goal is for us to learn from one another, not to become one another. The contrasts between my perspective and Hayes's perspective are not a matter of either/or, oppositional argumentation. Our perspectives are two sides of one womanist coin. Womanists are both/and thinkers, Katie Cannon has long observed, not "either/or thinkers." There are times when I am a separatist like Hayes and Walker, for reasons of health, and times when I am more intercultural. Womanist reality is fluid within limits. Much depends on contexts and series of events.

## Walker's Work and Christian Womanist Spirituality

I sometimes refer to myself as an Alice Walker womanist, because of my commitments to an integrative understanding of God and creation. I do not share Walker's eclectic spirituality which is a combination of paganism, Buddhism, and shamanist-influenced experience. The fact that she identifies with Sojourner Truth, Harriet Tubman, and Rebecca Cox Jackson, black Christian feminists of the nineteenth century, however, gives me and other Christian womanists some sense of connection to Walker's mixed spirituality.[30] I am a Christian womanist. More precisely, however, I am what Howard Thurman called a follower of Jesus.[31] In the relationship between Alice Walker's womanism, the writings of Howard Thurman, and Whiteheadian metaphysics, I find common ground.[32] Walker's spiritual starting point is everyone's common ground—the earth. In *The Same River Twice,* Walker writes of the earth, Nature, and the Universe as a Trinity that opens her "to love, intimacy, and trust."[33] This is different from the Trinity in the type of womanist Christianity I propose, in which God is viewed as "creating Spirit, incarnate Spirit, and transforming Spirit" who is present in creation but not defined as Creation. Yet there is resonance between the Christian womanism proposed here and Walker's understanding that God is not absent from creation, but intimately related to it in some way.

It is the *Christian tradition*'s alienation of Jesus from creation and the folk that Walker most criticizes. Jesus, on the other hand, "coexists quite easily with pagan indigenous peoples," she writes, because they already know the love that he preached. In the twentieth century, Howard Thurman also found that God and creation are our literal common ground. Like Walker, he was influenced by his African and Native American heritages. Moreover, he was influenced by some of the insights of process metaphysician Henry Nelson Wieman.[34] Unlike Walker, however, Thurman did not view creation as God/Spirit. While I agree with Walker's assessment regarding an integrative relationship between God and creation, I do not share the *pantheism* (the understanding that God is all things) that she brings to the table. To the contrary, I share the panentheistic view of theistic process metaphysics. Like Thurman, I reject Wieman's nontheistic approach. In *panentheism*, particularly in theistic process interpretations, God is *in* all things. Our common ground is the omnipresence of divine, cosmic, love and creativity. This divine, loving creativity that is present in creation is the source of hope, that as Walker puts it, "anything that we love can be saved."[35] In Walker's Pulitzer prize–winning novel *The Color Purple*, the integration of creation and spirit is explicit. The sexually and physically abused Celie learns from blues-singer Shug that God is not an old white man in the sky:

> God is inside you and inside everybody else. You come into the world with God. But only them that search for it inside find it. And sometimes it just manifest itself even if you not looking, or don't know what you're looking for. Trouble do it for most folk, I think. Sorrow, lord.[36]

There is an implied metaphysics in Walker's work. Specifically, if God is "inside you and inside everybody else," then we have indications of a *panentheistic* worldview in which God is *in* all things. If God sometimes "just manifest itself even if you not looking, or don't know what you looking for," then God is omnipresent. On the next page, however, the text suggests that Shug's God may be *pantheistic*, the view that God *is* all things. The response to the question "But what do it look like?" is: "I believe God is everything, say Shug. Everything that is or ever was or ever will be. And when you can feel that, and be happy to feel that, you've found it."[37]

Here, Morris and I observe, Walker suggests a *pantheistic* understanding of God. God is everything. Feminist and womanist theologians sometimes gloss over this, writing as if Walker, who admits Shug's spirituality is her own, were clearly *pantheistic*. Beatrice Morris, a womanist Ph.D. student at the General Theological Union in Berkeley and an up-and-coming ecowomanist theologian, shares that she, independently, has made similar observations in a paper on the work of Alice Walker, postcolonial theory, and ecowomanism. She is an important colleague in the developing field of ecowomanism.[38] The narrative in *The Color Purple*, Morris and I observe, is ambiguous. Moreover, in various essays, Walker describes herself as a "pagan" who worships nature. Baptized at age seven, she was more fascinated by the leaves in the muddy creek than the preacher's words. "I was unable to send my mind off into space in search of a God who never noticed mud, leaves, or bullfrogs. Or the innocent hearts of my tender, loving people. . . . It is fatal to love a God who doesn't love you,"[39] she writes.

Walker's Shug says that her first step from the image of God as an old white man was "trees. Then air. Then birds. Then other people." Then, one day, she explains, "I knew that if I cut a tree, my arm would bleed."[40] God is everywhere. God in Walker's work is relational. When we recognize relationship with God, we realize that when we harm creation, whether human or the universe that sustains our bodies, we crucify God and ourselves. To love the Spirit is to love creation, not in the *pantheistic* mode that Walker often presents, but in the recognition that the Spirit is omnipresent, yet infinite in relation to the finite universe we have come to know. God is everlastingly creating "a new thing" in response to a perishing earth and its peoples. Our calling is not to worship nature itself, which perishes, but God, the Spirit who is present in nature but never perishes.

### NOTES

1. Gloria Hull et al., *All the Women Are White, All the Blacks Are Men, But Some of Us Are Brave: Black Women's Studies* (Old Westbury, NY: Feminist Press, 1982).

2. Alice Walker, *In Search of Our Mothers' Gardens: Womanist Prose* ( Diego: Harcourt Brace Jovanovich, 1983), xi.

3. Katie Cannon writes extensively about black women's moral agency in *Black Womanist Ethics* (Atlanta: Scholars Press, 1988).

4. Alice Walker, *In Search of Our Mothers' Gardens*, xi.

5. Alice Walker, *The Way Forward Is with a Broken Heart* (New York: Ballantine, 2001). The entire book is about Walker's 1960s interracial marriage and her journey to healing after her divorce.

6. Alice Walker, "Womanist," in *In Search of Our Mothers' Gardens,* xi–xii.

7. Alice Walker, "In Search of Our Mothers' Gardens," in *In Search of Our Mothers' Gardens,* 231–243.

8. Ibid., 240–243.

9. Alice Walker, "Womanist," in *In Search of Our Mothers' Gardens,* xi.

10. Charles Hartshorne, *Omnipotence and Other Theological Mistakes* (Albany: State University of New York Press, 1985), 14, 45, 86; *The Divine Relativity: A Social Conception of God* (New Haven: Yale University Press, 1948), 46. There have been debates about whether or not womanists ought to include contributions of white men and women in our work. See, for example, Katie Cannon and Cheryl Sanders, "Round Table Discussion," *Journal of the Feminist Study of Religion* 5, no. 2 (Fall 1989). My position, like Cannon's, is that we may draw on wisdom wherever we find it, learning from "the other" without becoming "the other." Monica Coleman, Henry James Young, and Theodore Walker are African American process metaphysicians. I share their appreciation for process metaphysics, finding it a helpful analogy for the dynamic nature of reality. Coleman is Director of the Womanist Religious Studies Program and Assistant Professor of Religion at Bennett College for Women, Greensboro, North Carolina. The first Whiteheadian womanist theologian, or "third wave black feminist theologian" as she sometimes puts it, Coleman is the author of *The Dinah Project: A Handbook for Congregational Response to Sexual Violence* (Cleveland, OH: Pilgrim Press, 2004). Publication of her revised dissertation on African American Yoruba and Whiteheadian metaphysics is forthcoming. See also the work of Hartshornian Theodore Walker, Jr., *Mothership Connections: A Black Atlantic Synthesis of Neoclassical Metaphysics and Black Theology* (Albany: State University of New York Press, 2004).

11. Alfred North Whitehead, *Process and Reality,* Corrected Edition, ed. David Ray Griffin and Donald W. Sherburne (New York: Free Press, 1978), 343–344, 351.

12. Alice Walker, *Anything We Love Can Be Saved: A Writer's Activism* (New York: Random House, 1997), 24–25, 106–107; "Everything Is a Human Being," in *Living by the Word* (San Diego: Harcourt Brace Jovanovich, 1988), 139–152. See also Chandra Taylor-Smith, "Earthling Embodiment: The Ecological Dimensions of the Spirituality of Alice Walker," paper presented at American Academy of Religion Annual Meeting, November 23, 1997. Taylor-Smith is an ecowomanist.

13. Hartshorne contrasts this concept of divine love with that of classical Christian writers. Quoting Alfred North Whitehead, he concurs that "They gave unto God the properties that belong to Caesar." See Hartshorne, *Omnipotence and Other Theological Mistakes,* 14–15, and Alfred North Whitehead, *Process and Reality,* 342–343. Whitehead's precise words are, "The Church gave unto God the attributes which belonged exclusively to Caesar." He refers to God as "the lure for

feeling" which in African American experience could be interpreted as "the call for response," the call to respond to experiences of God's initial aim for right relationship between God and creation.

14. John B. Cobb, Jr., and David Ray Griffin, *Process Theology: An Introductory Exposition* (Philadelphia: Westminster Press, 1976), 49.

15. Alice Walker, "Womanist," in *In Search of Our Mothers' Gardens*, xi.

16. Renita Weems, email correspondence, June 2, 2004. Weems, the William and Camille Olivia Hanks Cosby Endowed Professor at Spelman College, writes that it is "our task to go beyond [Walker's] lyrical parameters." She is the author of several volumes on womanist analysis of biblical literature.

17. Drawn from coursework taken from Cannon in 1983–84. See also the texts by Cannon noted above.

18. Diana Hayes, email correspondence, June 15, 2004. Hayes is Professor of Theology at Georgetown University in Washington, D.C. A renowned Roman Catholic womanist theologian, she holds not only a J.D. and a Ph.D. but is also the first African American to receive the Doctor of Sacred Theology degree (S.T.D.) from the Catholic University of Louvain in Belgium. She is the author of *Hagar's Daughters: Womanist Ways of Being in the World* (New York: Paulist Press, 1995).

19. Howard Thurman, *With Head and Heart* (New York: Harcourt Brace Jovanovich, 1979). See also Walter Earl Fluker and Catherine Tumber, eds., *A Strange Freedom: The Best of Howard Thurman on Religious Experience and Public Life* (Boston: Beacon Press, 1998), 131–147, 220–224.

20. Alice Walker, "Afterword," in *Now Is the Time to Open Your Heart* (New York: Random House, 2004). *Yage* or *Ayahuasca* is a South American medicinal plant and hallucinogenic. While its Western proponents claim it is not addictive, because of its brutal intestinal purging effects, they seem to miss the fact that we live in a world where people will abuse anything, adding addictive elements to it to make a profit. If we cannot recommend *yage*, for black youth, which no responsible person would, then it is of no use to black communities and it is irresponsible to recommend it to the Western world at all. *The Western world does not have the spiritual, emotional, or mental maturity not to abuse any form of hallucinogenic.*

21. Ibid., 1–6, 196–197.

22. Renita Weems, email conversation, June 2004.

23. I appreciate Weems's use of the term "lyrical" to describe Walker's words.

24. Joan Martin, who studied with Katie Cannon for her Ph.D., is Associate Professor of Christian Ethics at the Episcopal Divinity School in Cambridge, Massachusetts. She is the author of *More Than Chains and Toil: A Christian Work Ethic of Enslaved Women* (Louisville, KY: Westminster John Knox Press, 2000).

25. Gloria Anzaldúa and Cherríe Moraga, eds., *This Bridge Called My Back: Writings by Radical Women of Color*, 2nd ed. (New York: Kitchen Table—Women of Color Press, 1984).

26. Diana Hayes, email correspondence, June 15, 2004.

27. Diana Hayes, email correspondence, June 3, 2004.

28. Ibid.

29. Ibid.

30. Alice Walker, "Womanist," and "Gifts of Power: The Writings of Rebecca Jackson," in *In Search of Our Mothers' Gardens*, xi and 71–82; "A Name Is Sometimes an Ancestor Saying Hi, I'm With You," in *Living by the Word: Selected Writings, 1973–1987* (San Diego: Harcourt Brace Jovanovich, 1988), 97–98.

31. See Howard Thurman, *Jesus and the Disinherited* (Richmond, IN: Friends United Press, 1981), 13–35; *With Head and Heart: The Autobiography of Howard Thurman* (San Diego: Harcourt Brace Jovanovich, 1981). Schubert Ogden, in his Bultmannian analysis of scripture, refers to Jesus as one who is said to be Christ the apostolic tradition of the New Testament. See Schubert Ogden, *The Point of Christology* (Dallas: Southern Methodist University Press, 1982), 106–126.

32. Howard Thurman also suggested the earth/universe is our common ground. In his studies of the process metaphysics of Henry Nelson Wieman, he found Wieman's organic, relational understanding of God and world helpful, but rejected Wieman's nontheistic conclusions. I find commonality with *theistic*, process understandings developed by Hartshorne, Cobb, Suchocki, and Coleman. See Howard Thurman, *The Search for Common Ground: An Inquiry into the Basis of Man's Experience of Community* (Richmond, IN: Friends United Press, 1986), and Luther Smith, *Howard Thurman: The Mystic as Prophet* (Lanham, MD: University Press of America, 1981).

33. Alice Walker, "The River: Honoring the Difficult," in *The Same River Twice: Honoring the Difficult* (New York: Scribner, 1996), 43.

34. Thurman, *The Search for Common Ground*.

35. Alice Walker, *Anything We Love Can Be Saved*.

36. Alice Walker, *The Color Purple* (San Diego: Harcourt Brace Jovanovich, 1992), 166.

37. Alice Walker, *The Color Purple*, 167.

38. Beatrice Morris, email correspondence, June 2004. Morris's work is significant and distinctive in its synthesis of postcolonial theory and analysis of Walker to argue for the necessity of ecowomanism. We are exploring publishing venues for Morris's "Divine Reciprocity: Alice Walker, Ecowomanist," originally written for Rosemary Radford Ruether, Graduate Theological Union, Berkeley, California, May 5, 2003. I learned of Morris's paper after presenting similar analyses of Walker's ecowomanist spirituality at the "Fifth Annual Whitehead Conference," Seoul, Korea, May 22–29. See Karen Baker-Fletcher, "Why Womanist Theology: A Process Perspective," in *Process Thought and East Asian Culture: Keynote Lecture* (Seoul, Korea: The Whitehead Society of Korea and International Process Network, 2004), 87–109, and "Whiteheadian Metaphysics as a Resource for Womanist Theology," in *Process Thought and East Asian Culture: Process Theology* (Seoul,

Korea: The Whitehead Society of Korea and International Process Network, 2004), 79–94. Much of the work in this essay was originally presented in Korea.

39. Alice Walker, "The Only Reason You Want to Go to Heaven Is That You Have Been Driven Out of Your Mind," in *Anything We Love Can Be Saved*, 24–25.

40. Ibid.

# Chapter 11

# Quilting Relations with Creation
## Overcoming, Going Through, and Not Being Stuck

### Cheryl A. Kirk-Duggan

You have worked and prayed and begged and threatened
Through slave rebellion, reconstruction, and civil rights
You sang, you mourned; you were mother, daughter, sister
The tribe of your family with more extensions than any hairdo
Some can't spell college; some have a Ph.D.
You sit at the welcome table; you are prostitute; you're complex
You have instigated, ruminated: many thousands gone.

My essay explores components of relationality amid creation as critical to a creative, justice-motivated concept of *Womanist* thought and methodological strategy. After giving an overview of my definition of *Womanist* theory and relationship as covenant, I then consider *"overcoming,"* as the historical reality of black women's experience; examine *"going through,"* thus specifying how *Womanist* thought is a tool for unmasking the violence which impedes relationships; and I explore *"not being stuck,"* to question where *Womanist* thought *"goes from here."*

### Womanist Theory and Relationality

One touchstone of Alice Walker's seminal work, *In Search of Our Mothers' Gardens: Womanist Prose*, 1983, which *Womanist* scholars have used as foundational to their work, is the concept of relationships. Essentially, relationships undergird and weave through her essays, articles, reviews, and statements, reflecting her definition of "*Womanist.*" Relationships are broad-based ways of experiencing knowledge and life (epistemology, theology, and psychology), amid the particular topics that affect our daily lives (economics, politics, health, values, and symbols), and the attributes which pertain to ways of being (attitude, justice, and community). *Womanist* methodologies are my contextual lens for viewing the necessary relationships for a holistic life which honor the divine, the sacred in all persons, and which name that which distorts, thwarts, and disrespects that sacrality: violence. Violence denigrates and destroys ecosystems, individual and communal faith, health, and spirituality, thus negating respect and hospitality.

*Womanist theory* invites one to live in the present, while simultaneously being a student of history, engaging in radical discerning: to listen, see, know, challenge, analyze, and make a difference. *Womanist theory* is a field of study, a way of thinking and living that takes seriously the exposure, analysis, and transformation of societal and personal injustices and oppressions that affect those who usually matter least in society, as symbolized by poverty-stricken black women. *Womanist theory* is interdisciplinary and examines experience present in living, written, oral, visual, aural, sensual, and artistic texts to create its epistemology, hermeneutics, and philosophy, toward intellectual, spiritual dialogue to prepare individuals to experience life in a holistic manner. *Womanist,* derived by Alice Walker from the term "*womanish,*" refers to women of African descent who are audacious, outrageous, in charge, and responsible. In hope and transformation, a *Womanist* emancipatory theory engenders mutuality and community amid the responsibility and stewardship of freedom, and honors the *Imago Dei,* the image of God—the essential goodness within all persons.

The body of knowledge and research of *Womanist* thought includes, but is not limited to, issues pertaining to theology (divinity, dialogue, identity, sacrality, spirituality, and power); Bible and narratives (texts, authority, characters, rituals, language, and history); ethics (value, behavior, emotions, visibility, integrity, and praxis); and context (autobiography, culture, aesthetics, socio-history, ecology, and community). *Womanist* theory is a tool to name, expose, question, and help transform the oppression of women, of all people. *Womanists* champion the struggle for freedom, a gift and a right bequeathed by God. God is personal, not an abstract, philosophical construct. Engaging the politics of language, where words and expressions can inspire or subjugate, a *Womanist reading* takes seriously the multidimensional complexity of communication.

*Womanist* theology intentionally creates arenas where one makes visible the black African diasporic women's experience. *Womanists* expose cruelty, are serious, and commit to the survival, wholeness, and health of all people. As a *Womanist* scholar, storyteller, and performer, I have a deep appreciation for the richness of God's revelation in the world through many faiths, allowing for new avenues of reform, possibility, and communal solidarity. Consequently, my use of *Womanist* theology embodies reformation.

Such reformation confronts the many complex issues of individual and communal daily life amid the grace of God, and social justice issues toward a vision of life that champions immediacy, inclusivity, and self-love. My *Womanist* vision searches for a way to champion the freedom, dignity, and justice of *all* people, black, white, yellow, or brown, male or female, and old or young—a prelude to the praxis of morality; a prelude set to the music of life itself, to the rhythm of words, of poetics. Just as there are *Womanists* who have Christian faith traditions, there are *Womanists* who have non-Christian faith traditions. There are women who acknowledge an allegiance to this *Womanist* way of thinking across the world. In Austria several years ago, I met *Womanist* scholars from Amsterdam.

Acknowledging the past, being conscious in the present, and embracing the future, *Womanists* look toward the flourishing of the peoples of African descent, and of all peoples in the twenty-first century. Critical to this flourishing is a holistic understanding of relationality, rooted in Walker's definition of *Womanist,* along with the voice of *bell hooks,* and the Christian values of love for God, neighbor, and self.

Relationship concerns interdependence and connectivity: the state of being mutually interested or involved. In Walker's text on *Womanist* prose, there are at least three major categories for engaging or thwarting relationships: (1) a spirituality of aesthetics, (2) an incarnated holistic vision, and (3) parasitic oppression.

(1) *Womanist* spirituality is a vital, expressive, revolutionary, embodied, personal, and communal resistance-based way of life and theoretical discourse, based upon the rich lived, yet oppressed, experiences of black women descended from the African diaspora, who as social beings in relationship with the Divine, celebrate life and expose injustice and malaise. My theological aesthetics, grounded in a notion of Beauty, in dialogue with the God-given beautiful human expression, appreciate all of creation and the phenomenal art, which radiates that Divine Beauty, as communal,

and individual lived reality. Such a participatory, spirituality of aesthetics merges liberatory resistance and a notion of Divine Beauty incarnated in creation toward wellness and transformation. These aesthetics embody the hidden, radiant beauty of African peoples, a complete sense of one's undiminished blackness, a heritage of orality, revolution, and a search for wholeness and vital, life-giving love and truth. As one loves regardless, one knows a powerful sense of place that honors freedom, the poor, community, and reflective history. The undergirding spirituality of relationship connects human beings and the divine, honors self-recognition, and sees when grief becomes absurd, and laughter must emerge to reclaim sanity.[1]

(2) *Womanist* holistic vision builds on the context of an aesthetic spirituality to embrace an imaginative epistemology, and a transformative attitude, while building a concrete methodology. This methodology supports a perspective that can sustain DuBoisian doubles while honoring all voices and being intentional about economic development. Such an epistemology takes serious academic learning and the mother wit of great grandmothers, transcending larger society's move to control blacks as the disinherited. A transformative attitude lives in the tension of contrariness, hate, and miseducation, while drawing on a spiritual richness of love and beauty, communal resourcefulness and generosity, and justice with tolerance. One engages the many practices of justice out of a sense of care, where one can give of self out of freedom, knowing that in working one can make mistakes, and making mistakes is not failure. A liberatory methodology concretized in the daily tasks of life understands the need for the courage to change and the import of setting priorities. Living in a world of DuBoisian doubles and being part of the African diaspora in another country, embraces a vision where one does not allow the self to be diminished because of oppression. While twoness and threeness in everything exists from history and literature to people, the dichotomy arises when one has and uses power over another. A transformative *Womanist* vision appreciates the sacred voice within all persons, knowing that many of these voices remain silent and unheard. Ultimate change cannot happen without a press for economic development. This means creating work for poor women, "the least of these," and being aware of the intersection of economics, politics, and class as part of one's theological well-being.[2] When these values are not honored, but crushed, the result is parasitic oppression.

(3) *Womanist* aesthetic spirituality exposes personalities and practices

of parasitic oppression. These include any category of human interaction where those with power manipulate, abuse, and misuse another, including but not limited to classism, sexism, heterosexism, racism, ageism, and ableism. The heinous nature of oppression can be as blatant as legal slavery and Jim Crow or as perfunctory as environmental racism. With all of these *isms* comes the experiences of exploitation, pain and agony, the wild, creeping growth of weeds and kudzu, that grow faster than you can destroy it if you fail to keep removing it from its roots of deep fear and ignorance. The shame of it all occurs when the exploited have to wait incessantly for things to change at the convenience of someone else.[3] *bell hooks*'s notion of "*killing rage*" can be a tool for uprooting oppression and mining healthy relationships.

*hooks* reminds us that oppression is insidious; if we pretend it does not exist, that we do not see it or know how to change it, then the oppression never has to go away. Consequently, we never have to be in relationships of mutuality. To change the oppression requires major provocation. Denial permits us to be complicit. To transform denial and to transform complicit oppression requires "*killing rage*," as militant resistance. *Killing rage,* the fury and anger that bubbles up amid an experience of violation, is painful; without an outlet that rage can evolve into intense grief and destruction. The locus of this rage is a place of aliveness, of immediate presence. *Killing rage,* a source for metamorphosis and empowerment, helps us to name, unmask, and engage the self and others in profound politicization and self-recovery.[4] Such rage, a catalyst for courageous action and resistance, helps one grow and change. Pathological, addictive, and dysfunctional behaviors dull the pain and the rage. *Killing rage,* a destructive or creative force, gives us the choice to comply or resist, being pessimistic or hopeful; to stay stagnant or work for healthy relationships. Because rage can be consuming, it must be tempered "by an engagement with a full range of emotional responses"[5] to move toward self-determination. Sharing rage spawns communication and facilitates connections; shutting down rage leads to "assimilation and forgetfulness."[6] The antithesis of engaged rage is consensual victimhood. To defy such victimhood, we must engage in a language of self-determination, as we struggle to end racist, sexist, classist, and heterosexist domination.[7] *Killing rage* is an electrifying tool for change, a catalyst viable for public and private sectors; for nurturing healthy relationships, relationships rooted in love.

In the West, we speak of three kinds of love, which emerge from Koine Greek,[8] the language of the New Testament: *agape, eros,* and *filia.*

αγαπε, *agape*

1. *Christianity.* Love as revealed in Jesus, seen as spiritual and selfless and a model for humanity.
2. Love that is spiritual, not sexual, in its nature.
3. *Christianity.* In the early Christian Church, the love feast accompanied by Eucharistic celebration.

ερoσ, *eros*

1. *Greek Mythology.* The god of love, son of Aphrodite.
2. Often *eros* Creative, often sexual yearning, love, or desire: "The new playful eros means that impulses and modes from other spheres enter the relations between men and women" (Herbert Gold).
3. Psychiatry. Sexual drive; libido.
   a. The sum of all instincts for self-preservation.

φιλια, *filia*

1. The Greek term for friendship or amiability.
2. In the philosophy of Empedocles, the constructive principle counteracting the destructive influence of *neikos* [*neikoV*]; that is, benevolence over against the spirit of discord or strife.
3. Aristotle regarded friendship as a crucial component of the good life.

In sum, we generally talk about love in three ways: *filia*—brotherly, sisterly love; *eros*—erotic, romantic love; and *agape*—unconditional love—that sense of we are in relationship and I am here unconditionally for you. The noblest form of love, however, was *agape.* William Barclay noted that *agape* concerns the mind, not only an emotion arising reflexively in our hearts; rather, it becomes a committed way of life. This is the kind of love that we must have for all people—even our enemies (Matt. 5:44). Though rooted in the Christian tradition, this term encapsulates the *Womanist* motif to always act out of love, that is, in the best interest of one's fellow human beings;[9] ultimately, self-love.

A most exhaustive treatment of this kind of love ethic is found in I Corinthians 13. The apostle gives more than a dozen descriptives that regulate the operation of *agape* or unconditional love, and it honors the Niebuhrian disinterested love of the neighbor. I Corinthians 13 celebrates the qualities of love: patient and kind; not jealous or boastful; not arrogant or rude; is not selfish, irritable, or resentful; does not rejoice at wrong, but rejoices in what's right. Love bears all things, believes all things, hopes all things, endures all things—all things of relationship that create or that arise out of mutuality and Grace. The essence of love is God who gives graciously and wants to be in relationship with us. Believing, hoping, and enduring all things is not permission to do any and everything that is wrong in a relationship. Love may or may not include affection. We can be generous and kind to someone without being intimate or having physical contact. Jesus taught the great commandment, saying: "Love the Lord your God with all you heart, mind and soul, and love your neighbor as yourself" (Matt. 22:37–40). To study *agape* is to realize how far we fall short of attaining the divine ideal of concern for others.

The paradox of this love is that one must have the capacity to love one's self to love the neighbor, to see the sacred, the divine image in another regardless of their behavior. This kind of radical love is essential for transforming relations in creation. Loving the neighbor grants the other respect and the responsibility of freedom. Love embodied presses us to respect other individuals and to be good stewards of ourselves and of creation. Relationships become more important than the acquisition of things. Love as an energy of connectivity fuels community that embraces the divine and the human as incarnation personified. When such a love and the resulting relationships are first and foremost in our lives, then envy, greed, hate, fear, anxiety, and self-loathing become trivial and are greatly diminished. Since the first slave ships traversed the Atlantic with black cargo in the bowels of the ships, black women have had to live amid oppression, quilting together the emotional and spiritual wounds and scars of their families, so that we might continue to live. The experience of these women has been that of "overcoming."

## "Overcoming": Black Women's Historical Experience

Birthed centuries ago in
Mothers/sisters/girl-children ancient, strong, determined
Across the Atlantic, codified by the papal bull of 1441
Come the moans and groans of protest
You: discounted, ridiculed, yet triumphed in these Americas.

Black women of African descent have known the wounds of oppression sown in slavery, sanitized by Jim Crow, and taunted by internalizing the hurt, and venting the injury on others. Within the anathema of slavery, the deep oppressions emblazoned on the psyche of black folks caused much trauma, to the point that even today, many distant children of Africa experience posttraumatic stress disorder that has reduced many communities of African descent to crack dens, poverty, abuse, and invisibility. Though court decisions and legislation, including *Brown v. Board of Education* and the Civil Rights Acts of 1964 and 1965, are the law of the land, the poisons and prisons of racism, sexism, classism, ageism, and heterosexism have gone high-tech, and left in their wake deep pathologies of pain, self-hatred, self-defeatism, insatiable desire, and rage. For example, Toni Morrison's Breedlove Family, in *The Bluest Eye*,[10] experience difference, tragedy, dissonance, racism, sexism, and patriarchy run amuck. The concept of ugliness is the metaphor for all of their self-loathing, pain, deceit, hatred, and crippling codependency, rooted in racism. Ironically, their name emblazons their shortcomings, for the family does not breed love, but hate. The ugliness, one indicator of self-hatred, is a dialectical mark of difference: it sets them apart and makes them unique, while creating a predisposition for tragedy, pain, oppression, and ridicule. Echoing the mantras of ugliness and hatred, rooted in United States soil—the ugliness of white privilege, intraracial racism, and external racism, personify the ugliness that traps, defiles, and ultimately kills Pecola, psychologically and spiritually, in her quest for the bluest eyes; eyes that will make her desirable and lovable.

In the twenty-first century, regardless of her life context, a black woman of African descent cannot avoid oppression. Some people assume that a black woman of African descent *must* be inferior, because she is black. Society tells black women that they cannot *really* be made in God's image; consequently, they are either a servile machine or a sexual, exotic, and erotic thing. As machine or sex object, dominant culture tries to reduce her to a commodity. Many people choose to see her blackness, her gender, her age, and her class, as sanctions to control her. Her daily reality of multiple, complex oppression embodies violence, used to subjugate her as the objectified "other."[11] Both interracial and intraracial attitudes create problems for black women and cause a gross imbalance in families and societies, an otherness, like an incurable disease. Within and outside of African-American culture, the issue of skin color is profound.

*Intra*racial racism, or colorism, is alive and well. There are situations where a dark skinned person wants to relate only with other darker skinned African Americans, and lighter-skinned African Americans may only associate with those of a paler hue. Consider the racism of Du Bois's legendary conflict with Booker T. Washington about the education of the 10% versus industrial education for the other 90%, and the comparisons between the lighter skinned Thurgood Marshall with the field hand hues of Clarence Thomas. The outsider, the one who is lighter or darker, is the *other*. Some live in the denial of "*passing*." Even within the larger black community, while "*passing*" [for white] is considered a form of opprobrium, few within the larger black community "out" a *passer* who is successful. Clearly, societal injustice and prejudice warps the spiritual aesthetics and health of people and whole communities. Such pathologies pervert human sensibilities and create an environment of communal and self-deprecation and hurt. The systemic tyranny of racism has become so internalized, so embodied by some within the race, that any difference in skin hue within the race provokes hatred of self and gives permission to make other those that do not resemble themselves.[12]

This *otherness*, shared by all persons of African descent, concretizes profoundly in the African-American female experience, which uses control to make black women invisible.[13] The *Womanist* perspective seeks to make the invisible visible in a movement to garner freedom in love, for all people, regardless. In sum, from a theological ethics perspective, *Womanists* engineer epistemological revolution, as they seek to name and help others know significant issues and resources, to expose inconsistencies, and transform the compounded, interrelated wrongs of sexism, classism, racism, ageism, and heterosexism in narrative and in society.

The history of black women in the African diaspora reveals abuse, exploitation, separation, and suffering. Nevertheless, thousands of black African peoples have continued to agitate for justice, have overcome tremendous odds, and have made a difference. Many slave women had a theology of suspicion, resistance, redemption, remembrance, and retelling that undergirds the Spirituals and is present in their stories, poems, novels, and other art forms. Stories of slave women document their belief in a "mighty God," the brutality, violence, and sexual abuse from their arrogant male slave masters, and the resentment, rage, hatred, and persecution from their ambivalent slave mistresses.[14] Yet, many slave women quilted together their religious, spiritual, and aesthetic resources to survive, to develop self-esteem, to protect them, to bolster their total health, to speak the truth, and to love themselves regardless. These women, who used their suspicion to explore situations and to be leery of naïve idealism that did not support their realities and values, are the ancestors of *Womanist* scholars. They celebrated God's redemptive nature, resisted their incarceration, and developed their own sense of Christianity in deference to the religious hypocrisy practiced by their owners. They invoked the language of re-telling and re-membering. Like these nineteenth-century women, twenty-first-century black women continue to wrestle against oppression, against larger society, and against their own pastors and church leaders who use biblical texts to brainwash them into believing that women ought not preach, that women have no business in the pulpit, that women must be subservient to men. How is it that certain folk think they have the inside scoop on what God knows, wants, and does? The complex oppressive experience of black women pushes *Womanist* thinkers to develop an epistemology that is (1) eschatological or goal-oriented; (2) concerned with physical, mental, emotional, spiritual, and economic health and liberation, and loving the individual and communal mind/soul, spirit, and body; (3) committed to relational, historical black experience; (4) based on real feelings, experiences, actions; and (5) a transformational, life-changing process that enhances everyone. *Womanist* vision brings identification and healing in communion with a living God. Such power helps one to "overcome," and "go through."

## "Going Through": Exposing Violence

And so you toiled, wet-nursed, did back breaking work,
They sold you at auction
Yet, you triumphed amidst degradation, malnutrition, mutilation
Loved life, loved roundness, were outrageous, audacious
You have continued to "lift as you and your people climb"
You have hope in the holler, despite misbegotten anguish;

*Womanist* scholarship and social activism have done much to expose the violence that is so rampant in many black communities that its intense presence makes it invisible. Women of African descent have not taken oppression lying down. They have strategized and organized for the uplift and survival of their people since coming to the United States, as individuals and in community. They have embodied Womanist sensibilities through surviving, following a "making a way out of no way" God, and helping their poor destitute families deemed chattel to feel like somebody. Throughout the nineteenth century, many unnamed women worked for revolution. They worked in the freedom and civil rights movements and worked in the areas of education and social change. Nationally, black women's organizations relied on the work of nineteenth-century women to acknowledge the victimization of black women and the connection between black sexuality and white violence, particularly lynching. For example, Anna Julia Cooper saw the connection between American racism and African American sexism. Ida Wells-Barnett documented tremendous prevalence of southern lynchings of Blacks and Whites and showed the economic and sexual reasons for lynching.[15] Many such women worked against racism, sexism, and classism. They were not always supported by women or men of African descent, but they did not let that reality stop them. These women have persevered and been instrumental in creating change at home and in society. Often women's work and women's revolutionary acts of transformation go unrecorded in mainstream historical documents. Nevertheless, there are so many women who have exposed the violence and worked to make a difference.

The 1960s Civil Rights movement could not have happened without the music and without the women. Women organized and strategized behind the scenes, for example, as they waited for the right test case in Montgomery, Alabama. Montgomery protest grew out of the organized efforts of the *Women's Political Council*, a black professional women's organization which had organized to protest injustice prior to Rosa Parks's arrest and used Parks's arrest to launch an all out protest. When Parks sat down on the bus and was arrested, the women went to their ministers who conscripted Dr. Martin Luther King, Jr., to lead the boycott that lasted for 381 days. Some of the named women who helped lead that movement include Ella Baker, Septima Clark, Fannie Lou Hamer, Coretta Scott King, Bernice Johnson Reagon, Joanne Robinson, and Ruby Doris Smith Robinson.

Today women of black African descent continue to protest and organize for change. Some do their work by "teaching to transgress," in the school room and the board room. Twenty-first-century black women's organizations organized for political empowerment continue the adage of those early twentieth-century black club members whose motto was "lifting as we climb." Modern day novels, poems, songs, paintings, sculpture, and dance portray the realities of black women's lives and often inspire women and men across the globe to change their lives; to know that they can make a difference. Moreover, it is in *Womanist* scholarship, which has just passed its twenty-year mark, that has helped bring these women's stories to light and to expose the violence, from a religious, spiritual, theological, sociological, psychological, ethical, and aesthetic perspective. We are now into the second and moving toward the third generation of *Womanist* scholars, and in tribute, I mention a few trailblazers here.

Katie Cannon reminds us that when she does ethics, it is like Ezekiel's wheel in the middle of a wheel. On an epistemological trajectory, she places the wheels of (1) the traditional, typically European male patriarchal canon that masks the existence of black women; (2) the nexus, history, and experiences of Afro-Christian culture and the Black Church community; in concert with (3) women's experiences and the interpretation of these experiences. In the process, Cannon can name the power relationships and debunk the myths that often produce and support the violence that continues to plague our society. Thus, *Womanist* ethics as liberation ethics demystifies, unmasks, and untangles the ideologies, theologies, and systems of value operative in a particular society to evaluate the myths that sanction oppression, where the oppressed can make responsible decisions that support the well-being of humanity.[16]

Theologian Delores Williams[17] juxtaposes the Hagar story (Genesis 16, 21) and matters of atonement to shake us from our lethargy about viewing violence as perfunctory in the biblical texts and in life. She states that the crucible of atonement lies in the *ministerial* vision of Jesus. Such a vision teaches, loves, and empathizes, but does not subjugate, exact violence on, or defile creation. Intraracial oppression, pathological white racial arrogance and narcissism, and stereotypical socio-political symbolism affect black women's survival and resistance in the wilderness. Williams's notion of the *"wilderness"* experience symbolizes the place where Hagar, women of African descent, and their children meet, identify with, and are cared for by God. This *wilderness* is the place of "risk-taking faith," exercised in a crisis when a woman meets and receives individual direction from God.[18]

Emilie Townes reminds us that in doing *Womanist* ethics, ethics from a nondominant cultural perspective, we must ask ourselves questions about the nature of authority and obedience. Particularly we must see how one moves toward authority in community as people live out their lives as moral agents; deal with pain and suffering, toward an experience of justice; engage in a quest of liberation and reconciliation; attend to prophetic voices. In constructing an ethics of protest, Townes sees the struggle for social equity amid social activism as *Womanist* spirituality. The works of Cannon, Williams, and Townes epitomize some of the groundbreaking work of *Womanist* scholarship. This scholarship exposes the violence, as women of black African descent move through life toward transformation. Other scholars, like Jacquelyn Grant, Karen Baker-Fletcher, Cheryl Townsend Gilkes, Renita Weems, Diana Hayes, Evelyn Parker, Stacey Floyd-Thomas, JoAnne Terrell, Kelly Brown Douglas, M. Shawn Copeland, Marcia Riggs, Carol Duncan, Lynne Whitfield, and me, use *Womanist* theory to explore the life experience of persons of the African diaspora, exposing violence and offering hope toward transformation in areas as diverse as ecology, Christology, sexuality, moral theology, Christian education, psychology, and the sociology of religion. The violence is no longer able to be invisibly visible. The question is where do we go from here?

### *"Not Being Stuck": Taking Next Steps*

With your legacy, our mandate too, to lift as we climb
Is covenant with you, all of you:
The ancestors, the young, the in-between
To write your stories, construct new ways of seeing, doing, knowing
The years of oral traditions, became organically canonized
When doors of ivy leagues and seminaries finally opened the doors to Nubian
giants of intellectual prowess
They said, we say: "We are here! Deal with us!!

As we move further into the twenty-first century, *Womanist* scholarship will continue to build and expand on Walker's definition. This scholarship will help women to celebrate all women, without exception,[19] but first appreciating ourselves: our physicality, our sexuality, and our mental, emotional, spiritual selves. This involves Townes notion of spirituality as a social witness born out of people's struggle and determination to continue to find ways to answer the question: Do you want to be healed? This spirituality is the deep kneading of humanity and divinity in one breath, one hope, and one vision. A healthy sense of self stands in tension with a rejection of idolatry.

Such spirituality challenges *Womanists* to live in hope and justice. To do so, requires that we understand the dominant ethics model which Katie Cannon notes makes a virtue of those qualities which lead to economic success: industry, frugality, and self-reliance. The freedom and choices required to do and live theological ethics is often not available to white women, and women and men of color; nor to the poor, nor other marginalized groups in the United States. The existence of white supremacy and the related hate crimes forces all of us to live in varying levels of freedom. Note that under oppression, freedom nor self-reliance are choices. Part of standing in this tension successfully is to listen to prophetic voices, but who are our prophets? How do we learn to listen to the God-voice within ourselves and those unacknowledged prophets within the community?

There may be times when we will have to work from both the center and the periphery, facing systemic and institutional evils, exposing, dialogical, liturgical, confessional, pedagogical, and ecumenical oppression. As black diamonds in the rough, we will need to speak our truths, for we cannot live whole if we do not take responsibility for our gift of freedom. We must continue to make the invisible visible and to use our indignation and anger in creative ways. For Audre Lorde reminds us that hate destroys; anger does not. When anger is community based as distorted grief, it can desire change. We are called to love and love well, framed in an aesthetic spirituality of love and communal vision. As we channel our anger, all of our emotions creatively, we can become more inclusive. We can understand the privilege of education and that it can be a useful tool to deal a death knell to oppression. When tapping into such freedom, we come alive to the point of having a revitalized, life-affirming relationship with God. We can have true sisterhood and brotherhood, having a more egalitarian, communitarian model of community/family. This one clear trajectory for *Womanist* theory, wherein we quilt complex relationships creatively toward wholeness, then becomes a witness to the awesomeness of God, the power of Creation, the gift of life, and the honor of doing this work.

### NOTES

1. Alice Walker, *In Search of Our Mothers' Gardens: Womanist Prose* (San Diego: Harcourt Brace Jovanovich, 1983), 155, 241, 85, 27, 199, 48, 49, 5, 198, 86, 4, 51, 115, 67, 56.

2. Ibid., 14, 17, 19, 21, 25, 32, 38, 43, 57, 77, 123, 125, 132, 137, 141, 176, 215, 237.

3. Ibid., 165, 208, 213, 234.

4. bell hooks, *Killing Rage: Ending Racism* (New York: Henry Holt, 1995), 12, 16.

5. Ibid., 19.

6. Ibid., 47.

7. Ibid., 4, 8, 11, 19, 47, 57, 61.

8. The New Testament was written in *Koine* Greek. The word *Koine* denotes "common," because this style of Greek was the language of the common man-on-

the-street during the time of Christ. *Koine* Greek came into vogue about 300 years before the birth of Jesus, and it became an obsolete language about three centuries after his death. *Koine* Greek, the most precise instrument for the conveyance of human thought that the world has ever known, has several words representing different aspects of love. *Eros* generally had to do with sexual love. From this term derives the English word "erotic." This word, however, is never found in the New Testament.

Then there was the noun *storge*. This term was primarily employed in family affection. Paul used a negative form of it in describing the base traits of certain pagans of his day. He spoke of those who were "without natural affection" (*astorgous*—Rom. 1:31). A very common word for love during the apostolic age was *philia*, meaning genuine affection—heart love. It is seen in the place name *Philadelphia* (City of Brotherly Love). Jesus had this kind of love for his closest disciple, John (John 20:2), and for Lazarus (John 11:3). See Wayne Jackson, *The Challenge of "Agape" Love*, Christian Courier: Archives, Thursday, June 10, 1999; http://www.christiancourier.com/archives/agape.htm.

9. Ibid.

10. Toni Morrison, *The Bluest Eye* (New York: Penguin/PLUME, 1970).

11. James H. Cone, *For My People: Black Theology and the Black Church* (Maryknoll, NY: Orbis Books, 1984), 125, 128–29.

12. For some of the impetus behind such a pathology, explore its roots in the divide-and-conquer motif of the "Willie Lynch Letter" debacle.

13. Ibid. Deborah Gray White, *Ar'n't I a Woman: Female Slaves in the Plantation South* (New York: W. W. Norton, 1985), 14, 23.

14. M. Shawn Copeland, "Wading through Many Sorrows": Toward a Theology of Suffering in Womanist Perspective," in *A Troubling in My Soul: Womanist Perspectives on Evil and Suffering*, ed. Emilie Townes (Maryknoll, NY: Orbis Books, 1993), 109–29.

15. Cornel West, "The Prophetic Tradition in Afro-America," *The Drew Gateway* 55 (Winter 1984/Spring 1985): 104–6.

16. Katie G. Cannon, *Katie's Canon: Womanism and the Soul of the Black Community* (New York: Continuum, 1996), 138.

17. Delores Williams, *Sisters of the Wilderness: The Challenge of Womanist God-Talk* (Maryknoll, NY: Orbis Books, 1993), 164–67.

18. Ibid., 108–9, 113, 117. The *wilderness* is the place where God meets black women in times of trouble, impending death, or destruction; where God cares and gives the believer personal direction, which helps her make a way out of no way, a religious *wilderness* experience of transformation. *Wilderness* had a different connotation for the dominant white American culture. Early pioneers envisioned the *wilderness* as a hostile place that required conquering, not living in. The *wilderness* was a remote, strange place of solitude and freedom for European Romanticism.

19. Walker, *In Search of Our Mothers' Gardens*, 145.

# Chapter 12

# The Sweet Fire of Honey
## Womanist Visions of Osun as a Methodology of Emancipation

### Shani Settles

## Introduction

African Derived Religions (ADRs) have been and continue to be an absent presence within Womanist discourses. Blatantly omitted and often
deemed inconsequential under an Orthodox Christian hegemony, ADRs
are an "extra-church" and extra-theological subject. Unfortunately, the re-
pudiation of ADRs within Womanist signifying activities denies their historical place and meanings within the plural religious landscape of Black
communities past and present. When fully considered, ADRs may be understood as complimentary/additional religious affiliations that have provided mental/emotional/physical/spiritual frameworks not available within Judeo-Christian and Islamic traditions yet necessary for the survival
and success of/for Black women, their families, and communities.[1] ADRs
were and continue to be powerful oppositional and differential resources
for liberation projects because they embody and engender a "methodology
of the oppressed," methodologies for emancipation that create models of
revolutionary modes of being.[2]

Speaking wholly and embodying Alice Walker's vision of Womanism,
ADRs implicitly and explicitly circumvent western system of thought to
perceive and understand Black women's subjectivity and personhood
holistically. By contextualizing standpoint within a universal (visible and
nonvisible) matrix of relationships, communities, and institutions, ADRs
present women's culture, emotional flexibility, sexual and nonsexual relationships, activist commitments, and courageous willful behaviors as

vehicles establish good character, acquire knowledge, and foster/direct *ashe*, the power to make things happen for the benefit of self, the community, and the universe.[3] Moreover, the belief systems and praxis of ADRs demand revolutionary forms of "loving" that discursively produce conscientization.[4] To love the spirit, self, folk, music, dance, the moon, struggle, food, and roundness "*Regardless*" is to walk the path of light with enlightened ancestors and Spirit while fulfilling one's given destiny.[5] This essay seeks to provide a critical semiotic analysis of the popular representation and attributes of Osun, a highly visible and contested Orisa, and in so doing explore the formation and function of hegemonic/oppositional identity politics that may be discerned while discerning a Womanist theology centered on revolutionary love.

## ADRs as Methodologies for Emancipation

Any attempt to cogently argue that Osun is a significant resource for expanding or advancing Womanist thought and praxis must begin by briefly yet systematically detailing those salient conceptual and ritual systems that undergird an understanding and conceptualization of this figure as a theoretical space/place for emancipation/liberation projects. I suggest that two dimensions of ADRs—(1) a holistic/referential "Afro-centric cosmology" that encompasses/permeates all life, and (2) "communo-theistic" relations between humanity and a divine community of beings—allow individuals to give "birth to themselves as [whole] persons" and secure a symbolic and real haven for self.[6]

## Cosmology/Divine Communities

As a worldview and ethos, Afro-centered cosmologies not only inform individual and collective perceptions and orientations to the natural/physical world, but they also ascribe ultimate meaning and significance to shifting social and psychological realities; they are the cornerstone of all belief and practice. While the exact nature and expression of Afro-centered cosmologies may vary across and within ADR traditions, they remain centrally premised on envisaging "the whole universe [visible and invisible] as sacred."[7] The entire cosmos—the heavens, earth, and underworld—are immanent realms infused with and connected by a divine essence/spirit/presence.[8] This cosmology becomes particularly meaningful when embraced by Africans in the Diaspora engaged in the quest to establish and legitimate the world as real and sacred in the face of alienation, dislocation, and dispossession. Every moment, experience, and subject-object becomes imbued with ultimate significance through a homology-house-body cosmos principle, a spiritual rearticulation of space and time.[9] All psychic, physical, and material spaces/places reflect and reveal the governing principle, the order of the world: "The life is an altar, the living is the prayer."[10] The embodiment of the sacred is experienced in living.

For humanity, this explicitly entails establishing and cultivating relations with the divine, whether manifest in nature, energies, or a community of beings/spirits. Through ritual postures, individuals and communities become priests of the cosmos who "awaken the universe [and their consciousness]" by speaking, listening, and maintaining mythical and real harmony and balance.[11] Through a cyclical process of "externalization," "objectivation," and "internalization," devotees or practitioners of ADR are able to project human conditions onto a divine landscape, establish an objectified social matrix, interrogate it, and then recapitulate it to express a new and profound sense of place in thought and action.[12] As such, the divine community may be viewed as a sort of "plausibility structure" that encapsulates and embodies hegemonic discourses as well as resistance narratives to provide individuals and communities with the opportunity to apprehend, articulate, and mitigate their "ontological insecurity" within a neocolonial matrix of oppression.[13]

## Divine Community

The Orisa may readily be viewed as the central figures/energies within the divine community that equip individuals with a differential attitudinal infrastructure to form counternarratives.[14] Reflecting on them allows one to view the process by which "normative" definitions of reality are disrupted and subjective conceptions are centered so that a sense of somebodiness is realized and given a value that is beyond the "contingencies of human meanings and human activities."[15]

Although typically presented in literature as intercessors or mediators, who periodically intervene in human affairs to bring luck, offer protection, and to initiate healing, the Orisa primarily function as paradigms of ontology.[16] As beings/energies with multiple guises, paths/roads, or personalities, they celebrate and hold paradox/contradiction/ambiguity in complexity; they "mirror and map" the patterned disorder that marks the divergent sources, goals, points of origin, and destinations of life.[17] Indeed, through speech and gesture the Orisa elaborate and express the contested experiences of the subaltern attempting to succeed in a world that is structured for failure and dispossession by offering a visible template of/for differential movement. They communicate to practitioners that humanity has the ability to direct if not wholly control/manipulate the outcome of any given situation. By being flexible and responsive to the constructive and destructive dimensions of life, that is, by adhering to/harmonizing, melding, or flowing with oppositional forces rather than overtly resisting them, one can survive and thrive. The ability to bend the self through code switching is a mechanism, movement, and spiritual quality that invests practitioners with *ashe,* the power to make things happen. Empowered by learning how to control the self, individuals may in turn arrive at an understanding of how to live in the world while ultimately transcending those things which seemingly constitute the human condition. "Striving for" an alignment with an Orisa and their corresponding spiritual qualities/attributes "in this world" then becomes a testament to right faith and action.[18]

Naturally, a formal reciprocal relationship with an Orisa cannot be entered into lightly or superficially maintained. ADR traditions predicate the intimate fusion of a divine consciousness in a devotee's head and heart, the articulation and embodiment of idiosyncratic attributes/characteristics, and regular propitiation through offerings and sacrifices. For practitioners, the integral feature of humanity's relation with Orisa is ultimately the identification and cultivation of attributes associated with them; "You are your *Orisa* and your ancestors and they are you."[19] Through identification and internalization, individuals transform the small "I" into the "total Self."[20] They move from a state of fragmentation, disassociation, alienation, and isolation toward a level of being that engenders wholeness and community.

Ultimately, Afro-centric cosmologies and relationships with Orisa may be viewed as political tools that foster the inner and outer technologies of semiology, mythologizing, meta-ideologizing, and differential movement. By definition, these modes of resistance equip individuals and communities with an idiom to discern, deconstruct, transcode, and rebuild the basic structures of consciousness and meaning production.[21] In ADR, the language, images, and ideologies surrounding the Orisa must first be apprehended and perceived as contingent products versus circumscribed reality.[22] Once this first level reading is acquired, the multiple meanings or realities of imposed and internalized ideologies become divested of their totalitarian/normalizing powers. The "surface phenomena" or superficial understandings of the Orisa/self are perceived as "false constructions" and movement into a deeper reading ensues.[23] For devotees, this means proclaiming to self and the dominant hegemony: I am not who you say or imagine me to be and then reconstituting or constructing the Orisa/self through an Afrocentric lens. When this is accomplished, individuals may begin to authentically speak, think, and feel their existential history and current reality as Africans in the Diaspora. Individuals attain a sort of inner wholeness, a superhuman ontology that ascribes a sense of ultimate freedom.[24]

## Semiology of Osun

Engaging in a semiotic exploration of Osun may explicitly impart how ADRs, can be utilized by Womanists as a medium or vehicle for engendering the decolonization of consciousness and the emergence of a revolutionary being. Indeed, because Osun's representations and attributes are read as cultural artifacts or texts within sign reading exercises, the contesting relational discourses on identity, sexuality, and standpoint are illuminated and become powerful sources for enacting a politic of affirmation. Black women, implementing the inner and outer technologies which constitute a methodology of the oppressed, a methodology for emancipation, are able to discern the creation and enforcement of hegemonic definitions of Black womanhood and resist the "skin deep" and "skin tight" nature of neocolonial discourse so that a counternarrative may be produced and enacted at every visual and interpretive level.[25] I suggest that it is through these "biomythography" processes of deconstruction and reconstruction, that Osun's iconography and attributes become extricated from an ethnocentric and reductive referential frame and reinscribed with Afrocentric conceptions of wholeness, personhood, and agency.[26] Yet, because Osun is one brilliant and multidimensional Orisa in a pantheon of divine beings and many Orisa in one, the following analysis should by no means be considered comprehensive or exhaustive.[27]

Osun as an assemblage of metaphorical, mythical, and aesthetic representations is the owner of cool air and water, the vital source that sustains and heals all life, the principle of creativity, and the leader of the Aje-

witches who take power and knowledge without asking.[28] Her power is soothing, softening, disarming, and dangerous. Like the ripples of a flowing stream Osun can bring happiness, joy, and well-being, or like tidal waves she may unleash a dangerous, noiseless, amniotic terror.[29] Nevertheless, this multiplicity, her essential nature, is denied in dominant culture. Too often appropriated and diminished to one scripted representation, Osun is popularly imaged as a young, rich, beautiful, loving, light-skinned coquette.[30] This prevailing signification effectively establishes Osun as a prototypical "love goddess," an "African Venus" or "Afrodite," who presides over the erotic component of human nature.[31] As such, Osun is simply the essence of passion and beauty itself.

## Osun—A Colonized Divinity

A first level reading of this representation clearly demonstrates the emblematic historical mythicizing or branding of Black female imagery by a dominate gaze that has "power over."[32] Denigrated to a passive sociopublic body, Osun becomes a site of disassemblance on which a nexus of sexed and raced interests, structures, and agendas are inscribed.[33] Situated within the motif of Aphrodite, a white "love goddess," Osun's worth, her beauty, is essentially constructed vis-à-vis the white cultural standards. On the surface, she appears as a "dusky" white woman in color and feature, her cultural origins lost and unknown.[34] Because of this ethnic masking, Osun becomes an honorary white woman who possesses the traditional attributes associated with this veil of color: beauty, power, and being. In this popular view, Osun foregrounds the hegemonic imperative to eradicate Blackness as a color and ontology. Yet, this raced imagery is secondary to Osun's reduction to a hypersexual being. Exalted as a divine courtesan or harlot, Osun's body and her sexuality become synonymous with commodification and prostitution. She is depicted as exotic, erotic, wild, deviant, and available to all. The quintessential "pornographic object," Osun in this representation extends the exploitation, commodification, and othering projects of the white male majority.[35]

The power and import of a first level semiotic reading of Osun as a colonized figure is the ability to "focus viewers' attention on the relationship between the portrayed individual and the general qualities ascribed to a class of individuals."[36] As a visibly raced and highly sexed figure, Osun allows Black women to scrutinize the hegemonic/neocolonial social matrix to view shifting realities of cultural devaluation, social segregation, political exclusion, and economic degradation. Indeed, the benefits derived from conforming to prevailing social, patriarchal, and capitalistic politics are ultimately negligible for the Black female "other."[37] This understanding compounded with a second level reading that delves deeper into the popular representation to interrupt or turn out the "turnstile of form and meaning" allows individuals to further interrogate the true purpose and meaning of this construction as well as its impact on Black womanhood.[38] Osun, as she is popularly presented, becomes apprehended as a false construction. Her raced and sexed imagery then are not considered to be dreadful or detrimental in and of themselves. It is the "thing," the meanings and the values attached to them, that make the dominant representation of Osun dangerous for establishing and maintaining a healthy Black female subjectivity.[39] Furthermore, in a second level reading individuals acknowledge that it is only when the "conventional notions of sexuality and desirability" are divested that hidden underlying meanings may be identified or comprehended. Through a demystification process which shifts the white patriarchal gaze so that individuals can see through and beyond these interpretive lenses, Black women begin to see themselves and each other in a different landscape.[40] One transformative and empowering reading that emerges through this process posits Osun as a template of the erotic as a source of/for power.[41] Her degraded sexuality is transformed into revolutionary love which creates new possibilities of "being and living for" black women.[42]

## The Erotic as Power

Through the demythologizing process, individuals begin to discern that the systematic suppression, repression, and manipulation of the many forms of the erotic by the dominant system are both a symptom and product of a deep-seated fear of revolutionary capabilities.[43] Indeed, by reducing the erotic to sexualized forms, the power of revolutionary love is routinely misread and misunderstood. Rather than being presented as passion and intimacy in its truest and "deepest [forms and] meanings," the erotic is simply imaged as a constellation of physical-interpersonal experiences.[44] The wide, deep, divine (nonsexual-*agape*), and profane (sexual-*eros*) aspects of the erotic then remain relatively unacknowledged and unused resources which could potentially provide the necessary energy or direction for personal and social change.[45] Decoding Osun's sexuality in a second level reading allows individuals to go beyond the superficial ruminations on her body to address the metaphysical, spiritual nature of eroticism and its portent in affirming Black women as Black, "female and spiritual."[46]

Instead of being imaged as a vain coquette whose energy and power is automatically relational, heterosexual, and directed outward, Osun becomes perceived as a highly reflexive and spiritual being whose eroticism is foundationally rooted in cherishing self. Indeed, her detailed attentions to self are not enacted for the love or benefit of others. They are executed for the empowerment of self.[47] In "loving" herself deeply and fully, Osun is posited as undertaking the quest to manifest self-respect and self-determination in a world that fosters the internalization of hatred and contempt.[48] Through continual reflection, she is able to find in herself that magnificent, pure, and true light of being that cannot be eradicated.[49] Over time, she slowly builds upon and expands this essential self so that it is released from the "borderlands" and becomes the center of her being, her "blood and bone."[50] Through this representation, Osun articulates a radical liberationist project to Black women: in loving self at all costs, one is ushered into transformative ways of seeing and being regardless. Equipped with this new faculty, individuals are enabled to "evaluate those aspects [of being] honestly in terms of their relative meaning within our lives" and live with new sensitivity and strength.[51] From family, education, career, to play, Osun's model of revolutionary love challenges us to be conscious, ethical, and authentic in all spheres of reality.

In addition to being a developmental vehicle for consciousness, revolutionary love is the "lifeforce" or mechanism of action that challenges Black women not only to celebrate themselves but also to exalt each other mind-bodyspirit.[52] In practice, revolutionary love is an oppositional posture that demands both the inward and outward emanation of love that should "lead us into greater communion with the world."[53] I suggest that in a second level reading, Osun clearly illustrates that loving self incites one to fully and deeply love one another, humanity, and life itself. This is particularly significant for Black women seeking to establish bonds of "sisterhood." By loving and respecting ourselves as hybrid composites, an authentic community or coalition may be established that spans across socio-economic-cultural-political difference.[54] Indeed, through the mutual respect of an individual's multiplicity and an acknowledgment of an immanent divine presence, a revolutionary community may emerge that becomes an empowering space for the transformation of love into libera-

tion. Like breath, love in this new space/place is able to flow freely and differentially between people so that all are equally nurtured and sustained.[55]
It manifests and intersects at all levels so that a new social matrix is manifest. Moreover, because this new framework of self and communal love
complicates, even mitigates traditional conceptions of reality, identity, and
power, humanity is able to "incite, shape, empower, and *sustain* [real]
social change."[56] While this is only one possible second level rereading of
Osun, it illustrates the ways in which a divine figure may be employed as a
mirror for revisioning conceptions and relations at micro, intermediate,
and macro levels. However, the meaning-making process cannot stop here.
In addition to finding oppositional spaces within dominate discourses,
Black women must also sustain "an independent consciousness as a sphere
of freedom" to continually engage in additional forms of resistance.[57] We
must learn to pivot the center and create a third level of meaning by establishing our own myths, images, or scripts to support this newly formed
consciousness.[58] I suggest that the many other representations of Osun
denied in dominant culture are well suited for this endeavor. Lasyrenn,
one of the lesser explored paths of the Vodou Ezili—a constellation of
female deities—is particularly useful because she communicates the
necessity of differentially employing meaning to articulate and enact hybridity.[59] Indeed, because her identity is constituted "within [a hybrid]
representation," she invites us to go beyond the existent colonial forms of
representation that exist to constitute a new radical subjectivity.[60]

### Lasyrenn as a Meta-Ideologizing Principle

Typically envisioned as a mermaid and sometimes a whale, Lasyrenn is a
large, dark, silent, elusive creature that hovers just below the surface of the
deep sea, at "the back of the mirror."[61] Metaphorically speaking, she is an
absent presence that resists objectification as the other because she is
never fully exposed in her entirety, and yet, her presence hints at the re-
splendent and magnanimous nature of Blackness and to a lesser extent
femininity.[62] Gazing at and identifying with Lasyrenn then allows Black
women to articulate their standpoints as Black women. Through her we
are able to apprehend our multiple identities at the "zero degree," or the
"crossroads," and reestablish meaning to survive endemic systems of oppression.[63] In doing so, Lasyrenn assists us in explicitly puncturing the
everyday narratives of being to become resituated as new Africans.

Reading Lasyrenn as an embodiment of "connectivity" shows how individuals and communities may mitigate the psychic suicide implicit in their subjugated standpoints. Through a politic of flexibility, that is, embracing duality and ambiguity, Black women may survive and thrive.[64] Similar to an ecstatic or mystical union in which one falls, flows, and melts into a void of nothingness, Black women immerse themselves in liminality, in nothingness to ultimately transcend socio-political boundaries and topographies. Indeed, the conscious choice to use the imposed emptiness of their standpoint as an "occasion for insight rather than as one more indication of their worthlessness" renders liminality as a vehicle for liberation.[65] Black women are enabled to live and survive only through a constant and differential movement "betwixt and between" trajectories of being.[66]

In addition to affirming hybridity and differential movement, Lasyrenn also restores a sense of presence, ontological Blackness. In Vodou, she beckons devotees to "Ginen," the ancestral home and dwelling place of the Iwa beneath the water, connecting individuals to the culture and wisdom of Africa.[67] Africa here becomes a historical, terrestrial, and psychic place/ space; it is a distinct frame of reference that is inscribed on every reality. On every person, fantasy, desire, or goal, Africa becomes omnipresent. As such, Black women are affirmed as children of Africa; their Blackness (ethnicity/culture) or ontology is valued and significant.[68] Moreover, I suggest this projection further situates Black women in a liminal psychic space/ place marked by unity and dissonance. "African influenced value systems" explicitly allow Black women "to live with the contradictions" inherent in existence and make meaning of their lives.[69] They turn out the "dark continent trope" and empower Black women because they reinvest meaning to race, culture, and oppositional perceptual modes.[70] Knowing and perceiving Africanisms at every level of being then is ultimately a transformation of a culture of "power and death into a culture of life and rebirth."[71] Through a meta-ideologizing process, Black women create an autonomous space in which reality may be experienced and named in one's own words without the disruption and interjection of another's interpretation.

## Conclusion

In conclusion, a critical exposition of ADR as a methodology of emancipation and a semiotic analysis of the many representations and attributes of one Orisa, Osun, illustrate the contestation, negotiation, and transformation of Black womanhood. Through mystical identification with the Orisa, Black women are able to discern and challenge the construction and manipulation of controlling/devaluing "public images" that hold up distorted mirrors or "public images" of white hegemonic mores and values.[72] Indeed, we are enabled to view the paths of surveillance and oppression and how to work within and without to annihilate them. As a result, Black women are ushered into modes of self-definition and self-actualization; we move from a narrative of madness to one of healing, wholeness, and hybridity. The key to spiritual liberation becomes then the internal and external deconstruction of Eurocentric patriarchal codes and structures. We must rescue Black womanhood from the omnipresent and powerful gaze of white-male supremacy that explicitly colonizes our consciousness. Rather than being a void upon which the dominant culture attempts to establish one mode of perception as fact, Black women become reflective spaces, both/and figures that hold organic conceptions of seeing and being. This process is particularly significant for Womanists seeking to establish autonomous epistemologies. Since Black women have been "so long unmirrored, we may have forgotten how we look. Nevertheless, we can't theorize in a void, we must have evidence."[73] Osun and other Orisa become the evidence that assist Black women in becoming actors, who define our situations and employ internally produced gazes. We begin to see ourselves oppositionally by imagining, describing, and inventing self as a transformative whole being rather than the perpetual other.

"We have been beggars at the table of a religion that sanctioned our destruction. Our own religions denied, forgotten; our own ancestral connections to All Creation something of which we are ashamed."
—Alice Walker[74]

"Well, I say . . . we all have to start somewhere if us want to do better, and our own self is what us have to hand."   —Alice Walker[75]

NOTES

1. Tracey E. Hucks, "'Burning with a Flame in America': African American Women in African-Derived Traditions," *Journal of Feminist Studies in Religion* 17, no. 2 (Fall 2001): 89–90.

2. Chela Sandoval, *Methodology of the Oppressed* (Minneapolis: University of

Minnesota Press, 2000), 10. I speak here of those religious complexes (particularly Santeria, Vodou, and Yoruba/Orisa) emerging within the context of the Atlantic slave trade and developing/flourishing in the United States through a process of localization. Although there are significant conceptual/ritual differences present in each system, the representation and understanding of the reciprocal relations between devotees and Orisa are analogous. Thus, when I speak of ADR I am generally referring to the consistencies found across these traditions.

3. Alice Walker, "Definition of Womanist," in *In Search of Our Mothers' Gardens: Womanist Prose* (San Diego: Harcourt Brace Jovanovich, 1983), 1.

4. Ibid.

5. Ibid.

6. Gloria Wade-Gayles, *No Crystal Stair: Visions of Race and Sex in Black Women's Fiction* (New York: Pilgrim Press, 1984), 184. Sandoval, *Methodology of the Oppressed,* 27.

7. Michael N. Dash, Jonathan Jackson, and Stephen C. Rasor, *Hidden Wholeness: An African American Spirituality for Individuals and Communities* (Cleveland, OH: United Church Press, 1997), 19.

8. The superimposed layers of the cosmos—which broadly reflect Eliade's generalized functionalist presentation of the sacred—of reality function as containers of and conduits for a salient neutral mystical power that lives and speaks. This power may be harnessed by humanity or a divine community of beings to positively or negatively impact destiny. Mary Cuthrell Curry, "Making the Gods in New York: The Yoruba Religion in the Black Community (Black Community, Santeria)," Ph.D. diss., City University of New York, 1991, pp. 61.

9. Mircea Eliade, *The Sacred and the Profane: The Nature of Religion* (San Diego: Harcourt Brace, 1959, 1987), 172. Donna Danette Daniels, "When the Living Is the Prayer: African-Based Religious Reverence in Everyday Life among Women of Color Devotees in the San Francisco Bay Area." Ph.D. diss., Stanford University, 1998, p. 95.

10. Daniels, "When the Living Is the Prayer," 13.

11. John S. Mibiti, *Introduction to African Religion* (Chicago: Heinemann, 1975), 36.

12. Peter L. Berger, *The Sacred Canopy: Elements of a Sociological Theory of Religion* (New York: Anchor Books, 1969, 1990), 2.

13. Mary Douglass, *How Institutions Think* (Syracuse: Syracuse University Press, 1986), 13–14. Zora Neale Hurston, *Mules and Men* (London: K. Paul, 1935), 79.

14. I do want to note here that ancestors are particularly important in constructing identity, but that the patterning process is primarily formed on the figures of the Orisa.

15. Berger, *The Sacred Canopy,* 32.

16. Gary Edwards and John Mason, *Black Gods: Orisa Studies in the New World*

(Brooklyn, NY: Yoruba Theological Archministry, 1998), 1–11. Curry, "Making the Gods in New York," 85–88.

17. Karen McCarthy Brown, *Mama Lola: A Vodou Priestess in Brooklyn* (Berkeley: University of California Press, 2001), 221.

18. Aja, personal interview, Decatur, Georgia, April 13, 2002.

19. Ibid.

20. Gloria Anzaldúa, *Borderlands/La Frontera: The New Mestiza*, 2nd ed. (San Francisco: Aunt Lute Books, 1999), 105.

21. Semiotics moves power through the faculty to read signs in culture as cultural, historical, and human productions; mythologizing challenges ideological forms by deconstructing them to unveil deeper levels of meaning; revolutionary examination or meta-ideologizing appropriates dominant forms whole to transform them by inscribing new meanings; and differential movement makes it all possible through the revolutionary love of self and community (Sandoval, *Methodology of the Oppressed*, 83).

22. Sandoval, *Methodology of the Oppressed*, 92. Roland Barthes, "Myth Today," in *Mythologies* (New York: Hill and Wang, 1957), 113–115.

23. I do acknowledge that the prevailing cultural milieu is an externally and internally reproduced paradigm that cannot be destroyed or erased in its entirety. This however does not imply that the matrix of oppression is a model "from which there is no exit," rather it is a limiting ideology/structure of relations that perpetuates dehumanization and domesticity. Paolo Friere, *Pedagogy of the Oppressed* (New York: Continuum, 1970), 34. Spaces of autonomy (not wholly implicated or repressed by the milieu) may and do exist to challenge the dominant ethos/worldview. Additionally I liken this process to Berger's cyclical model of project and internalization (Berger, *The Sacred Canopy*, 15). Individuals project the cosmologies of Africa onto the existential landscape to establish a new social matrix. Then through a process of internalization, these alternative constructions become recapitulated and expressed through individual consciousness. As such, the Black Sacred Cosmos of ADR maintains the thought styles of Africa by internalizing and sacralizing its social order (Douglass, *How Institutions Think*, 13, 42).

24. Anthony B. Pinn, *Varieties of African American Religious Experience* (Minneapolis: Fortress Press, 1998), 189.

25. Kimberly Wallace-Sanders, ed., *Skin Deep, Spirit Strong: The Black Female Body in American Culture* (Ann Arbor: University of Michigan Press, 2000), 6.

26. Elizabeth Alexander, "'Coming Out Blackened and Whole': Fragmentation and Regeneration in Audre Lorde's Zami and The Cancer Journals," in ibid., 219. The dominant gaze is turned out, and Black women can claim and realize radical epistemologies. Patricia Hill Collins, *Black Feminist Thought: Knowledge, Consciousness, and the Politics of Empowerment*, 2nd ed. (New York: Routledge, 2000), 252; Sandoval, *Methodology of the Oppressed*, 316.

27. I'm really employing only two figures for analysis. Osun Kole and Lasyrenn may be considered a dualism that proffers a distinctly hegemonic and indigenous understanding of Black women's standpoint and identity.

28. Sandoval, *Methodology of the Oppressed*, 1–9.

29. Rowland Abiodun, "Hidden Power, Osun the Seventeenth Odu," in *Osun Across the Waters: A Yoruba Goddess in Africa and the Americas*, ed. Joseph M. Murphy and Mei-Mei Sanford (Bloomington: Indiana University Press, 2001), 25.

30. Layli Phillips and Dionne Stephens, "Freaks, Golddiggers, Divas, and Dykes: The Sociohistorical Development of Adolescent African American Sexual Scripts," *Sexuality and Culture* (Winter 2003): 1–48. Like Phillips and Stephens, I denote "image" broadly; it goes beyond a visual representation or "two-dimensional symbol of people or objects. The reality is that these are more than pictures that guide behavior," they are scripts of thought and action (5).

31. Luisah Teish, *Jambalaya: The Natural Woman's Book* (San Francisco: Harper and Row, 1985), 58, 221.

32. Chris Weedon, *Feminist Practice and PostStructuralist Theory*, 2nd ed. (Oxford: Blackwell, 1997), 14.

33. Elizabeth Alexander, "'Coming Out Blackened and Whole,'" 223; Terri Kapsalis, "Mastering the Female Pelvis: Race and Tools of Reproduction," 231; Lisa Collins, "Economies of the Flesh: Representing the Black Female Body," all in *Skin Deep, Spirit Strong*, ed. Wallace-Sanders, 109.

34. Hill Collins, *Black Feminist Thought*, 89, 91.

35. Ibid., 69, 139. bell hooks, *Black Looks: Race and Representation* (Boston: South End Press, 1992), 61–73. Rather than being heralded as a wife or a mother, traditional elements that comprise true womanhood, Osun, a divinized Black female is only considered valued as a lover. I suggest this speaks to the contested discourse surrounding Black womanhood, her emasculating "nature," and inability to provide for her children. See Angela Y. Davis, *Women, Race, and Class* (New York: Routledge, 2000); Hill Collins, *Black Feminist Thought*.

36. Hill Collins. *Black Feminist Thought*, 136.

37. Eric C. Lincoln and Lawrence H. Mamiya, *The Black Church in the African American Experience* (Durham, NC: Duke University Press, 1990), 99–278. Franklin E. Frazier, *The Negro Church in America* (New York: Schocken Books, 1963, 1974), 80–85.

38. Sandoval, *Methodology of the Oppressed*, 104.

39. Hill Collins, *Black Feminist Thought*, 96.

40. I suggest here, as many Black feminist scholars have, that Black women's gazes can most viably pierce the objectification of Black women (ibid., 104).

41. Hill Collins, *Black Feminist Thought*, 113. hooks, *Black Looks*, 65. Again, there are many possible alternative understandings that may be discovered through a second level semiotic reading, but I choose to speculate and present the one which I visibly see. The erotic as a source of power because it is through Black

women's bodies and our sexuality that the dominant hegemony tends to reduce and control.

42. Carol P. Christ, *Diving Deep and Surfacing: Women Writers on Spiritual Quest*, 3rd ed. (Boston: Beacon Press, 1980, 1995), 23.

43. Hill Collins, *Black Feminist Thought*, 150, 167. bell hooks, *All About Love: New Visions* (New York: HarperPerennial, 2001), 93.

44. Audre Lorde, *Sister Outsider: Essays and Speeches by Audre Lorde* (Berkeley, CA: Crossing Press, 1984), 54, 56. Hill Collins, *Black Feminist Thought*, 150.

45. Even this duality is misleading as in the figure of Osun what is considered *eros* and *agape* are experienced simultaneously so that the very definition of love that we so often employ is shattered.

46. Lorde, *Sister Outsider*, 54–56, 174.

47. June Jordan has noted that the self-love of the hegemony requires suicide. June Jordan, "Where Is the Love?" in *Women's Consciousness, Women's Conscience: A Reader in Feminist Ethics*, ed. Barbara Hilkert Anderson, Christine E. Gudorf, and Mary D. Pellawuer (San Francisco: Harper and Row, 1985), 204.

48. Jordan, "Where Is the Love?" 203. JoAnne Marie Terrell, *Power in the Blood? The Cross and the African American Experience* (Maryknoll, NY: Orbis Books, 1992), 118.

49. I can't help but note that I was reminded here of Ntozake Shanges's quote "I found god in myself and I loved her fiercely" (Christ, *Diving Deep and Surfacing*, 97).

50. Gloria Anzaldúa, *Borderlands/La Frontera: The New Mestiza*, 2nd ed. (San Francisco: Aunt Lute Books, 1999), 101. Lorde, *Sister Outsider*, 165.

51. Lorde, *Sister Outsider*, 57. hooks, *All About Love*, 88.

52. Lorde, *Sister Outsider*, 55, 57. Hill Collins, *Black Feminist Thought*, 131, 150. Although not explicit in this reading, women's love of women (sexual and nonsexual) is nevertheless legitimized and nurtured. Christ suggests that a black woman in loving a woman through the figure of Osun, "learns to love self" (*Diving Deep and Surfacing*, 94).

53. hooks, *All About Love*, 76.

54. The complexities of difference and its threat to community have been duly noted in the writings of Black feminists including Barbara Omalade and Barbara Smith.

55. Toinette M. Eugene, "While Love is Unfashionable: Ethical Implications of Black Spirituality and Sexuality," in *Women's Consciousness, Women's Conscience*, ed. Hilkert Anderson, Gudorf, and Pellawuer, 126.

56. Hill Collins, *Black Feminist Thought*, 171, my emphasis.

57. Ibid., 205.

58. Sandoval, *Methodology of the Oppressed*, 270.

59. In Vodou, a trinity of beings is often acknowledged, Erzulie Freda, Erzulie Dantor, and Lasyrenn. Interestingly Lasyrenn is an ambiguous figure with connec-

tions to both Mami-Wata and Yemoja and may be described as such by practitioners. However, in this context, I claim Lasyrenn the Siren/mermaid as a representation of Osun. One must note that the figure of the whale is sometimes identified as a separate entity, Labelynn, and in oral tales is considered her mistress the Amazonian, who accompanies/supports the bisexual Lasyrenn (Conner, 59) As such, she epitomizes the borderlands. See Randy P. Conner and David Hatfield Sparks, *Queering Creole Spiritual Traditions: Lesbian, Gay, Bisexual, and Transgender Participation in African-Inspired Traditions in the Americas* (New York: Harrington Park Press, 2004), 59.

60. hooks, *Black Looks*, 131. Lasyrenn is alternately represented as white and black. When you see "her with your eyes in the sea, she's white; when you dream her, she's black" (Brown, *Mama Lola*, 222).

61. Brown, *Mama Lola*, 223. Metaphorically speaking, this is interesting as the mirror is a reflective surface that allows one to see, think, and act in many ways. Lasyrenn at the back of the mirror suggests she is the image, the essence that is an absent presence in all others.

62. Hill Collins, *Black Feminist Thought*, 101.

63. Sandoval, *Methodology of the Oppressed*, 140.

64. A myth exists in which attempting to "try to get too close or hold on too tightly" to any one vision of Lasyrenn ensures an erasure of self (Brown, *Mama Lola*, 223). Individuals may drawn wholly into her seductive depths drown.

65. Christ, *Diving Deep and Surfacing*, 17.

66. Victor Turner, "Betwixt and Between: The Liminal Period in Rites of Passage," in *The Forest Symbols: Aspects of the Ndembu Ritual* (Ithaca, NY: Cornell University Press, 1967), 95.

67. Brown, *Mama Lola*, 224.

68. As such, individuals are affirmed further, situated within a liminal psychic space marked by unity and dissonance, yet affirms their unique glory as children of Africa.

69. Hill Collins, *Black Feminist Thought*, 207.

70. Lola Young, " 'Race,' Identity and Cultural Criticism," in *Feminism and "Race,"* ed. Kum-Kum Bhavnani (Oxford: Oxford University Press, 2001), 172.

71. Christ, *Diving Deep and Surfacing*, 75.

72. Hill Collins, *Black Feminist Thought*, 166.

73. Evelynn Hammonds, "Black (W)holes and the Geometry of Black Female Sexuality," in *Skin Deep, Spirit Strong*, ed. Wallace-Sanders, 306.

74. Alice Walker, "The Only Reason You Want to Go to Heaven Is That You Have Been Driven Out of Your Mind (Off Your Land and Out of Your Lover's Arms)—Clear Seeing, Inherited Religion, and Reclaiming the Pagan Self," *On the Issues* 6, no. 2 (Spring 1997).

75. Alice Walker, *The Color Purple* (Orlando, FL: Harcourt Books, 1982, 2003), 278.

# Part IV

# Critical Engagement

CRITICAL ENGAGEMENT—[the fourth tenet of womanism] 1. the epistemological privilege of Black women borne of their totalistic experience
with the forces of interlocking systems of oppression and strategic options
they devised to undermine them.

"Taking seriously the expansiveness of [Black women's] particularity
means employing an integrated, interstructured analysis [that] helps pry
open the dynamics of oppressions"   —Townes

"[Taking] into account the complexity of black women's experience of
interrelated oppressions including (but not excluding) racism, classism,
sexism, and heterosexism, and consider[ing] how this analysis can be
interpreted theologically and ethically while embracing the depths of religious plurality."   —Harris

2. an unequivocal belief that Black women hold the standard and normative measure for true liberation; the capacity of Black women to view
things in their true relations or relative importance; and while expected to
be among the chief arbiters of accountability, advocacy, and authenticity,
they, too, must be faithful to the task of expanding their discourse, knowledge, and skills.

"The conscious and intentional appropriation of one's knowing and
the orientation of that knowledge toward the achievement of authentic
and moral human living . . . an internal requirement toward excellence."

—Copeland

3. a hermeneutical suspicion, cognitive counterbalance, intellectual in-
dictment, and perspectival corrective to those people, ideologies, movements, and institutions that hold a one-dimensional analysis of oppression; an unshakable belief that Black women's survival strategies must
entail more than what others have provided as an alternative.

"[A] certain poignancy that characterizes Black women's intellectual
positioning"   —Copeland

# Nevertheless, in Stark Contradiction

*Nancy Lynne Westfield*

The first time I saw my own reflection
Was in the buckle of the boot
That was stepping on my neck
Though contorted I thought myself beautiful
With this paltry glimpse of myself
Covered with sweat & cunning
My attention is focused toward the smug ones
My eyeballs remain fixed on them lest we die
My slog provides profit for them/I am yet a cotton picker
As I toil they stare watching my lips, hips, my hair
Comparing mine/me to them/theirs
Brown, course, & thick always comes up short, lacking, inferior
Thought to be too much, too extra, too deeply Amethyst
To their lavender pale the High-falutin' folk
Assume themselves better cuz they different
The RevDoctorBishops, The Miss Annes, The Mrs. So'nSos
Think the Gleaning women, the Hagars, the Celies
To be discardable, disrespectable, disgusting

Nevertheless, in stark contradiction,
These Uppity folk panic . . . they can't be without us,
Saditty folk can't do
What we do:
See something where others have thought everything worth taking was took
Create fresh possibilities in heaven & hell & the planets in-between
Stretch hope where anguish & misery thought it ruled supreme
Sister-girls who be like us pioneer in foreign lands

Adapt easily to new terrain
Build homesteads with steely foundations from leaves of new trees
While others scurry 'round for water, sustenance, in scarcity & want
Black women sniff out the untapped
Plumb pauper graves for wisdom
Call on the ancestors to fulfill their promise
We be Black women who know what tradition say & fight to uphold
    support her
We'ns also know uprightness is bundled with innovation
Keeping the law must be done with creativity
A bent over back don't mean she can't see the sun
Divinely dependent upon Mama-n-d'em, Us-ins', All y'all
Our survival continues

# Chapter 13

# Womanist Humanism
## *A New Hermeneutic*

## *Melanie L. Harris*

## *Introduction*

Celebrating twenty years in the academy, womanist theology and ethics survive and thrive through the published pens and activism of several generations of womanist writers, scholars, artists, and activists. The discipline has now reached a level of academic maturity whereby critiques offered, but previously tabled, are now being fully addressed and embraced. Among those critiques include questions concerning the lack of attention womanist theological scholarship has given to Alice Walker's own religious and ethical voice.

To date, limited careful analysis of Walker's nonfiction work revealing her own religious and ethical perspectives has been conducted in the field of womanist theology and ethics. While most womanist religious scholars cite Walker's definition of womanist, only some reference her fiction work, and only a few reference her nonfiction work to examine her own religious presuppositions.[1] This observation is important, since Walker's term "womanist," adopted by womanist religious scholars, derives from her work and her own socio-cultural religious perspectives. Alice Walker is a self-proclaimed pagan. In her essay, "The Only Reason You Want to Go to Heaven,"[2] she explains paganism as an Earth-centered religion and writes, "in day-to-day life, I worship the Earth as God—representing everything —and Nature as its spirit."[3] Overlooking Walker's paganism expressed in her fiction and nonfiction work exposes a significant gap in the discipline of womanist theological scholarship because of the important task of uncovering black women's voices, including Walker's.[4]

Why hasn't womanist theology and ethics taken Walker's pagan identity seriously? Is it because, until recently, womanist theology has been identified as solely Christian and limited to using methodologies that assume Christian presuppositions and associate with Christian categories? Do those categories limit womanist theology's ability to reach and liberate black women who have religious experiences outside the Christian tradition? As the debate ensues about the nature and future direction of womanist theology, new methodologies are being developed to address these and other critiques. This essay introduces a new hermeneutic, womanist humanism, designed to move womanist theology into position to face these critiques and accept the challenge of religious plurality. It also takes into account the current limitations expressed in black humanist thought.

## Facing the Critique: Womanist Humanism

Born of two schools of thought, womanism and black humanism, womanist humanism is a new hermeneutic that introduces a mode of fresh and hard inquiry into the "complex subjectivity"[5] of womanist identity in connection with the reality of religious pluralism. It combines a womanist theological approach and attention to black women's experiences with a black humanist "nitty-gritty hermeneutic."[6] The former, a womanist theological approach, centers on the theological reflections and ethical worldviews of black women that are shaped by their experiences of—and resistance to—racism, classism, sexism, and heterosexism. It uses race, class, and gender analysis to frame a lens through which these issues and other interrelated oppressions are examined in order to develop strategies and theologies of resistance and survival. Some of the important tasks central to a womanist theological approach include uncovering black women's stories and naming them as valid epistemologies, constructing liberating theologies and ethical worldviews, and giving attention to quality of life issues for black women across the African Diaspora.

The latter hermeneutic, a "nitty-gritty hermeneutic," derives from a philosophical school of thought, black humanism. Black humanism asserts human worth, agency, and responsibility, and envisions these themes as a part of the process toward black liberation. Black humanism also emphasizes an "increased sense of self,"[7] the empowerment for black individuals and black communities.[8] The "nitty-gritty hermeneutic," developed out of the strong black humanist position of Anthony B. Pinn, "often brings into question the theological and religious assumptions of Christian doctrinal structures and scriptures."[9] In its attempt to reveal the "rawest layer of truth,"[10] this hermeneutic centers on "problems of life" and existential questions about the meaning and dehumanization of black life and objectification of black bodies. The promotion of justice, the eradication of evil, the existence of God, and theodicy are other "problems of life" that a black humanist "nitty-gritty hermeneutic" attempts to address.

## Mutually Enhancing

A womanist humanist hermeneutic is unique in that it combines approaches from both womanist theology and black humanism to conceive of a mutually enhancing hermeneutic that helps to reveal shortcomings and strengths within both schools of thought. The black humanist lens of a womanist humanist hermeneutic helps womanist theology to confront theological "hard inquiries" and become more self-critical of its Christian categories. By working outside the scope of Christian categories, the black humanist lens points out the problematic assumption that a womanist perspective is synonymous with a Christian perspective. It pushes womanist theology to become more inclusive of religious positions beyond Christianity.

At the same time, a womanist lens of a womanist humanist hermeneutic presses black humanism to incorporate race, class, and gender analysis of black women's experiences and examine how these and other interrelated oppressions impact black women's theological and religious reflections. Recent work in black humanism identifies the work of only a few black women as having humanist sensibilities. The limited presence of black women's voices in black humanist scholarship exposes its lack of attention to gender in the construction of the sense of self. While a sense of self is a key tenet of black humanism, to date, it has not provided analysis of how interrelated race, class, and gender oppressions impact black women's sense of self. Overlooking the importance of black women's selves as gendered exposes black humanist thought to critiques of sexism. Furthermore, black humanist male-centered and nontheistic perspectives raise questions of its accessibility to black women who may have theistic belief systems.

## The Black Humanist Side of Womanist Humanism

One way womanist humanism helps womanist become more self-critical of its Christian constructions is a reexamination of the phrase "Loves the Spirit" in the four-part definition of womanist. Careful analysis of "Loves the Spirit" would suggest that Walker points to the nature of womanist spirituality as religiously pluralistic. This understanding would expand womanist theological discourse to include "womanist wisdom"[11] from a variety of religious, theistic, pantheistic, and nontheistic perspectives that are life-affirming and life-giving to black women.

To date, most womanist theologians and ethicists write from a theistic and Christian-centered perspective, using a Christian lens to express black women's experiences of religion and liberation.[12] While the traditional perspective of womanist theology is Christian, a womanist humanist lens shows that womanist, by definition, does not necessitate an adherence to solely Christian discourse. The black humanist lens that contributes to the womanist humanist approach enhances womanist theology by exposing the elevated and exclusive status Christianity holds within womanist theology. The humanist side of womanist humanism poses questions about whether that status fits the overarching goal of womanism to uncover *all* black women's stories and religious reflections.[13] It also investigates whether womanist, by definition, is inherently Christian. Examination of the definition provides evidence that the definition of womanist leaves room to embrace black women's reflections on a variety of religious experiences.

The phrase "*Loves* the Spirit"[14] is not inherently Christian nor theistic. In fact, the inclusive nature of the womanist definition celebrates a variety of colors and cultures and honors a fluidity of emotional expressions and religious identities. Womanist, by definition, includes the perspectives of black women who may understand the phrase "*Loves* the Spirit" in communal and universal terms, separate and apart from Christian or theistic understandings. In essence, one does not have to be a Christian to be a womanist. Womanists can identify as theistic, nontheistic, polytheistic, or pantheistic and participate in a variety of religious traditions.

"*Loves* the Spirit" has been the target of womanist debate before. In her initial response in the 1989 landmark essay, "Roundtable Discussion: Christian Ethics and Theology in Womanist Perspective," Cheryl J. Sanders raises a concern about the adoption of the term womanist to express black women's religious (read: Christian) experiences. In the essay, Sanders claims that the phrase "*Loves* the Spirit" is simply not strong enough to convey the Christian commitment, she believed, black women theologians and ethicists needed to express when writing about black women's theological and ethical reflection. The lack of "God-language" in the definition made use of the term womanist problematic for Sanders and she questioned whether womanist theology was appropriating a term that did not fit.

> The fact is that womanist is essentially a secular cultural category whose theological and ecclesial significations are rather tenuous. . . . Walker's definition comprises an implicit ethics of moral autonomy, liberation, sexuality and love that is not contingent upon the idea of God or revelation. . . . The use of black women's experience as a basis for theology is futile if that experience is interpreted apart from a fully theistic context.[15]

Although Sanders raises a critical point, one must ask what is to become of the stories and experiences of black women who do not function in these theistic or Christian contexts that Sanders alludes to? What, for example, is to become of Walker's spiritual story and perspective as a pagan black woman? Does womanist theology have no relation with or responsibility to honor black women's non-Christian religious experiences? A womanist humanist hermeneutic helps to address this question and examine other questions regarding womanist self-critique.

### The Womanist Side of Womanist Humanism

The mutually enhancing character of womanist humanism uncovers how a womanist approach challenges black humanism in two ways. First, the womanist side of womanist humanism acknowledges the importance of including black women's voices and providing race, class, and gender analysis crucial to understanding black women's sense of self. Sense of the self is a vital characteristic and tenet of black humanism.[16] Understanding the depth of how race, class, and gender identities (complex subjectivity) impact black women's sense of self is critical for black humanist scholarship to address. If black women's voices, perspectives, art, and writings are to be fully and equally integrated into black humanism, then the discipline must open itself to race, class, and gender analysis.

In addition, although womanism negates the religiously pluralistic nature of black women in its appropriation of the womanist definition, its theistic nature challenges black humanism to engage in a theistic orientation. To date, most theological scholarship and discussion involving a black humanist perspective comes from a nontheistic, "strong humanist," and male perspective. The absence of a female theological perspective in black humanism exposes it to questions concerning how a male lens may constrict the scope of black humanism. "Why are there so few 'daughters of Nimrod'?"[17] "Is there something inherently patriarchal about how black humanism is constructed that limits the expression of black women's voices?" "Is there any room for black women theists to identify themselves as black humanists or a womanist with humanist sensibilities to maintain her theistic beliefs?" These questions are important to address if black humanism is be accessible to womanists. Womanist humanism challenges black humanism and brings to light a theistic perspective buried inside black humanism.

Initially constructed along the hard boundaries of theistic and nontheistic beliefs, Anthony B. Pinn introduced two categories of humanism in his 1995 book, *Why Lord? Suffering and Evil in Black Theology*.[18] Explaining the rigid distinctions between strong and weak humanism he writes, "the former entails an increased sense of self and one's place in the human family. This position does not call God's existence into question. . . . For strong humanism, relatively sustained and oppressive world conditions bring into question the presence of any Being outside of the human realm."[19]

Theistic black humanism that includes some voices and experiences of black women entails more than "an increased sense of self and one's place in the human family."[20] Analysis conducted through a womanist humanist hermeneutical lens would suggest that embracing black women's voices obliges black humanism to reshape itself in order to allow breathing room for black women's perspectives that may also be theistic. One way the womanist side of a womanist humanist hermeneutic helps black humanism engage theistic perspectives is by proposing that black humanism adopt the inclusive and fluid nature found in womanist thought.

The inclusive and fluid nature found in the meaning and definition of the word womanist is one way the womanist approach helps black humanism expand its discourse. Womanist humanism enhances black humanism by meshing its hard boundaries into a more fluid, mutually enhancing one, allowing more space for a theistic humanist perspective.

Phrases within the womanist definition that point to the inclusivity of cultures and colors, sexual preferences, and emotional flexibility suggest that the term womanist was originally created as a fluid term. The diversity of perspectives and inclusive nature of the word is explained further by Walker herself, in an essay entitled, "Audre's Voice."[21] In the essay, Walker gives tribute to the acclaimed writer Audre Lorde and reflects upon the powerful impact Lorde's work has on her own work. Walker's reflections upon the distinctions between womanist and black feminist in the essay are telling of the inclusive nature of womanist. Recalling a conversation with Lorde, who respectfully disagreed with Walker's creation of the term, Walker clarifies that the term womanist was not created to divide ranks within black feminism, or separate black women from themselves, but rather to honor the rich diversity and wholeness of black women's experiences.

> She had questioned my use of the word "womanist" in lieu of "black feminist," saying that it appeared to be an attempt to disclaim being feminist. . . .
> I pointed out to her that it is a necessary act of liberation to name oneself with words that fit; that this was a position in her own work celebrated. . . .
> We talked until Audre seemed to understand my point about using the word "womanist": more room in it for changes, said I, sexual and otherwise. More reflective of black women's culture, especially Southern culture. . . .
> We ended our conversation amicably.[22]

The fluidity and "room for changes" suggested in Walker's interpretation of womanist support the adoption of a new womanist humanist hermeneutic that calls for a more nuanced and fluid boundary between strong and weak positions in black humanism.[23]

### Digging Deeper: A Womanist Humanist Hermeneutic

A womanist humanist hermeneutic is mutually enhancing in that it addresses and critiques two schools of thought, womanism and black humanism. Regarding womanism, the hermeneutic points out ways in which theological womanism can reach beyond Christian constructions and include a variety of black women's religious experiences as resources for womanist scholarship. The hermeneutic also contributes an analytical lens whereby black humanists can examine the interconnectedness between race, class, and gender, thus making black humanism more inclusive of black women's experiences and more accessible to black women religious scholars concerned with multilayered oppressions facing black women. A womanist humanist hermeneutic also uncovers an important theistic stance within black humanism and two shared themes found within each school of thought, self-love and human agency. Examination of these themes forms a basis upon which to enhance womanist and black humanist discourse, builds a wider base for the womanist humanist hermeneutic, and affirms the rich stories and religious diversity of black women.

## *Self-Love and Human Agency in Womanism and Black Humanism*

One of the theoretical bases for womanist humanism is comparative analysis of shared themes and values found within womanism and black humanism. The common themes of self-love and human agency in both schools of thought suggest that, in spite of the differences in philosophical and theological perspectives, both womanism and black humanism share some common ground. The elements of common ground are strengthened by Walker's four-part definition.

### Self-Love

Self-love and human agency are intrinsic threads within womanist and black humanist thought. These themes play an essential role in expanding womanist theological scholarship beyond Christian constructions and widening black humanism to work beyond its currently constructed, male-dominated, and nontheistic perspectives. Concerning the presence of self-love in womanist thought, it is the most well-known value exclaimed in a three-word phrase of the womanist definition. The phrase, "Loves herself. *Regardless*," implies a persuasive tone, encouraging black women, who identify with the term womanist, to embrace and love their whole selves, despite outer circumstances and interrelated social oppressions. Often interpreted as "love yourself. *Regardless*," the message of self-love captures the primary goal of womanism to empower and liberate black women across the African Diaspora, and all women of color. Each part of the four-part womanist definition supports the theme of self-love by evoking images of strength and describing womanists as black women who are self-assured and who take the path toward self-knowledge seriously.

For example, in part one of the definition the descriptive words "audacious," "courageous," and "willful" suggest a radical sense of self-knowledge, self-ownership, and self-acceptance. In black culture, the link between knowing the self, self-autonomy, and owning authority over one's self dates back to encounters of existing as a people whose humanness was not always assumed. Throughout American racial history, arguments for the dehumanization of black women and men were used to scientifically "prove" the inferiority of Blacks and the superiority of Whites.[24] These "proofs" were used to legalize slavery, lynch black people, and justify racial profiling. The embrace of self-love in Walker's womanist definition combats the historical message of dehumanization that has accompanied black life, and promotes the idea that black women should know and love themselves as fully human, having innate worth and value. Addressing womanists' humanness and human value is key to a womanist humanist outlook. This outlook pays particular attention to how black women and womanists are treated in humane ways in the wider society and recognizes the strivings of black women and womanists to live fully whole and fully human despite facing multiple oppressions.

The knowledge of and love of the self, emphasized in Walker's definition, supports a womanist humanist perspective and hermeneutic in that it leads womanists to embrace a variety of selves or identities that womanists represent. This includes acknowledging the diverse socio-cultural, sexual, and religious identities of womanists, while at the same time pointing to the shared humanness among womanists. Acknowledging the diversity of womanists' identities and the shared humanness of womanists help to expand womanist discourse.

Self-love is also a theme in black humanism. Evidence of this is found in the five principles of black humanism, revealing self-love as an aspect of self-determination and a key principle of black humanist identity. In his recent book, *African American Humanist Principles: Living and Thinking Like the Children of Nimrod*,[25] Anthony B. Pinn proposes five major principles of black humanism that reveal the values held and sensibilities associated with a black humanist position. They are:

1. understanding of humanity as fully (and solely) accountable and responsible for the human condition and the correction of humanity's plight;
2. suspicion toward or rejection of supernatural explanation and claims, combined with an understanding of humanity as an evolving part

of the natural environment as opposed to being a created being. This can involve disbelief in God(s);

3. an appreciation for African American cultural production and a perception of traditional form of black religiosity as having cultural importance as opposed to any type of "cosmic" authority;

4. a commitment to individual and societal transformation;

5. a controlled optimism that recognizes both human potential and human destructive activities.[26]

The theme and value of self-love in the black humanist principles can be seen most vividly in tenet number three. Appreciating and valuing the cultural production that comes from one's own people suggests that self-love is evident in the validation of black cultural modes of expression. Themes of self-respect, self-ownership, and self-determination undergird this understanding and value of self-love in black humanism. To appreciate and value black peoples and culture, to be accountable to the human condition, to correct humanity's plight, and to commit to individual and societal transformation implies that a tenet of black humanism is the eradication of racism, classism, sexism, and heterosexism so that human potential and self-love can be reached.

## Human Agency

Human agency is another theme found within the principles of black humanism. It is defined as a human's ability and right to exert power over one's own self. It includes having the power to take responsibility and make decisions for one's self. The emphasis on human responsibility in black humanism suggests the presence of human agency.

Making decisions for the good of one's self and an emphasis on black women's autonomy also suggests human agency is a major characteristic within womanism. Human agency is revealed most clearly in the womanist definition. Part one of the definition describes human agency as a womanist who has knowledge and wants "to know more," and "interested in grown up doings."[27] These attributes imply a black woman's knowledge and ability to exert power over her own self. Part two of the definition visibly illustrates human agency as a key theme in womanist thought by referring to a womanist as "traditionally capable."[28] The short story told in part two of the definition suggests that the daughter, mother, and community ("bunch of other slaves") have agency by "walking to Canada" in hopes of reaching freedom. Even the hope of achieving freedom can be seen as evidence of human agency.

The themes of self-love and human agency found in womanism and black humanism suggest that the common values held in both schools of thought serve as the foundation for womanist and black humanist discourse and establish the base for the construction of a womanist humanist hermeneutic. This hermeneutic identifies the limitations within womanist and black humanist thought as well as identifies their strengths. These strengths serve as a catalyst for the development of life-affirming methodologies and hermeneutics inclusive of religious plurality and race, class, and gender analysis. Further development of these methodologies and hermeneutics would widen womanist and black humanist scholarship to include the diverse life experiences and religious identities of black peoples and, specifically, black women.

## Conclusion

Facing the critique of outside theological perspectives that traditionally negate the validity of black women's voices and experiences as sources for alternative epistemologies comes at a cost for womanist theology. It requires womanist theology to mature. Beyond its comfortable settings of Christian categories and perspectives, womanist theology is now at a point whereby its voice must speak for the liberation and religious expression of black women in a variety of religious traditions. No longer does the Christian church or academic settings house enough space to embody where womanist theology must go. If we are to engage all of black women's religious experiences, womanist theology must break outside of its own western, Christian categories, be self-critical, and begin to embrace religious plurality.

Keeping black women's voices, experiences, and perspectives at the forefront of womanist theology is central to its approach. Giving special attention to race, class, and gender analysis and examining how other interrelated oppressions impact black women's theological and ethical perspectives continue to be important for womanist theology and womanist thought as a whole.

Twenty years after its inception, womanism is ready to enter dialogue with other schools of thought that can critique, enrich, and expand the scope of its discourse. Black humanism is one of these schools that contributes to and is mutually enhanced by a womanist perspective. Its sharp critique of Christianity informs womanist theology on how to move beyond Christian presuppositions and be more inclusive of other black women's non-Christian stances. True to its communal nature, womanist theology not only receives critique that will help its growth, but also supplies black humanism with critique that will honor black women's presence in black humanism. As such, womanist critique of black humanism informs the male lens of a strong humanist perspective of ways to be more inclusive of women and black women's experiences of religion. Developing race, class, and gender analysis within black humanist critique is essential to making black humanism accessible to black women. Likewise, uncovering a new kind of theism within black humanism is key for black women theists, who also identify as having humanist sensibilities.

A womanist humanist hermeneutic combines womanist methodology and attention to black women's experiences with a black humanist "nitty-gritty hermeneutic."[29] The new hermeneutic is mutually enhancing to both schools of thought and helps to provide critique that will enrich the future direction of both womanism and black humanism. Womanist humanism can be described as the personification of a combined womanist attitude of "wanting to know more and in greater depth than is considered 'good' for one,"[30] and the black humanist characteristic of "heuristic rebelliousness."[31] As such, it takes seriously hard theological critique of Christianity and forms a critical, descriptive, and prescriptive approach to black religion.[32]

Black women's stories have always remained central to the work of black womanism and the scope of womanist humanism is no different. Womanist humanism takes into account the complexity of black women's experience of interrelated oppressions including (but not excluding) racism, classism, sexism, and heterosexism, and considers how this analysis can be interpreted theologically and ethically while embracing the depths of religious plurality.

The common themes and values identified in both womanism and black humanism present a firm foundation for a womanist humanist hermeneutic. The shared association that both groups can and have made with the perspective and person of Walker also suggests that both groups share a common identity. It is this common identity that shapes the frame of womanist humanism. The future direction of womanist humanism includes analysis of Walker's theological voice and her religious and ethical reflections. By creating a space to engage religious plurality, through the use of a womanist humanist hermeneutic, womanist theology can now embrace Walker's paganism and discover how this religious stance reflects womanism. Uncovering Walker's theological voice will not only honor her position as the mother of the term womanist, but it will also fuel future work with an abundance of sources for the study of black religion.

N O T E S

1. Examples of some womanists' works that have cited Walker's nonfiction writings, beyond the definition, include Katie G. Cannon, *Black Womanist Ethics* (Atlanta: Scholars Press, 1988), and *Katie's Canon: Womanism and the Soul of the Black Community* (New York: Continuum, 1996). Delores S. Williams gives attention to Walker's fiction work, *The Color Purple,* in her text, *Sisters in the Wilderness: The Challenge of Womanist God-Talk* (Maryknoll, NY: Orbis Books, 1993). Emilie M. Townes also references *The Color Purple,* in *In a Blaze of Glory: Womanist Spirituality as Social Witness* (Nashville: Abingdon Press, 1995).

2. Alice Walker, "The Only Reason You Want to Go to Heaven Is That You Have Been Driven out of Your Mind (Off Your Land and out of Your Lover's Arms)—Clear Seeing, Inherited Religion, and Reclaiming the Pagan Self," in *Anything We Love Can Be Saved: A Writer's Activism* (New York: Ballantine, 1997).

3. Ibid., 9.

4. According to womanist ethicist Marcia Y. Riggs, there are at least four goals of womanist ethical scholarship. They are clearly outlined in her text, *Awake, Arise and Act: A Womanist Call for Black Liberation* (Cleveland, OH: Pilgrim Press, 1994), 2. One of the primary goals is "uncovering the roots of a womanist tradition through examination and reintegration of black women's experience into black history in particular and American history in general." In this first task of uncovering, Riggs suggests that studying the lives and ethical thought of historical and present-day black women is crucial for womanist scholarship.

5. I am building upon Anthony B. Pinn's notion of complex subjectivity articulated in his work, *Terror and Triumph: The Nature of Black Religion* (Minneapolis, MN: Fortress Press, 2003)

6. This hermeneutic is built to confront theologically "hard inquiries" from outside the scope of traditional Christian categories. For more, see Anthony B. Pinn, *Why Lord? Suffering and Evil in Black Theology* (New York: Continuum, 1995), 117.

7. Ibid., 141.

8. The relationship between the self and community in black humanism can be understood in a similar way to the way ethicist Peter J. Paris explains the relationship between the person and the community in his work. In *Virtues and Values: The African and African American Experience (Minneapolis, MN: Augsburg*

*Fortress, 2004)*, he suggests that the self (person) and the community are in an "integral person-community relationship" (20) and that this is possible because "the person's life has an ultimate goal . . . the preservation and promotion of community" (15).

9. Pinn, *Why Lord?* 180.

10. Ibid.

11. I am indebted to Emilie M. Townes for the use of this term. In her book *In a Blaze of Glory*, she describes womanist wisdom as having many sources saying, "Womanist wisdom springs out of the experience of African American women as they have been daughters, wives, partners, aunts, grandmothers, mothers, other mothers, comrades, worshipers, protestors, wisdom bearers, murderers, and saints in African American culture and society—and in the life of the church" (10).

12. An exception to this is the work by Debra Mubashshir Majeed, included in this anthology; see chapter 3, "Womanism Encounters Islam: A Muslim Scholar Considers the Efficacy of a Method Rooted in the Academy and the Church."

13. Uncovering black women's voices and experiences is named as an important task and proscribed as a methodological step in the work of many womanist scholars, including Alice Walker in her essay "Saving the Life That Is Your Own: The Importance of Models in an Artist Life"; Katie G. Cannon in her book *Black Womanist Ethics* (Atlanta: Scholars Press, 1988); Emilie M. Townes in her book *In a Blaze of Glory*; and Marcia Y. Riggs in her book *Awake, Arise and Act*.

14. Alice Walker, *In Search of Our Mothers' Gardens: Womanist Prose* (San Diego: Harcourt Brace Jovanovich, 1983).

15. Cheryl J. Sanders and Katie G. Cannon, Emilie M. Townes, M. Shawn Copeland, bell hooks, Cheryl Townsend Gilkes, "Roundtable Discussion: Christian Ethics and Theology in Womanist Perspective," *Journal of Feminist Studies in Religion* 5 (Fall 1989): 87.

16. Pinn, *Why Lord?*

17. The term "daughters of Nimrod" refers to the black women writers, referred to in Anthony B. Pinn, *African American Humanist Principles: Living and Thinking Like the Children of Nimrod* (New York: Palgrave, 2004).

18. Pinn, *Why Lord?*

19. Ibid., 141.

20. Ibid.

21. Alice Walker, "Audre's Voice," in *Anything We Love Can Be Saved* (New York: Ballantine, 1997).

22. Ibid.

23. Walker's understanding of womanist as a fluid term simultaneously supports a black humanist push for womanist theology to include black women's theistic, pantheistic, and even nontheistic perspectives on religion. Understanding these religious experiences as valid sources of womanist wisdom is an important task for womanist theology, especially because a major goal of the discipline is

to uncover black women's stories and mine these stories for womanist wisdom, moral and religious understandings.

24. George M. Fredrickson, *The Black Image in the White Mind: The Debate on Afro-American Character and Destiny, 1817–1914* (Middleton, CT: Wesleyan University Press, 1987).

25. Pinn, *African American Humanist Principles*.

26. Ibid., 7.

27. Walker, *In Search of Our Mothers' Gardens,* xi.

28. Ibid.

29. This hermeneutic is built to confront theologically "hard inquiries" from outside the scope of traditional Christian categories. For more, see Pinn, *Why Lord?* 117.

30. Alice Walker, *In Search of Our Mothers' Gardens,* xi.

31. Pinn, *Why Lord?* 117.

32. Some may argue that the theological critique of Christianity limits the scope of black humanism. Claims that black humanism's focus on critiquing this one religion make it susceptible to being considered a reactionary theology. Womanist humanism follows suit with the necessity to critique Christianity because of the stronghold Christianity, Christian categories, and Christian presuppositions have on the way black religion has been constructed. At the same time, womanist humanism is aware that adopting a black humanist approach makes it susceptible to having limited use. Still, the critiques of Christianity that it offers are necessary in order to widen the scope of womanist thought and black religion.

# Chapter 14

# A Thinking Margin
## *The Womanist Movement as Critical Cognitive Praxis*

## *M. Shawn Copeland*

The mind of the man and the mind of the woman is the
same, but this business of living makes women use their
minds in ways that men don't even have to think about.[1]

My folk . . . have always been a race for theory—though
more in the form of hieroglyph, a written figure which is
both sensual and abstract, beautiful and communicative.[2]

As a group, African American women remain underappreciated as critical
thinkers, that is, as intellectuals who can assess astutely, reliably, and com-
prehensively the breakdowns and collapses in religion and society as well
as generate creative and plausible alternatives. More than a decade ago,
Michele Wallace bemoaned the condition of black women thinkers, con-
curring with French feminist critics that "we are all functioning sym-
bolically as phallocentric, ethnocentric, and logocentric subjects, in other
words as 'white men [with] black women . . . the least convincing in this
role, the least trustworthy."[3] Thus, a certain poignancy characterizes black
women's intellectual positioning: Even those scholars with whom we share
the periphery, other outsiders committed to human flourishing, suspect
our intellectual ability. Put differently, womanists—theologians, ethicists,
scholars, and cultural critics—fight a never-ending battle against the
hegemony of the pseudo-universality of a deracinated male posited as the
Western standard of normativity.

Since the black woman's involuntary arrival in the West, her body and mind have been relegated to the margin, pressed to and beyond the limit. Down-pressed, she became a marginated being—living, breathing, bleeding, thinking, struggling, moving, and loving on the margin. She was reduced to an "exotic" outer edge against which men, white and black, tested physical and sexual power. Her body's heartbreaking fertility was manipulated to adjust the planter's margin of profit; her soul's longing for expression was thwarted against desperate and mimetic preference for the black male. Pressed to the margin, embodying outsider status in society and religion, black women became liminal. Standing outside conventional points of social, cultural, and religious reference, black women have learned to think on the margins, to think clearly and quickly before the blunt force of *ersatz*-reality. Black women intellectuals have taken up Zora Neale Hurston's keen razor-sharp oyster knife to cut through thick stuff, to apprehend and appropriate their own subjectivity in search of truth.

Alice Walker's definition of womanist captures the intensity, responsibility, and accountability of the vocation of black women situated on the margins with the denotation "serious."[4] The notion *serious* connotes a perspective or stance that is *resolute* or "strong-minded, unflinching, tenacious, persevering"; *critical* or "essential, pivotal, radical"; *responsible* or "far-sighted, reasonable, trustworthy."[5]

To be a serious thinking margin means to take up a *critical cognitive praxis*. The phrase *cognitive praxis* denotes the dynamic activity of knowing: questioning patterns and the sometimes jagged-edge of experience (including biological, psychological, social, religious, cultural, aesthetic); testing and probing possible answers; marshaling evidence and weighing it against cultural codes and signs, against imperious and subjugated truths; risking judgment; taking up the struggle. Such knowledge roots its accountability, its authoritative control of meaning and value in the cognitive, moral, and religious authenticity of the identity of poor, excluded, and despised black women.[6] Womanist critical cognitive praxis yields not only concrete embodied relatedness to truth, but a metaphysical one as well. For the human mind wants to know and wants to know that what it knows is *real*. But what is real is not necessarily what is "out-there," for the kind of "measure and standard of objectivity" that "out-there," empirical and observable represents is but a form of naïve realism.[7] Insofar as womanists enact a critical cognitive praxis in which the "fulfilling conditions are data of sense or data of consciousness," then what womanists know is real, is being.[8]

The term *critical* in womanist cognitive praxis refers to its intention to carry out a radical critique of what is. This critique encompasses both intellectual and practical aims, disrupts all habitual affirmation of the status quo, distinguishes appearance from reality, and exposes the roots of what is. To borrow Katie Cannon's definition of liberationist ethics, womanist radical critique engages in

> debunking, unmasking, disentangling the ideologies, theologies, and systems of value operative in a particular society . . . by analyzing the established power relationships that determine cultural, political, and economic presuppositions and by evaluating the legitimating myths that sanction the enforcement of such values.[9]

To be serious, then, calls for the conscious and intentional appropriation of one's knowing and the orientation of that knowledge toward the achievement of authentic and moral human living. To be serious means to acknowledge and accede to an *ethics of thinking,* that is, a surrender and commitment to the *eros* or integrity of the exigencies of the mind. An ethics of thinking has everything to do with what Audre Lorde named "an internal requirement toward excellence" that results in "an internal sense of satisfaction," which stems from "demand[ing] the most from ourselves, from our lives, from our work"; from holding onto our "honor and self-respect."[10]

As an expression of subjugated knowledge,[11] womanist analysis is *responsible* to the historical conditions of black folk—children, women, and men. Patricia Hill Collins offers a truism, although one that is neither trite nor meaningless, when she remarks: "On some level, people who are oppressed usually know it."[12] Subjugated knowledge emerges from ordinary people's reflection on their experiences of gender, race, and class oppression. Cannon describes the relation of womanist work to subjugated knowledge as "draw[ing] on the rugged endurance of black folks in America who outwit, outmaneuver, and outscheme social systems and structures that maim and stifle mental, emotional, and spiritual growth."[13]

Theologians and philosophers frequently equate the term *foundations* with the reduction of the act of knowing (or knowledge) to pure sense impressions or with the attachment of knowing to a priori first principles or with the search for absolute validity and total certainty so typical of Cartesian method in science and philosophy or Kant's categorical imperative in morals. The position I advocate locates womanist foundations not in propositions but in persons, in critically inquiring, thinking, probing, reflecting, judging, deciding, acting black women.

Womanists are their own foundations. When black women critically inquire, probe, reflect, judge, decide, challenge, and act in service of truth, they constitute themselves as critical knowers (and doers). Womanist critical cognitive praxis, as a mode of critical consciousness oriented toward emancipatory struggle (personal, communal, and social transformation), can trace its genesis to the earliest actuated meanings of resistance by captured and enslaved African women.

As a mode of critical self-consciousness, black women's cognitive praxis emphasizes the dialectic between oppression, conscious reflection on experience of that oppression, and action to resist and eliminate it. Thus, as an authentic intellectual movement, womanist analysis originates in asking and answering serious questions; in grappling with human existence confronted by the mix of greed, cruelty, and desire in struggle for life and love. Hence, black women know the meaning of human existence as capital, labor, collateral, medium of exchange, object of property. But black women also know themselves as subjects, as thinkers, as knowers, as actors. The matrix of domination responds to human agency: the struggle of black women suggests that there is choice and power to think, to theorize, to act—mindfully, seriously.

Womanists are their own foundations. This position welcomes Toni Morrison's insistence that the Ancestors are foundations.[14] We should recall that Alice Walker puts forward the definition of womanist in the context of remembering and honoring the Foremothers. Indeed, her search for a ground on which to stand and from within which to grow leads to and through our mothers' gardens. Here, audacious women tend and prune the trees of the knowledge of good and evil, of truth and life; plant and nurture magnificent flowers. The wisdom they possess grows from experience and struggle. Walker describes these mothers and grandmothers and great-grandmothers in lyrical, yet poignant language as

> exquisite butterflies trapped in an evil honey, toiling away their lives in an era, a century that did not acknowledge them except as "the mule of the world." They dreamed dreams that no one knew—not even themselves, in any coherent fashion—and saw visions no one could understand. . . . They forced their minds to desert their bodies and their striving spirits sought to rise, like frail whirlwinds from the hard red clay. And when those

frail whirlwinds fell, in scattered particles, upon the ground, no one mourned.[15]

Yet the Foremothers persisted in their dreams and "waited to pass on the creative spark, the seed of the flower they themselves never hoped to see."[16] They handed on to their daughters "a legacy of respect for all that illuminates and cherishes life, respect for the possibilities—and the will to grasp them . . . respect for strength [and] love of beauty."[17]

The release of subjugated knowledge constitutes a serious, even dangerous, activity. To question ideas and circumstances, to probe and understand and evaluate and judge those ideas and circumstances, begins a first and crucial moral step toward authentic liberation. Yet liberation springs not only from what human persons know, but also from their actions or showing what they truly are—human beings. Womanist critical cognitive praxis slices open the brutal oppressions of sexism, racism, classism, and heterosexism in order to advance being human and human flourishing.

Womanist analysis is not idealist, believing that to know the good is to choose it; rather, womanist critical cognitive praxis concludes in decision that leads to action, to transformation in religion and society. Audre Lorde warned us that "the master's tools will never dismantle the master's house. They will allow us temporarily to beat him at his own game, but they will never enable us to bring about *genuine change.*"[18] Tools for genuine change or transformation include nurture and interdependency; the acceptance, understanding, and appreciation of difference; and friendship.

Womanists share among themselves as well as with other subaltern scholars a fluid constellation of cognitive and religious commitments, methodological and theoretical practices. Over the past two decades, womanists have developed a wide-ranging and rich conceptual vocabulary that mediates meaning, even as those meanings may be contested and require negotiation and refinement. In considering the meanings of these nine notions —body, canon, death, know, mind, race, sass, survival, transgress—my hope is to suggest something of their protean meanings, repetitive and multilayered resonances; to suggest the curve and flow of the grammar of the womanist movement.

By sorting, labeling, and disciplining different types of human *bodies,* the notion of *race* simultaneously constructs, signifies, and symbolizes social conflicts and interests.[19] To understand race as a social construct is serious *knowledge*. For to consider race as ideology is to refuse to address the longevity, resilience, geographic irreverence, and egregious effects produced by biased race-thinking and race-acting. To dismiss race as illusion detaches it from human experience, that is, from human bodies and their situated-ness in particular social and historical circumstances.

In order to defuse these inaccurate conceptions of race, womanist analysis subverts the aesthetic taxonomy of the West, in which blackness is constructed as a deficient and negative signifier. Black bodies are stigmatized and marked as dangerous, diseased, pathological, sexually deviant, and coerced to assume an inferior ontological position. One way to re-order this aesthetic is to contest the *canon* and its attendant moral and religious connotations.

Canon [from the Greek, connotes standard or measure]: In academic contexts, canon refers to that set of texts that determine the standard by which epistemic, aesthetic, moral, and cultural decisions, as well as human acts, are adjudicated. Canonical texts constitute a course of study and, often, may yield a tradition of thinking. Too often canonical texts valorize or are distorted to valorize *one* culture and *one* experience to the detriment, even degradation, of differing cultural perspectives, insights, and values. To demonstrate the force of the implications of *the* canon in Western education, we need only mention the famous Britannica collection, "The Great Books of the Western World."

A canon coaches, sometimes seduces, but always intentionally forms a *mind*. It leads and trains a mind in an appropriation of a tradition of epistemic, aesthetic, moral, and cultural decisions, priorities, and desires. But, sometimes when coaching and seduction fail, in order to prime the mind and the soul, a *cannon* is turned on human bodies. Cheikh Hamidou Kane in his novel *Ambiguous Adventure* describes the impact of the cannon and the canon in a small African village. He writes:

> real power resided not at all in the cannons of the first morning but in what followed the cannons. Therefore behind the cannons was the new school. The new school had the nature of both the cannon and the magnet. From the cannon it took the efficiency of a fighting weapon. But better than the cannon it made the conquest permanent. The cannon forces the body and the school [the canon] fascinates the soul.[20]

As a serious thinking margin, womanists critique the canons of their various disciplines, not merely because they disapprove of the distinction between opinion and knowledge, nor because they reject the possibility of an objective transculturally valid rational standard.[21] On the contrary, black women *know* (in mind and body) just what it means to be the object of relativized opinion or stereotype, what it means to be excluded from or be regarded as the conspicuous exception within the community of rational discourse. Rejecting knowledge grounded in empiricism and idealism, womanists advance a critical realist way of knowing, in which human experience can be interrogated and differentiated seriously; in which differing and analogous experiences, questions, and judgments are engaged and weighed in the service of understanding reality and truth; and in which knowledge exists for the creation and development of the common human good as well as individual human liberation.[22]

As a serious thinking margin, womanists have adopted an archaeological approach to canon formation. Digging back and deep into black history, literature, and other expressive forms of culture, womanist scholars have unearthed the bodies of unknown or forgotten black women and bodies of unknown or forgotten texts. Katie Cannon brings the writing of black women's texts and the reading of black women's bodies together when she cites African American literary critic Mae Henderson, who identifies "black women's bodies as texts."[23] Thus, the crucial contribution that womanist analysis makes to canon (re)formation is the heretofore neglected subject of the experience of black women.

This does not mean that womanist theologians, for example, overlook Friedrich Schleiermacher or Karl Barth or Bernard Lonergan or Aristotle or Plato just because they may be dead white men. Rather, womanists take the *survival* and *flourishing* of oppressed, excluded, and despised humanity (children, women, and men of all races and classes) as criteria for evaluation in reading texts. As Katie Cannon explains, "Canon formation is a way of establishing new and larger contexts of experience within which African American women can attend to the disparity between sources of oppression and sources of liberation."[24] Insights that potentially enrich or correct our understanding of what is good and true can never be ignored. Reading in this way, womanists disentangle valuable and effective insights from thorny and ineffectual ones. Moreover, through this critical reading, womanists not only critique and (re)shape the canons of their disciplines but also rethink, revise, and transform whole areas in the common fund of human knowledge.

Another and crucial way in which womanists subvert the canon is through teaching. Education, bell hooks insists, must be the practice of freedom, to teach in this way is to teach to transgress. Transgression entails "movement against and beyond boundaries."[25] Transgressive teaching leads students to grapple with boundaries that constrict cognitive and moral growth; encourages them to explore new intellectual terrain; and models for them compassionate solidarity with the poor in the advance of justice.[26] Transgressive teaching grasps and communicates the difference between life and death.

Another form of transgression is *sass.* Sass is the use of mother wit and verbal dexterity to resist insult or assault. It denotes impudent, uppity speech; sharp, cutting back talk—sharp, cutting talk thrown at the back. Sass is a gift from the Ancestors. Enslaved black women took up verbal warfare in order to regain and secure self-esteem, to gain psychological distance, to tell the truth, and, sometimes, to protect against sexual assault.[27] The word "sass" derives from the bark of the poisonous West African sassy tree. Deconcocted and mixed with certain other barks, sass was used in ritual ordeals to test, punish, or absolve those accused of witchcraft. For our enslaved Foremothers, sass was a ready defense that allowed them to "return a portion of the poison the master . . . offered."[28] The sass is strong and threatening in the lines of a song women cutters sang in the Louisiana cane fields: "Rains come wet me/Sun come dry me/Stay back, boss man/Don't come nigh me."[29]

These nine terms—body, canon, death, know, mind, race, sass, survival, transgress—form part of a large and complex conceptual vocabulary that overlaps discussion in other fields, including anthropology, epistemology, literary criticism, philosophy, sociology, Africana and post-colonial studies. This chapter has attempted to interpret and engage some of the notions and terms pertinent to womanist cognitive praxis, and what has been accomplished is by no means definitive or exhaustive. My basic concern here was to turn a light on womanist cognitive praxis and to demonstrate its necessity in the realization of our dreams.

## NOTES

1. John Langston Gwaltney, *Drylongso: A Self-Portrait of Black America* (New York: Vintage Books, 1981), 33.

2. Barbara Christian, "The Race for Theory," in *Making Face, Making Soul: Haciendo Caras,* ed. Gloria Anzaldúa (San Francisco: Aunt Lute, 1990), 336.

3. Michelle Wallace, *Invisibility Blues: From Pop to Theory* (London: Verso, 1990), 7.

234 M. SHAWN COPELAND

4. Alice Walker, *In Search of Our Mothers' Gardens: Womanist Prose* (San Diego: Harcourt Brace Jovanovich, 1983), xi.

5. Robert A. Dutch, ed., *The Original Roget's Thesaurus of English Words and Phrases,* rev. ed. (New York: St. Martin's, 1965), 350, 376.

6. Bernard Lonergan, "Cognitional Structure," in *Collection: Papers by Bernard Lonergan,* ed. Frederick E. Crowe (Montreal: Palm Publishers, 1967), 221–239; idem, *Insight: A Study of Human Understanding,* vol. 3, *Collected Works of Bernard Lonergan* (1957; University of Toronto Press, 1992). My account of womanist cognitive praxis relies on the work of Bernard Lonergan, who offers the best transcultural account of the human mind that I have come across in more than twenty-five years of study. Its significance for the cognitive praxis of all persons forced to the margins of society is found in its ability to pose an ethics of thinking and to expose the emergence of bias when that ethics is violated. To illustrate: Racism, sexism, heterosexism are structural forms of bias that result from *scotoma* or blindness that results from the more or less conscious refusal to admit new insights, questions, discoveries, and to repress the insights or questions that continue to disturb. Thomas Jefferson's ambivalence toward slavery provides a good concrete example.

7. Lonergan, "Theories of Inquiry: Responses to a Symposium," in *A Second Collection,* ed. William F. J. Ryan and Bernard J. Tyrrell (Philadelphia: Westminster Press, 1974), 39. The "out-there" or "the already-out-there-now-real," Lonergan explains in "An Interview with Fr. Bernard Lonergan," in *A Second Collection,* is " 'already'—prior to any questions; 'out'—extroverted consciousness; 'there'—spatial sense organs have spatial objects; 'now'—the time of the observer is the time of the observed" (219).

8. Lonergan, "Insight Revisited," in *A Second Collection,* 274; see also idem, "Metaphysics as Horizon," in *Collection: Papers by Bernard Lonergan,* 202–220; and John Phillips, *Contested Knowledge: A Guide to Critical Theory* (London: Zed Books, 2000).

9. Katie G. Cannon, *Katie's Canon: Womanism and the Soul of the Black Community* (New York: Continuum, 1996), 138.

10. Audre Lorde, "Uses of the Erotic: The Erotic as Power," in her *Sister Outsider: Essays and Speeches by Audre Lorde* (Trumansburg, NY: Crossing Press, 1984), 54.

11. My use of the term "subjugated knowledge," coined by French philosopher Michel Foucault, *Power/Knowledge: Selected Interviews and Other Writings, 1972–1977,* ed. Colin Gordon (New York: Pantheon, 1980), follows Patricia Hill Collins's reformulation of the term to more adequately represent black feminist thought. Foucault defines subjugated knowledge as "a whole set of knowledges that have been disqualified as inadequate to their task or insufficiently elaborated: naïve knowledge, a differential knowledge incapable of unanimity which owes its force only to the harshness with which it is opposed by everything surrounding it" (82).

With Patricia Hill Collins, I suggest that womanist knowledge is neither "naïve," nor incapable of "unanimity," in her *Black Feminist Thought: Knowledge, Consciousness, and the Politics of Empowerment,* 2nd ed. (New York: Routledge, 2000), 291n. 2.

12. Hill Collins, *Black Feminist Thought,* 8.

13. Cannon, "Appropriation and Reciprocity in the Doing of Womanist Ethics," in *Katie's Canon,* 135.

14. Toni Morrison, "Rootedness: The Ancestor as Foundation," in *Black Women Writers, 1950–1980,* ed. Mari Evans (New York: Anchor Press, 1984), 344–345.

15. Walker, *In Search of Our Mothers' Gardens,* 232.

16. Ibid., 232, 240.

17. Ibid., 241–242, 243.

18. Audre Lorde, "The Master's Tools Will Never Dismantle the Master's House," in *Sister Outsider,* 112 (author's italics).

19. Michael Omi and Howard Winant, *Racial Formation in the United States* (New York: Routledge, 1994), 55.

20. Cheikh Hamidou Kane, *Ambiguous Adventure* (1962; New York: Collier Books, 1969), cited in Ngugi wa Thiong'o, *Decolonising the Mind: The Politics of Language in African Literature* (1986; London: James Curry/Heinemann, 1989), 9n. 10, 32.

21. Joseph Wagner, "The Trouble with Multiculturalism," *Soundings* 77, 3–4 (Fall/Winter 1994): 410.

22. Joy James, "Teaching Theory, Talking Community," 118–135, esp. 133, in *Spirit, Space, and Survival: African American Women in (White) Academe,* ed. Joy James and Ruth Farmer (New York: Routledge, 1993).

23. Cannon, "Womanist Perspectival Discourse and Canon Formation," in *Katie's Canon,* 74.

24. Ibid., 76.

25. bell hooks, *Teaching to Transgress: Education as the Practice of Freedom* (New York: Routledge, 1994), 12.

26. Ibid., 13–22.

27. See Joanne M. Braxton, *Black Women Writing Autobiography: A Tradition within a Tradition* (Philadelphia: Temple University Press, 1988).

28. Ibid., 30, 31.

29. Dorothy Sterling, ed., *We Are Your Sisters: Black Women in the Nineteenth Century* (New York: W. W. Norton, 1984), 25, 26.

# Chapter 15

# The Womanist Dancing Mind
## *Speaking to the Expansiveness of Womanist Discourse*

### *Emilie M. Townes*

There is a certain kind of peace that is not merely the absence of war. It is larger than that. The peace I am thinking of is not at the mercy of history's rule, nor is it a passive surrender to the status quo. The peace I am thinking of is the dance of an open mind when it engages another equally open one—an activity that occurs most naturally, most often in the reading/ writing world we live in. Accessible as it is, this particular kind of peace warrants vigilance. The peril it faces comes not from the computers and information highways that raise alarm among book readers, but from unrecognized, more sinister quarters.

### *Toni Morrison,* The Dancing Mind

Morrison's essay is based on her acceptance speech for the National Book Foundation's Medal for Distinguished Contribution to American Letters in 1996. As such, Morrison focuses on the dangers, the necessities, and the pleasures of the reading/writing life in the late twentieth century. For her, the dangers are captured in two anecdotes she tells. In one, it is the danger that "our busied-up, education-as-horse-race, trophy-driven culture poses even to the entitled."[1] In the second, she teases out "the physical danger to writing suffered by persons with enviable educations who live in countries where the practice of modern art is illegal and subject to official vigilantism and murder."[2]

Morrison's essay is instructive for womanist thought in the religious disciplines. It is in the dancing mind that we meet each other more often than not. It is in our books and essays and lectures and papers that those who are not womanists most often meet us for the first, if not the only time and way. It is in this dancing mind—where we tease through the possibilities and the realities, the hopes, the dreams, the nightmares, the terrors, the critique, the analysis, the plea, the witness—that womanist work is done in the academy, in the classroom, in the religious gatherings of our various communities, in those quiet and not so quiet times in which we try to reflect on the ways in which we know and see and feel and do.

This womanist dancing mind is more than our attempt to make sense of the worlds surrounding us—sometimes enveloping us, sometimes smothering us, sometimes holding us, sometimes birthing us. It is more than our desire to reconfigure the world in our own images and then invite others to come and inspect the textures, the colors, the patterns, the shapes, the sizes of this new order, and this new set of promises.

No, the womanist dancing mind is one that comes from a particular community of communities yearning for a common fire banked by the billows of justice and hope. As such, our particularity marks us with indelible ink. Our task is to explore the twists and turns of the communities from which we spring and have our very life and breath. It is to be very particular about the particular—and explore the vastness of it.

The womanist dancing mind—the one that weaves in and out of Africa, the Caribbean, Brazil, the U.S. South, North, East, and West, the Christian, the Jewish, the Muslim, the Santeria, the Vodun, the Native American, the caste of color, the sexuality, the sexual orientation, the socioeconomic class, the age, the body image, the environment, the pedagogies, the academy—has before it an enormous intracommunal task. This task is one in which we are trying to understand the assortments of African American life. If we do this task well, we will realize the ways in which Black life is not our life alone, but a compendium of conscious and unconscious associations with others whose lives are not lived solely in the Black face of United States life.

## The Epistemological Mind Field

As a Christian social ethicist who uses an interdisciplinary framework as part of my method, I understand that all epistemologies lead us to ethical issues. This is because knowing is, itself, an act that has consequences—for the knowing subject and for the community. This ethics of knowing has extraordinary relevance as we leave behind a vexing twentieth century and as we unfold ourselves into a troubling twenty-first century.

Our new century has images of planes crashing into twin towers that have been seared into the collective consciousness of the U.S. and global publics by CNN, Fox News, ABC, NBC, CBS, CNBC, CNBC World, CNNfn, CSPAN, CPSPAN2, CPSPAN3, and MSNBC over and over and over with flags that continue to wave, representing patriotism, memory, horror, honor, vengeance, jingoism, violence, history, and a studied amnesia twined with a stunning ignorance of other peoples, cultures, and countries. The images of starvation from American shores—North and South —from the Sudan, from Afghanistan, from Iraq (before and after its "liberation" by the Bush administration) have become so common that many of us are tempted to live in a chilling numbness as defense and offense. The images of democratically elected presidents being overthrown and assassinated in Iran, in the Kongo, and in Chile as the CIA ranges around like shadow boxers in the miasma have become daily fare with the images of torture and murder from El Salvador, Guatemala, Nicaragua, Northern Ireland, Iraq, and from the urban and rural United States. Images of hatred being spewed as "sensible" discourse from Germany, Italy, and from our neighbors are parts of the standard text of many of our conversations.

The act of knowing is always contextual and fraught with our best and worst impulses. It is never objective and it is never disinterested— regardless of how many rational proofs we come up with to argue to the contrary. This is an important methodological, theo-ethical, and political insight when taking seriously working in the varying contexts within womanist thought. A key question that emerges for me is *who* (as opposed to what) is left out of the conversations about liberation in our various contexts? This is a large question and I only propose some preliminary thoughts on this in this essay. Certainly as a womanist ethicist, I am aware of the various ways in which Black women's experiences have been left out of the theoretical and material constructs of both Black and feminist theologies in the United States. It remains irritating to me that this weary state of affairs continues—often as though inclusion in the laundry list of "isms" will get the clothes washed, let alone cleaned.

I begin to conjure images of the Hottentot Venus (Saarti Baartman) of the early 1800s in Europe. She was the Black African woman who was put on public display because of the "immediacy" of her sex to European audiences—male and female—who had never seen such an ass as hers. Lost was her tribal name, Khoi-Khoi. Obsequious was the scientific opinion of the time that considered the Khoi-Khoi the missing link between advanced (read White, European) human being and apes. When she died, Baartman was dissected by Napoleon's surgeon-general and "preservers" made a plaster cast of her cadaver and *that* ass and *those* breasts were put on display in the Musee de l'homme (the Museum of Mankind) so that White folks and other passersby could look at her sex from the safety of their own cultural, economic, theo-ethical, and sociopolitical mud huts. She even achieved sardonic immortality in the comic opera, "The Hottentot Venus."[3]

I see images of Black children and men and women on auction blocks —contemporary and historical—with slave masters and mistresses inspecting their eyes, their teeth, their arms, their penises, their vaginas, their intellect, their coloredness, their anuses to see if this would be good brood stock, good field stock, good darkies in the melodrama of violence and race and sex and money that enfolds the story of slavery and the academic life. These images from beyond Black life, but voyeuristically controlling Black life, trouble me because they keep Black folks as objects and do not plumb the depths of our materiality. They are, however, markers for why it is so important for the womanist dancing mind to explore the particularities of blackness in the United States.

Yet before going further, it is important that I insert a confessional note: for many years, I have been a somewhat reluctant Christian. From childhood, I listened to and took seriously what the older folks told me about what being a Christian meant and I watched with equal care as almost no one ever came close to being one. It was for me, as a child, a strange disconnect and in many ways I thought (and continue to think) that Christianity is a wonderful religion but hardly anyone is actually doing it.[4]

What I found far too often, however, is a Christianity that sanctions oppression as holy or a religiosity that separates spirituality and social witness. This has spawned and continues to spawn oppressions that are rude cultural and political productions that are ever changing and historically situated. Oppressions are rude because they simply do not give a damn about people or the rest of creation, they are only concerned with the acquisition of power that dominates and bullies. Those who participate in it will sell their souls and anything else they can get their hands on or snatch out of someone else's hands to possess such power because oppressions work to make all of us commodities that can be bought and sold, discarded and annihilated. Moreover, it is of no help that we often dress this in theo-ethical drag and mince around in people's lives or stomp around on people's cultures in the process. Whatever the dance that is done the effect is the same—degradation, denial, and perverted decency that we often call "status quo" or "normal."

The dilemma is one of being—not so much in the dense ontological sense, but in a more mundane one. What is the difference for me when I say "I am a Christian" and "being Christian?" This is more than rhetorical ruffles and flourishes for me because as a womanist Christian ethicist, I am deeply concerned about the ways in which our actions and values line up or not. And the knowledge that oppressions are cultural and political constructs that vex us every time we offer unitary or intersecting analyses and critique as the sole mavens for libratory praxis means that when I engage feminist and Black theologies it is not only in the academic sense that I do so. I am also deeply concerned about the impact and fall out of intellectual musings.

I find it highly problematic that there remains such a far distance to go in feminist and Black theologies in the rigorous integration of the world-views and insights of darker skinned and poor women. This integration is absolutely necessary for good scholarship and methodologies within feminist theologies. There would be no womanist, mujerista, Asian, or African women's theologies if Christian feminist theology was deep and rigorous in scope. Frankly, what I experience in most feminist theological gatherings is not diversity but being part of a "subpopular" form of theological reflection, in which Black women's religious lives receive only qualified attention and respectability, while the profound challenges these lives present to a totalizing feminist discourse remain largely unmet.

Turning to the particularity of Black life and scholarship, a similar but more painful parallel exists. Some Black male colleagues in the liberationist tradition go about their intellectual work as though womanist discourse is a fad, a passing fancy, or a momentary bout of theological indigestion. This comes in a variety of practices from consistently leaving womanist thought out of their courses or consigning this body of work to secondary or supplemental reading lists. Some lecture on the faddishness and soon-to-be-deadness of womanist thought. Interestingly, these colleagues fail to say these same things to those of us who are their peers. Some Black male scholars refuse to offer a rigorous and thoroughgoing critique of womanist thought when asked to do so—demurring with the response "I don't want to get into trouble." As scholars, we all know that refusing to critique is a sign of devaluing and disrespect or worse—ignorance. Given that academic womanist thought has been around since at least 1985, this is stunningly supercilious.

These anecdotes are compounded in print. Early volumes on African American religion produced by Black male scholars of religion after the rise of womanist thought are telling in how they conceive of and include (or not) Black women's religious experiences. Perhaps the most egregious example is the 1990 volume by C. Eric Lincoln and Lawrence Mamiya, *The Black Church in the African American Experience*.[5] Although much heralded at its release, it is a troubling volume in that there is only one chapter that deals extensively with Black women and it confines our world to that of the pulpit and the pew. This kind of ghettoization of Black women's religious lives is problematic at best and questionable scholarship at worst. In a volume that is sweeping in its scope—considering sociology, black denominations, rural and urban churches, Black Nationalism, politics, economics, youth, and music—a chapter that deals with women in one sense makes sense, but on the other hand, it is puzzling why there is no complimentary chapter on men. Unfortunately, the implicit methodology of the book is that men shape the world of the other chapters. This is not true to the religious lives of Black folk in general nor Black women in particular. What begins then as an attempt at inclusion results in the reification of male hegemony—long a topic of concern and critique by womanist thought.

The internal debate among Black female and male scholars of religion about this volume has resulted in good progress, however. In the 2003 Cornel West and Eddie Glaude edited volume, *African American Religious Thought: An Anthology*, there are 44 essays—10 of which deal with Black women's religious lives. This includes the more "traditional" approaches of using gender relations and public speaking (preaching and orating) as well as considerations of heterosexism, homophobia, the public sphere, and race. Unfortunately, key womanist scholars such as Katie Geneva Cannon, Delores S. Williams, and M. Shawn Copeland are strangely absent. Other recent anthologies have incorporated the womanist critique of such marginalization into their methodologies such that Black women's voices are represented in a variety of tones and textures beyond the "women's topics." Notable among these is the 2003 edited volume by Alton Pollard and Love Henry Whelchel, *"How Long This Road": Race, Religion, and the Legacy of C. Eric Lincoln*.[6] These progress notes are mixed, however, when one mines the footnotes of many Black male scholars. Footnotes reveal the intellectual conversation partners and stimulators for most scholars. Here one finds few women's voices. There is much work to be done to develop an interstructured and rigorous integration of Black women's intellectual thought and experiential insights in Black malestream thought.

## Demurring Expansiveness

Given this contextual and intellectual mind field for the womanist dancing mind, heeding premature calls for expansiveness must be the absolutely last thing we think about in doing our work. What I am interested in is exploring the depths of African American life—female and male. For it is in exploring these depths, in taking seriously my particularity—not as a form of essentialism, but as epistemology—that I can meet and greet others because we are intricately and intimately interwoven in our postmodern culture.

In this particularity, I must stand toe-to-toe with the damaging and destroying effects of the African American color caste hierarchy—even as I—a relatively light-skinned Black woman—am a natural inheritor of its toxic benefits. Color and colorism places us in a tenuous and ultimately death-dealing place as Black folks in the United States. We make ourselves vulnerable *and* marked (if not targeted) for ideologies and practices that define darkness and blackness as lesser forms of creation—barely human, if human at all. A key task is to understand that the battle against racism cannot be successfully or effectively fought without also contending with color caste hierarchies internal and external to Black folks. Black folks must also be concerned about how we maim and devalue each other and it is crucial that this come from Black scholars of religion—female and male—as well. We must be clear about how we use (or not) color in our work and constantly check our methodological tool kits to make sure that we have not allowed someone else's notion of beauty and ugliness and/or salvation and sin to seep into our work such that we reify the legacy of denoting darkness and blackness with evil and light and whiteness with salvation. We are dim trumpets for anti-racism if we cannot address and seek to eradicate the insidious nature of color caste within ourselves.

Exploring this particularly means exploring gender—sexuality, sexual orientation, sexism—to get at not only my hope for wholeness, but also to understand the ways in which age and body image, and a history that contains the castrating matriarch, the ultimate mammy, and the lascivious whore continue to ooze from the pores of videos and magazines and television and radio and music and the pulpit. The Black body has long been a site of contention. We have endured hypersexualization that spans both genders and all age levels. In short, Black bodies are viewed as icons for sexuality—usually "deviant" sexuality. From the disgrace of auction blocks, young black children of the late 1800s and well into the 1900s were portrayed as pickaninnies with overly large genitalia for children of their age. Usually, these children were portrayed with ripped and frayed clothing designed to suggest wantonness and not childhood. Black men were the strong black bucks who were "known" for sexual prowess and therefore dangerous to the larger (White) culture. Internally, the Black community kept and keeps its secrets about GLBT folk in a disfiguring "don't ask, don't tell" ideology. Again, it is problematic enough what is visited *on* Black folks; it is deadly what *we* do to ourselves.

Because I sit in the academy, the church, the classroom, and the community, I must explore socioeconomic class as it moves in and out of Black life with blazing speed—taking the poor *and* the wealthy out of sight. This is an important tension to hold in that there are many conversations and studies about the poor and poverty. Often, these studies are located within Black communities. What is woefully lacking, however, is turning that same analytical lens to consider the rich and wealthy. There are momentary bouts of pointing to celebrities of all kinds, but what has not been as clearly or meticulously catalogued is the way in which the rich and wealthy function such that there can be a multibillion dollar tax give-away to the wealthy that is touted as a middle-class tax cut as more frays develop in the social welfare system already sagging loose at un- and underfunded seams.

Because we all have to live somewhere, the environment is something we cannot forget to call continually back into our consciousness and work —to broaden the Black community's understanding of what is at stake in the atmosphere we breathe beyond the pristine and irrelevant images of Sierra Club calendars that rarely, if ever, put people in nature. But to help us understand that postmodern culture and the air it spawns will kill us if we do not start paying attention to and then strategizing for a more healthy environment for all of us to live in.

### The Expansiveness of Particularity—Coherence and Incoherence

Turning to deal more directly with the expansiveness of womanist discourse through the lens of particularity, I am challenged to deromanticize the African continent by coming to know its peoples on their terms, not from my own. I am compelled to search out and recover my Caribbean and Afro-Brazilian streams of consciousness and memory to understand the different ways in which Black folk have survived and not survived our own Diaspora and the different manifestations of the latent Middle Passage in our historic and contemporary lives. I must listen to the different rhythms of blackness that come from the different geographies that shape peoples bodies and health. I am drawn, sometimes with enormous reservation and circumspection, to understand the different ways in which the religious, beyond my own Christian identity, have shaped my communities and me. Moreover, I must understand what is at stake when we have lost, forgotten, or been stolen away from the rich medleys of the religious in Black life. As I reach further into my particularity, I am brought face-to-face with the tremendous loss of touch with Native American peoples.

It is through the particularity of the womanist dancing mind that I can meet and greet those parts of myself that have been lost through neglect, ignorance, well-practiced amnesia, or malicious separation. I am challenged to look at those places that the "isms" that I impose on others are turned back at me and I am asked to see myself through the eyes of those whom I would and do reject. It does not matter that this rejection is not intentional or malevolent. What does matter is that if I say, as a womanist, that I am engaged in race, gender, class, and environmental interstructured analysis, then I must face those places within myself and within my work that ignore the ways in which that interstructuring takes place.

Examining and naming this incoherence of oppression is what womanist thought is about in many ways. Certainly as an ethicist, I see this as a key feature behind Marcia Riggs's call for an interstructured analysis and Katie Cannon's articulation of the dance of redemption as a socioanalytical tool for critique and action.[7] To confront, directly, hierarchies and hegemonies such as the ones named and unnamed in this essay is no small task because we are often caught in competing/complementing manifestations of oppression. Lamentably, the need to develop, maintain, and deepen interstructured analysis gets lost and bodies go missing. To continue to insist on a ranking of oppressions makes it difficult to address the multiplicity of oppression when the all of the incoherence of oppression is not being fully addressed.

As someone who lives and breathes in the interstructuredness of oppression, placing any part of oppression's incoherence at the forefront for me becomes risky business. For example, when I hear and experience the phrase "transnational or global capitalism," it is quickly followed by elite White males, not only the poor in El Salvador or the sweatshop workers in Singapore or the un- and underemployed in Lansing, Michigan. Right there in the incoherence of the interstructuring I cannot pull this body apart and lift up one dynamic of its is-ness from another. No, not the sex or the class, or the race alone—but all of these make up the problematics of wealth and poverty, sexism and heterosexism, race and ethnicity, nation and nationality and nationalism.

Taking seriously the expansiveness of particularity means employing an integrated, interstructured analysis that helps pry open the dynamics of oppressions—both the incoherent *and* the coherent. There is an undeniable deadly logic and coherence to oppressions that are not only theological, ethical, political, socioeconomic, and cadaverous, but most importantly intentional and structural.

## Dancing in the Expansiveness of Particularity

Morrison's essay is instructive when doing womanist work in such a complex mind field of "unrecognized, more sinister quarters," for it is in the dancing mind that we can meet diversities—cultural, racial, ethnic, class, gendered, national, age, and religious. As we allow our mind and our scholarship to dance, we can come to welcome the unknown rather than rush to name it, control it, and dominate it. This openness allows the richness of religious life and thought beyond what we know and do not know to fill our scholarship with deeper meaning, more piercing analysis, and more trenchant critique. This becomes intimate activity, then, for in the classroom, in religious gatherings of our various communities, and in those quiet and not so quiet times in which we try to reflect on the ways in which we know and see and feel and do; we are confronted with the smallnesses of our training and disciplines and the wearying shortcomings of our categories not as judgment, but as challenge.

As a reluctant Christian who is also womanist, I believe that it is crucial that we not stop at the gate while peering at religious worlds outside of the one or ones we know well by deeming them too hard to comprehend or worse—"interesting." What arrogance we commit when we allow the inadequacies of our training to determine what we can come to know and how. When any of us who do this intellectual work are candid, we know that there are wide gaps and large chasms in the methodologies we have

been trained to use in our disciplines. The mere fact that liberation theologies exist signal that something or someone is being left out of "normative" theo-ethical discourses. Indeed, for the Black scholars of my generation and those older, we trained ourselves to be scholars of Black religiosity. Few, if any, of us had mentors who knew the worlds of blackness as
subjects for scholarly investigation.

Addressing the expansiveness of particularity helps us hold as methodological compass points Africa, the Caribbean, Brazil, the U.S. South,
North, East, and West, the caste of color, sexuality, sexual orientation, socioeconomic class, age, body image, the environment, pedagogies, religious communities, and the academy. We have before us an enormous
intracommunal task in which we are trying to understand the assortments
of Black religiosity and scholarship. If we do this task well, we will realize
the ways in which no one form of theological reflection is the ultimate
arbiter of Black religiosity. It, like the Black life that creates it, is a compendium of conscious and unconscious associations with other religious
expressions. We see this in our larger culture all the time. Why continue to
shy away from approaching this as scholars of religion or practitioners in
the field? It certainly, I hope, is not because we have begun to think that to
study and understand the (un)popular is to do less rigorous scholarship. It
should not, I think, be because we allow our lack of expertise in one or
some areas not engage in meaningful apprenticeships. It would be tragic if
we fail to see this as important or necessary to appreciate the awesome
task we take on when we claim that our work be liberating as we seek to
survive. This worrisome conundrum is a challenge that faces all forms of
liberatory thought within the theological disciplines. This is *not* work that
womanists can or should do alone. Yes, to have a womanist dancing mind
means listening to the different rhythms of the sacred that come from the
different geographies that shape peoples' bodies and health—you do not
two-step to the electric slide. This womanist dancing mind requires "an
intimate, sustained surrender to the company of my own mind as it
touches another."[8] For Morrison, this is done in reading. For me, it is in
reading and listening. It is my own need, which Morrison names so well,
"to offer the fruits of my own imaginative intelligence to another without
fear of anything more deadly than disdain."[9] For Morrison, this is writing.
For me, this is writing, speaking, and working to bring in justice. As I
engage my work within communities of communities, I find both celebration and anguish. But mostly, what I hope to find is that peace of which
Morrison speaks. This is the peace of my mind as it dances, and dances,

and dances into a new future that I have had some small part in helping craft. A future (and a mitigating hope-filled present) that is more vibrant, more life-bringing and giving, more welcoming, more humane. What is at stake in womanist discourses is deadly serious—it is challenging the ways we know (epistemology) and the ways we think (orthodoxy) and the ways we act (orthopraxy). In addition, we make judgments on these.

I suspect such a task may be appealing to those who seek to reconfigure our worlds in the task of justice-bringing transformation. I welcome allies in this enterprise. However, my work cannot be their work and *vice versa*. Where we meet and touch and spark and burn—this is good. However, we each have our own communities, as well, that we must be responsive and responsible to as we challenge old paradigms of hegemony within them. As we learn from each other's struggles, so we better engage in more rigorous and thoughtful scholarship and action. Nevertheless, our work must stand on its own integrity. This peace of the dancing mind, this peace of the womanist dancing mind is not a panacea nor is it arcane intellectual camouflage. It is a peace that is only found in hard work, in close and respectful listening, in an openness to learn and grow, in a willingness to admit—if not confess—one's limitations and awfulnesses, to grow our lives, our scholarship, our teaching large. For as we stretch into this twenty-first century, there isn't anybody else who will do this for us.

NOTES

1. Toni Morrison, *The Dancing Mind* (New York: Alfred A. Knopf, 1996), 13.

2. Ibid., 13–14.

3. It was only in April 2002, after a protracted battle, that the French government returned her remains (her skeleton and bottled organs to South Africa as a symbolic gesture of reconciliation).

4. Yes, I include myself in this muddling crowd.

5. C. Eric Lincoln and Lawrence Mamiya, *The Black Church in the African American Experience* (Durham, NC: Duke University Press, 1990).

6. Alton B. Pollard III and Love Henry Whelchel, Jr., eds., *"How Long This Road": Race, Religion, and the Legacy of C. Eric Lincoln* (New York: Palgrave, 2003).

7. Marcia Y. Riggs, *Awake, Arise, and Act: A Womanist Call for Black Liberation* (Cleveland, OH: Pilgrim Press, 1994). Katie G. Cannon, *Katie's Canon: Womanism and the Soul of the Black Community* (New York: Continuum, 1995).

8. Morrison, *The Dancing Mind*, 15.

9. Ibid.

# Part V

# Appropriation and Reciprocity

APPROPRIATION AND RECIPROCITY—[a postscript to womanist allies] The intentional and concomitant effort of others to participate in solidarity with and on behalf of Black women who have made available, shared, and translated their wisdom, strategies, and methods for the universal task of liberating the oppressed and speaking truth to power

"the creation of a new, radical intellectual space"   —Kwok Pui-lan

"the heavy responsibility of untired presence, demanding of us the sacrifices that integrity and accountability always exact"   —Isasi-Díaz

"to have relevance in the larger struggle for justice and the collective good"   —Machado

"a theological anthropology of hope for all humanity where a better world is possible—of course, grounded primarily in right relations of balance and justice among all of the created order"   —Hopkins

"following the best of the womanist tradition, will give the notion of liberation greater depth and epistemological balance"   —Pinn

"affirming [a] social shift toward a more just and compassionate world, and [giving] special attention to those who are victimized"   —West

"bringing heaven down to earth"   —Russell

# they came because of the wailing

### *emilie townes*

they came because of the wailing
   the wailing of so many voices
   who had a strong song
      but were choking from the lack of air
they came because of the weeping
   the weeping of so many tears
   that came so freely
      on hot but determined faces
they came because of the hoping
   the hoping of the beating heart
      the fighting spirit
      the mother wit tongues
      the dancing mind
      the world in their eyes
they came because they had no choice
   to form a we
   that is many women strong
   and growing

*Chapter 16*

# Womanist Visions, Womanist Spirit
## *An Asian Feminist's Response*

### *Kwok Pui-lan*

Alice Walker came to my university in the mid-1980s for a reading when I was a graduate student. At one point, she said that she had visited China and met with the writers there, and she had written a poem, "Song," for the Chinese people: "The world is full of colorful/people."[1] After the reading, I greeted her and thanked her for writing that beautiful poem. I took out the book I had brought with me and asked her to sign it.

She smiled and autographed my book, *In Search of Our Mothers' Gardens,* with the color purple.

Walker's definition of the term "womanist" in this important book[2] has sparked a critical discourse in religion and theology among Black women scholars and activists. Womanist critiques of white supremacy and the complicity of white women, as well as androcentrism in the Black church and leadership, have called for the creation of a new, radical intellectual space. During the last two decades, womanist scholarship has provided much insight for my work, and I feel very honored to join my womanist friends and colleagues to celebrate their accomplishments and contributions to the religious communities, churches, academy, and society.

Womanist scholarship emerged on the scene with a radical critique of the study of religion and theology, which has long marginalized the voices of Black women and other women of color. The arduous process of creating a new body of knowledge requires the claiming of Black women as the theological and speaking subject, the gathering of relevant data and overlooked resources, the development of appropriate hermeneutics, the interface with other disciplines that are studying Black women's lives, and the delineation of culturally specific norms in an academy still largely defined by white criteria, methodologies, and frameworks. As the rich, complex, and multilayered conversations in this current book have amply testified, womanist scholars have provided something like a model, a mirror, or a pathway, inviting other multiply marginalized women to dialogue and debate, and to reflect and rejoice.

My engagement with womanist thought prompts me to delve deeper into the problematics of "race" and to note its power and tenacity in political and academic discourses. "Race" and "gender" are both social constructs, but the discourses on these two categories had evolved into quite different routes and trajectories in the American academy. In some quarters, women's studies or feminist studies have been absorbed or co-opted into gender studies and subsequently challenged by queer studies in the 1990s. Queer and poststructuralist theorists have called into question and destabilized "women," "gender," or "subjectivity." But what about "race"?[3] Although womanists believe that "race" is not biologically determined and is socially constructed, no one has yet to suggest that American society has reached a point in which we can downplay "race" and advocate "color-blindness." To the contrary, they insist that "race" must be foregrounded and sharpened in any womanist or feminist discourse on religion and theology.

White racist society at times considers it "hip" and "cool" for women to perform gender and to try out different roles (Madonna comes to mind). White privilege may be an enabling factor for Judith Butler and others to posit a performative understanding of gender. Butler acknowledges that she has not taken into full consideration racial gender norms or racialized sexuality in her influential work *Gender Trouble*.[4] The racial divide is much harder for Black and other feminists of color to transgress, given the current backlash against affirmative action and the right-leaning cultural politics of the neoliberal academy. The essays in part 1 of this book remind us that Black women's radical subjectivity is forged in the crucible of racist-sexist-classist oppression faced in their daily lives, as well as their perseverance in speaking truth to power.

A critical understanding of race theory is indispensable in my work as an Asian postcolonial feminist critic and theologian. Womanist scholarship as a "serious thinking margin" (Copeland) is crucial in clarifying the entanglement of race, gender, class, religion, and power. While womanist scholars debunk racist, sexist, and classist ideology in North America, postcolonial feminist scholars investigate how this ideology plays out or mutates and takes shape in another form in the larger global arena. As purple is to lavender, womanist scholarship adds a darker and richer layer to the analysis of religion and society in America, offering a much fuller picture by its inclusion of voices at the bottom of the social hierarchy. At a time when white America dominates the information highway and media outlets, and white theological and religious scholarship is more readily accessible across the globe, it is critically important to hear and promote the cutting-edge scholarship of womanists.

The title of Walker's book *In Search of Our Mothers' Gardens* serves as a guiding metaphor, as womanists look high and low for their inheritance, their history, and their cultural belonging. They have recovered Hagar's inheritance in the Bible, lifted up the works of Zora Neale Hurston, Anna Julia Cooper, Ella Baker, and Ida B. Wells-Barnett, reconstructed the moral insights of enslaved women, and charted Black women's leadership in social activism, in reform movements, and in the Black churches. The critique in this body of scholarship of white religious institutions and the roles played by white women is especially significant for cross-cultural comparison, for it sheds light on the racist dimension of white women's participation in the so-called civilizing mission during the colonial era.

An example of fruitful cross-cultural comparison concerns Frances Willard and the work of the Women's Christian Temperance Union (WCTU). Formed in 1874, the WCTU was an influential women's organization with a branch in every state in the United States and a membership of 200,000 members. Under the motto "For God and Home and Native Land," Frances Willard, the national president, mobilized women to protect their homes against social evils and Demon Rum. Willard was widely seen as a progressive social reformer, but Emilie Townes has documented how Willard was unable to see lynching as an institutional racist practice, when challenged by Black reformer Ida B. Wells. Wells also criticized the work of the WCTU as lacking a racial and economic analysis.[5]

The work of WCTU was brought to other countries, such as China, in the late nineteenth century. The temperance movement's strategy to protect homes against alcohol was limited in scope, at a time when China was confronted with more systemic issues of government corruption and foreign domination. The temperance groups attracted mostly middle-class Chinese women and failed to see why social ills could not be solved by moral influence or personal temperance alone.[6] A cross-cultural comparison of Black and Chinese women's experience of the temperance movement will enable us to see the multiple layers of history, the impact of white women's reform at home and abroad, and the limitation of "saving the home" as a reform strategy. While postcolonial critics have attended to the gender constructions and ethnocentrism of white colonial officials, Christian missionaries, diplomats, and foreign personnel, it is important to look at the racial assumptions of these people as well.

Womanist scholarship has also pointed to the inseparable relation among race, gender, and sexuality. Womanists have elucidated how racist stereotypes have helped to maintain white hegemony, and such stereotypes often include a gender dimension with overt sexual overtones. During slavery, white slave owners portrayed Black slave women as lustful and promiscuous to cover up their illicit desire and sexual advances. Such genderized racial myths and stereotypes continue to function today, as for example, in the discussion of the Black family and "welfare queens." The portrayal of women of other racial and ethnic groups as loose and promiscuous is also rampant in colonial discourse. The fantasy of a Suzie Wong, a Miss Saigon, or a Madame Butterfly falling for the heroic white man serves to bolster the egos and the superiority complex of the colonizers.

While white feminist scholars sometimes isolate the sex/gender system of a given society to study, womanist and other feminists of color challenge the separation between the private and the public and the myth of "sexual liberation" without the concomitant liberation of other forms of oppression. Sex cannot be separated from economics or politics. During slavery, Black women's bodies and sexuality were systemically violated to breed more slaves for the economic gains of the slave owners. Today, we witness the ugly and institutionalized exploitation of Asian women and girls in the form of sex tourism and child prostitution, especially in Southeast Asia. In their study of the exploitative use of women's sexual labor in both the United States and Asia, Rita Nakashima Brock and Susan Brooks Thistlethwaite dissect and analyze the myriad connections between patriarchy, militarism, violence, and economic domination.[7]

Alice Walker includes in her definition of womanist "a woman who loves other women, sexually and/or nonsexually."[8] Many readers of this book are undoubtedly familiar with the work and poetry of Audre Lorde. Lorde's prose and poetry evoke the beauty, joy, and ecstasy of Black women loving other women. Lorde's language about the power of the erotic and bodily pleasures points to a new sensual possibility that inspires and captivates a generation of feminists and persons of color.[9] Yet, the areas of homoeroticism and lesbian love have been underexplored in womanist work. While Kelly Brown Douglas, Renée L. Hill, Irene Monroe,[10] and others have helpfully criticized the homophobia of the Black churches, more work needs to be done in delving deeper into the various shades of purple in Black women's sexual and erotic lives. Under the burden of the white gaze and homophobia in American churches and society, it is often difficult to criticize and transform Black culture at the same time. Some of my lesbian womanist friends have chosen to be out among their family and friends, but not out in public. The frustration and marginalization of such an existence is not hard to imagine. Sadly, this is also the case for some of the Asian and Asian American lesbians whom I have come to know. Sexuality is also a taboo subject in the Asian religious communities, and I have increasingly felt the need to call attention to the struggle of gays and lesbians in Asia and Asian America.[11]

Alice Walker has a broad and expansive understanding of her spiritual roots and inheritance. Although her family brought her to church when she grew up, she feels increasingly alienated from Christianity. Walker has practiced Buddhist meditation, learned from Native tradition, and celebrated the movement of the ever-present spirit. Several authors in this volume also push for imagining the spiritual life of Black women in broader scope, to include Islam, African wisdom traditions in the diaspora, humanism, and shamanic and hybrid spiritual practices. One of Walker's books that has touched me deeply is *The Same River Twice*, in which she talks about the spiritual lessons of honoring the difficult in life.[12] During a time when she experienced physical exhaustion, emotional upheaval, and criticism from inside and outside the Black community, Walker described the resilience of her spirit and her sustained hope in the grand Universe. I am glad to see that the same practice of self-love and the embrace of the spirit can be seen in numerous essays collected in this volume. Walker's challenge of Black women to "love herself. *Regardless*" is not taken as a moral exhortation but has been transformed into a daily spiritual practice.

Since September 11 and the so-called war against terrorism, we need to hear much loudly the dissident voices, which represent the conscience of America, for we have witnessed the arrogant display of military aggression and the will to dominate in a time of rising American imperialism. Some of the pundits, such as Samuel P. Huntington, want to turn back the clock and move the nation back toward an Anglo-Protestant white culture and country.[13] At the same time, liberal religious figures bemoan the fact that the conservative religious right enjoys growing political power, and discussion on "moral values" often narrows down to hot-button issues such as abortion and same-sex marriage. Womanist discourse and movement will face new challenges at such a time.

First, it is important for womanists to continue to be a critical voice in the Black churches and other religious organizations. Historically, the Black religious communities have played important roles in the struggle for the dignity of Black people in society. As the leaders of the Civil Rights movement will soon have to pass the baton to the next generation of Black leaders (as evidenced by the recent deaths of Rosa Parks and Coretta Scott King), womanists need to ensure that these leaders, both male and female, be informed about womanist concerns. During the past several years in Boston, I have observed how the white media have used some Black clergy's opposition to gay marriage to drive a wedge between the Black and gay communities. I support Traci West's appeal to womanists to challenge heteropatriarchy and to speak on behalf of the marginalized members of the Black community, such as Black single mothers and Black gay, lesbian, bisexual, and transgendered persons.[14]

Second, given the current political climate, womanists and other progressive sectors in the society will need to work much closer together to effect social change. I understand that womanists need to have a space to define themselves and continue their critical work in searching for and interpreting the heritage that their foremothers have bequeathed to them. Yet, an insular approach or a single-minded focus on one's own "archive" will be counterproductive in finding meaning in the past, discerning the signs of the present, and envisioning the future. I would like to see a more rigorous and multileveled conversation and comparison of the religious lives and struggles of women of color. For example, how do Native American feminists look at the womanist theology of survival? What can Asian American feminists share with and learn from Muslim womanist philosophers? To what degree have womanists participated *en la lucha* side by side with Hispanic and Latina feminists? What are the linguistic, cultural, and institutional barriers for feminists of color to delve deeper into purple or whatever color they have chosen? How can womanists make room for or extend hospitality to other feminists of color whose voices are just beginning to be heard?

Third, I hope womanist scholars would pay closer attention to the struggles of Third World feminists, so that new dialogues and coalition work can flourish. Several womanists have already taken the lead to do this kind of work: Linda Thomas's anthropological study in South Africa,[15] Emilie Townes's research work in Brazil, and Karen Baker-Fletcher's visit and lecture in South Korea. On the one hand, womanist scholarship has much to share with other disenfranchised women in the world, and such scholarly exchange enables women overseas to have a much fuller picture of the women's movement in America. On the other hand, women in the Third World can broaden the scope of womanist analysis, so that it can make concrete connections between racism in the American domestic situation and America's dominance in the world.

In *Inheriting Our Mothers' Gardens*, Alice Walker celebrated and rejoiced that she had a child, Rebecca, of her own.[16] Today, Rebecca Walker, as a grown woman, has continued her mother's legacy and published her own work.[17] As I have grown older and cherish fond memories of twenty years of friendship with some of the pioneering womanists, I have begun to think of how we can pass our legacy to the next generation. I rejoice that the womanist group has increased in number and is growing strong. I pray and am confident that they will continue to "act womanish" and desire to "know more and in greater depth than is considered 'good' for one."[18]

## NOTES

1. Alice Walker, *Horses Make a Landscape Look More Beautiful* (San Diego: Harcourt Brace Jovanovich, 1986), 68–69.

2. Alice Walker, *In Search of Our Mothers' Gardens: Womanist Prose* (San Diego: Harcourt Brace Jovanovich, 1983), xi–xii.

3. Trevor Eppehimer raises this question in his review of *The Cambridge Companion to Postmodern Theology*, ed. Kevin J. Vanhoozer, *Union Seminary Quarterly Review* 58, no. 3–4 (2004): 238.

4. Judith Butler, "Preface," *Gender Trouble* (New York: Routledge, 1999), xvi and xxvi.

5. Emilie M. Townes, *Womanist Justice, Womanist Hope* (Atlanta: Scholars Press, 1993), 142–50.

6. Kwok Pui-lan, *Chinese Women and Christianity, 1860–1927* (Atlanta: Scholars Press, 1992), 120–26.

7. Rita Nakashima Brock and Susan Brooks Thistlethwaite, *Casting Stones: Prostitution and Liberation in Asia and the United States* (Minneapolis: Fortress Press, 1996).

8. Walker, *In Search of Our Mothers' Gardens*, xi.

9. Audre Lorde, *Sister Outsider: Essays and Speeches* (Trumansburg, NY: Crossing Press, 1984); and idem., *The Collected Poems of Audre Lorde* (New York: W. W. Norton, 1997).

10. Kelly Brown Douglas, *Sexuality and the Black Church: A Womanist Perspective* (Maryknoll, NY: Orbis Books, 1999); Renée L. Hill, "Power, Blessings, and

Human Sexuality: Making the Justice Connections," in *Beyond Colonial Anglicanism: The Anglican Communion in the Twenty-First Century,* ed. Ian T. Douglas and Kwok Pui-lan (New York: Church Publishing, 2001), 191–203. Irene Monroe writes a regular online column "Queer Take" for *The Witness* (www.thewitness.org).

11. Kwok Pui-lan, *Introducing Asian Feminist Theology* (Cleveland, OH: Pilgrim Press, 2000), 120–22; and my online article, "Gay Activism in Asian and Asian American Churches," *The Witness* 87:28 (May 21, 2004), www.thewitness.org/agw/kwok051904.html.

12. Alice Walker, *The Same River Twice: Honoring the Difficult* (New York: Scribner, 1996).

13. Samuel P. Huntington, *Who Are We? The Challenges to America's National Identity* (New York: Simon and Schuster, 2004).

14. Traci C. West, "Visions of Womanhood: Beyond Idolizing Heteropatriarchy," *Union Seminary Quarterly Review* 58, no. 3–4 (2004): 138–39.

15. Linda E. Thomas, *Under the Canopy: Ritual Process and Spiritual Resilience in South Africa* (Columbia: University of South Carolina Press, 1999).

16. Walker, *In Search of Our Mothers' Gardens,* 361–83.

17. Rebecca Walker, *Black, White, and Jewish: Autobiography of a Shifting Self* (New York: Riverhead Books, 2001).

18. Walker, *In Search of Our Mothers' Gardens,* xi.

# Chapter 17

# Lavender Celebrates Purple

## A White Feminist Response

### Letty M. Russell

Alice Walker's 1983 definition of womanism was not only political prose and poetic sass, but also truly prophetic, as Lynne Westfield has reminded us![1] Here we are twenty years later and the womanists in this book, as well as all other womanist scholars, show that the four parts of the prophecy have become a garden of riotous variety, yet still in four-part harmony! The creators of the Atlanta AAR celebrative panel and this collection were wise in following her four parts and asking us to discuss common questions, just to make sure the writers would not wander too far into their own gardens.

My response includes keeping the questions about Walker's prophecy in mind, addressing them to myself as an older, white, lesbian feminist, and lifting up a few of the challenges of womanism in the panel presentations. My four parts are entitled: When and Where We Enter; Critical Lenses for Serious Work; Naming, Claiming, Changing; Postcolonial Subjects.

## When and Where We Enter

Just to make it clear "when and where I enter,"[2] let me just say that I enter with the fourth part of Walker's prophecy: "Womanist is to feminist as purple is to lavender."[3] Each one of us has entered the reality and struggles of womanism at a different place or from many different places. For instance, Carol Duncan celebrates her heritage as a transatlantic black woman, born in London, raised in the Caribbean and Canada, by lifting up Walker's recognition of the Canadian diaspora. "Mama, I'm walking to

Canada and I am taking you."[4] Her connections of womanish from her African tradition and force ripe from her Caribbean tradition confront us all with the question of not only when we entered but also from where (Duncan, 31–32)? In our postcolonial world, our entry points are not always so clear, for colonialism and globalization have brought about an intermingling of peoples and culture and hybridized identities.

I began accompanying African American women in their struggles for liberation when I went to live and work as a pastor in an East Harlem Protestant parish in New York City in 1952. The development of liberation, black, feminist theologies of all colors, and queer theologies along with years of advocacy for justice did not make the struggle against my white racism and unearned privilege any easier. It did help in 1983, however, to discover that I could at least name myself, and one of my entry points, as "lavender"!

## Critical Lenses for Serious Work

Twenty years have gone by and we can see from book stores, academic appointments, and the contributions to this book that the first part of Walker's prophecy is writ large. Not just the part about "outrageous, audacious, courageous," what Lynne Westfield calls "acts of audacity," but the ending, "Responsible. In charge. Serious."[5] The womanist theologians leave us with no doubt that womanism provides critical lenses for serious work.

As we read, we discover that even the desire to know and to search for one's own foundational truth is what Lynne calls "an act of purple" (Westfield, 130). Shawn Copeland leaves no doubt in our minds about the problems of womanist theologies and ethics in the academy as they "—fight a never-ending battle against the hegemony of the pseudo-universality of a deracinated male posited as the Western standard of normativity" (Copeland, 226). Next to that "mouthful" she posits an alternative foundation for the womanist movement, the "emancipatory struggle . . . of resistance by captured and enslaved African women" as it connects to the continuing struggle and resistance of black women (Copeland, 229).

Whether the Mother's garden is the Ivory Coast, a plantation, a sweat shop, a white woman's home, Wall Street, or the academy, the foundation is the mining of the "motherlode" of the Mothers' lives, including the conceptual language that flows from it. For instance, in the early 1980s, some of us who were working with the Women's Theological Center in Boston invited Audre Lorde to speak at a lecture series on "Naming, Claiming, Changing." Inspired by her lecture and by the Walker definition, the women of the WTC created an empowerment program for African American women in Boston entitled, "Loves herself. *Regardless.*"[6]

## Naming, Claiming, Changing

Walker's third prophecy is that women who love themselves, regardless will be able to love just about everything else, even the struggle to name oppression and to change it. This is shown very clearly in Katie Cannon's work on Zora Neal Hurston's powerful reporting of the Ruby Jackson McCollum trial.[7] Mining the Zora Neal Hurston motherlode is Kate's way of grounding theology in the lived reality of struggle and advocacy; what she calls "bringing heaven down to earth."[8]

Even the definitions of womanism and the struggle for identity itself are slowly changed by this grounding, as "identity politics" gives way in womanist writings to understanding the word "womanist" itself as an advocacy for justice, now! Thus, for instance, Kelly Brown Douglas no longer bothers to argue about whether or not womanism is identified with lesbianism. Instead, in her book *Sexuality and the Black Church*, she takes on the thorny issue of sexuality in a racist society, and makes the case for justice within the Black church as well as in a racist society.[9]

"Naming, claiming, changing" continues to expand our ways of justice making in amazing ways. For instance, who of us nowadays can ignore the global, ecological, interreligious, and economic dimensions of advocacy work? "Loves herself regardless" leads us to work with women in Africa to fight the HIV/AIDS pandemic; to join the majority of the world in crying out against U.S. imperialism; and so much more. We serve a God whose middle name is justice![10] This is what the changing is all about.

## Postcolonial Subjects

In the second part of her prophecy, Alice Walker tells us that a womanist is "traditionally universalist" and that "the colored race is just like a flower garden." This advocacy for global "emancipatory difference" has drawn women to join the womanists from every part of the globe and to follow their courage in "inventing their lives."[11]

Womanists, along with the Mujeristas and Asian feminist theologians, have been pioneers in reinventing themselves as subjects of their own lives and future. Right now we can see how this prophecy of universalism has born fruit in the eruption of postcolonial feminist religious perspectives. The power of this critique and gendered rewriting of colonialism and neo-colonialism comes not only from the critical analysis but also from the reality of the presence of these scholars at the table with feminists of all colors from around the world.

And their message is again both universal and particular, recognizing that we are postcolonial subjects because we share in a global colonial history as members of imperialist and dominated nations, who are both oppressed and oppressors within those nations. The hybridity of our reality is so clear that Katie Cannon has declared, "My purple becomes lavender when I am in the African context with all the power of a U.S. citizen."[12] Our complicities are "complexified," but our justice work is never done. Womanists are about that work as they join Lynne Westfield in a praxis "epistemology of hope"!

This praxis of hope has been part of our lives together as women of all colors for some time. And the time of its birthing for me was soon after 1983. For I had been an opponent of white racism for many years, but without women of color as partners with me in that struggle within the academy. All of a sudden this became a possibility and we could write our Mothers' lives together for the first time. In 1987, Katie Cannon, Ada María Isasi-Díaz, Kwok Pui-lan, and myself wrote our first theology book together and entitled it *Inheriting Our Mothers' Gardens*. We were partners then and still continue to struggle together.[13]

A number of years ago Margaret Farley and I were teaching Feminist Theology and Ethics at Yale Divinity School. My colleague is an ethicist who is really into choice! One day she assigned us each to choose our favorite color and I decided that as a white feminist it was time to give up my long-term attachment to blue and opt for pink. Having declared my intentions to take back pink, I bought myself a pink suit to wear to the American Academy of Religion and another striped pink suit for Easter. My students responded by painting my office door pink and covering all the dead white male paintings in the common room with plump, pink paper goddess figures.

All of which is to say, I have wanted to resist Walker's metaphor of lavender and simply be pink. But now I see that purple and pink together make lavender! What better color for a white lesbian feminist? I am lavender, and Walker's prophetic words ring true again!

## NOTES

1. Alice Walker, *In Search of Our Mothers' Gardens* (San Diego: Harcourt Brace Jovanovich, 1983), xi–xii.

2. Paula Giddings, *When and Where I Enter: The Impact of Black Women on Race and Sex in America* (New York: Bantam Books), 1984.

3. Walker, *In Search of Our Mothers' Gardens*, xi–xii.

4. Ibid.

5. Ibid.

6. Ibid.; Beverly D. Johnson, "Loves Herself . . . Regardless: A Journey toward Self-Discovery/Rediscovery," *WTC Newsletter*, Sept. 1991, 3. Available from the Women's Theological Center, P.O. Box 1200, Boston, MA 02117.

7. Katie G. Cannon, "Race, Sex, and Insanity . . . ," in *Liberating Eschatology: Essays in Honor of Letty M. Russell*, ed. Margaret A. Farley and Serene Jones (Louisville, KY: Westminster John Knox Press, 1999), 75–89.

8. Telephone conversation, October 2003.

9. Kelly Brown Douglas, *Sexuality and the Black Church: A Womanist Perspective* (Maryknoll, NY: Orbis Books, 1999); Cheryl J. Sanders, "Roundtable Discussion: Christian Ethics and Theology in Womanist Perspective," *Journal of Feminist Studies in Religion* 5 (1989): 83–91, 109–112.

10. Walker, *In Search of Our Mothers' Gardens*, xi–xii.

11. Mary Helen Washington, *Invented Lives: Narratives of Black Women, 1860–1960* (Garden City, NY: Anchor Press, 1987); Iris Marion Young, *Justice and the Politics of Difference* (Princeton, NJ: Princeton University Press, 1990).

12. Telephone conversation, October 2003.

13. Letty M. Russell, Kwok Pui-lan, Ada María Isasi-Díaz, Katie Geneva Cannon, eds., *Inheriting Our Mothers' Gardens: Feminist Theology in Third World Perspective* (Philadelphia: Westminster Press, 1988).

# Chapter 18

# Womanists and *Mujeristas,* Sisters in the Struggle

## A Mujerista *Response*

## *Ada María Isasi-Díaz*

The struggle womanist and other racial/ethnic theologians and ethicists have been engaged in for now more than two decades is an awesome responsibility as well as a precious gift. *La lucha,* the struggle, is an awesome responsibility because it has been an inspiring struggle for the marginalized and minoritized, a creative struggle discovering and bringing forth new possibilities for ourselves and for members of our communities, opening up new areas for those who have eyes to see and to carry on carrying on. It is awesome also because it has saddled all of us racial/ethnic theologians and ethicists committed to liberation and fullness of life with the heavy responsibility of untired presence, demanding of us the sacrifices that integrity and accountability always exact.

This struggle has been a precious gift for three reasons. First, through our work we have been able to provide a platform for the voices of grassroots women from our communities that no one ever listens to because they are not valued. This has been our small but important contribution to unearthing the history of those who have been abused and oppressed, it has been our way of saying to the powers that be, your victory is hollow: in attempting to destroy us you in reality have been destroying yourselves. Second, the struggle has put us to the test time and again and, in our attempt to be responsible to the struggle for justice and liberation, we have had to press on to be our better selves. Of course, we have failed at times. Of course, at times we have been selfish, at times more preoccupied with self than with our communities, more concerned with protecting our privileges than with the struggle. But repeatedly we have responded to the call of our people and have forgiven ourselves and tried once again to be faithful to our own selves, to *la lucha,* and to our communities. The third reason the struggle for justice and liberation is a gift to us is because it has provided us the opportunity to contribute, I believe in a significant way, to the field of theology and ethics, to the theological enterprise, to a theological praxis focused on explaining the faith of our people, that is, an understanding of who God is and what God is like for African American, Latina, Asian American, and Native American women. We have acted not just for the pleasure of contributing to knowledge, but particularly for the privilege of being able to give back to our communities knowledge about their own faith in a way that supports them in their struggles for survival.

In no way am I attempting to romanticize the struggles of our communities and our own. Neither do I say all this for personal glorification. In reality, the opportunity to be involved in struggles for justice and liberation is most humbling in that it calls us to face our weaknesses and limited abilities, experiencing in the flesh the fact that, if we have accomplished anything, it is because grace has abounded more than our shortcomings and failures. I say this because, as we stop to look back at the developments of womanist theology, it is important to recognize the context of these developments. They have not happened apart from our lives. Our lives are enmeshed in the development of the theologies of struggle and liberation emerging from our communities. The theologies that we have elaborated, womanist theology, *mujerista* theology, and others coming from minoritized and marginalized communities, are entwined with our own personal histories, with our struggles to live as fully as we can day in and day out.

This long introduction is grounded in one of the elements that Alice Walker's coinage and definition of "womanist" brought to the fore: the identification of subjectivity, the fact that it is out of the histories of our communities that womanist theology and all liberation theologies emerge. There are three points that I believe important whenever we talk about subjectivity. First, we need to take into consideration what Beverley Harrison said years ago: the objectivity we claim from the perspective of liberation is rooted in critical subjectivity, not in the illusion of someone standing in no place, with no worldview, with no personal interest in what is going on or in its outcome. Subjectivity has to do with accountability and responsibility to the community. Subjectivity is not a screen behind which to hide selfishness or a liberal individualism that has people so set in a competitive mode that they cannot even imagine any reality beyond their world. However, the only assurance we have of not falling into a selfish and antagonistic mindset depends upon our own specific ways of being accountable to specific communities, to specific persons within our communities.

When it comes to responsibility I think we need to remember that we are not responsible *for* others (except, of course, for those who because of age or capabilities cannot be responsible for themselves). We are responsible *to* others for what we do. We are responsible to our communities for our work—and I do think that the academic community is one of those communities. However, since being ethicists and theologians is integral to who we are, then, yes, we are also accountable and responsible *to* our communities for who we are. I think this is what Shawn Copeland refers to in her article when she talks about womanists being their own foundation. This echoes Carol Duncan's embracing of the radical valuation of the quality of womanishness in Walker's definition. Identifying one's subjectivity, as Duncan said, means asking questions that are grounded in and lead to a discovery of the social relations that are intrinsic elements of ourselves and our theo-ethical enterprise.

Second, subjectivity has to do with understanding that power belongs to the community and not to individual persons within the community, and that those of us who on some occasion or other exercise power have to be accountable in specific ways to our communities about how we have used power. We have entered into the twenty-first century without dealing sufficiently with power. We seem content with repeating what we have heard about oppressive power and enabling power. This is not enough. I think we need to analyze and conceptualize power philosophically, theologically, and ethically from a critical perspective, having the experience of the oppression of our communities as the entry point and liberation as the goal. The issue of recognizing subjectivity and the role of subjectivity in theological elaborations is linked to how we understand and exercise power. This is why African American women theologians and ethicists embraced and expanded Walker's "womanist" to form "womanism." As Stacey Floyd-Thomas and Lynne Westfield explain, to create and define such a word is revolutionary—to seize power and exercise authority. Only from within such exercise of power and authority can we participate in clarifying what power is and how it is used. We have to name, rename, define, and redefine, to use Westfield's phrase, the worlds we inhabit, worlds in which power is ever present, in which power is used by a few to exclude the many.

Both of these two points, critical subjectivity and the issue of power in our subjectivity, require what Copeland highlights: responsible, serious thinking that in turn requires responsible, serious living. We need to engage, as she points out, in an ethics of thinking, in a cognitive praxis that seriously inquires, analyzes, reflects, and judges. Only then will one be able to debunk, unmask, and disentangle power.

Third, Kwok Pui-lan has pointed out how nonsensical the never-ending discussion about essentialism has become. I agree wholeheartedly with her! The best way to hold off the useless conversation about essentialism is to be grounded in the specificity of our communities of accountability and to pay attention to the personal and subjective in *lo cotidiano*. This is the best way not to fall into essentialism or into useless denunciations of essentialism. In the definition of "womanist" proposed initially by Walker and then taken hold of by womanist theologians and ethicists, one finds a commitment to put into words the day-to-day practical experience of the African-American communities: it is an attempt to construct an epistemology from the bottom up.

Yes, what Alice Walker did and African American women ethicists and theologians have done in inventing and defining "womanist" and "womanism" is to embark in an important epistemological journey. Womanist theology is not only knowledge about the religious faith of African American women. It is not only elaborating a discourse based on the religious experiences of African American women. Womanist ethics and theology is about creating meaning. Womanist ethics is about defining what ethics is, about what it should be. Womanist theology is about what theology is, about what it should be. Womanist theology and ethics is about defining what knowing is. The word "womanism" has provided womanist ethicists and theologians with the contours and the vision to move ahead in taking hold of their lives and facilitating the same for African American women at large. Taking hold of one's life, Alice Walker told us in gifting us with the word "womanist," has to do with creating meaning, with not only helping to highlight what we should know but also clearly pointing to what it means to know. Yes, womanist epistemology is an epistemology of hope, as Lynne Westfield indicates. Westfield points out that hope is an element of knowing. Choice is also an element of knowledge for womanists because it is a going beyond what is given. Shattering expectations is an element of knowing.

For Katie G. Cannon and Kelly Brown Douglas, as well as for many other womanists, knowing is a threefold process permeated with the virtues of hope, choice, and shattering expectations. First, to know is to be in the midst of the situation one is trying to know. Womanist ethics and theology emerge from the communities to which they refer, about which they speak. Womanists are their own foundation. This is why all womanist ethics and theology is pastoral theology, not an afterthought but a central element, because it is entrenched in the lives of African American women. Second, to know is to take responsibility for what one knows, for engaging in what one knows. This is not learning from afar, this is not knowledge gathered from anonymous theologians and ethicists. No! Learning requires involvement with what we know, taking responsibility for what we know. Knowing and creating meaning is always an ethical task. Third, all knowing has to do with changing what is. Nothing that we come to know passes through us as if we were a funnel. All that we come to know is changed in the process of our knowing it. In not only claiming that they know but also adding key insights into what it means to know, womanist ethicists and theologians have indeed changed what is known, changed how we should engage what we know, changed how we must define and redefine what we know.

Alice Walker gifted all of us with this wonderful epistemological task of naming and renaming, of defining and redefining. What she did not know was that there would be committed African American women who would take what she did and run with it, not walk with it but run with it. The communities of scholars created around the struggles for liberation have much for which to thank Alice Walker. But we also have much for which to thank womanist ethicists and theologians. They have challenged us to go ever deeper in our work, not only to enunciate but also to define. For this, many of us are deeply grateful and indebted to womanist ethicists and theologians.

*La lucha* continues. Let those who have ears to hear, hear. Those who do not hear, shame on you, shame on you.

Chapter 19

# Mining the Motherlode
## *A Latina Feminist Response*

### *Daisy L. Machado*

For more than two decades the theological community has witnessed the emergence of womanist theology, which, simply stated is the very particular expression of the theological and ethical voice of black women living in the United States. Through womanist theology, black women have been able to articulate their experience and have explored the issue of justice as it relates to the realities of life in the United States for black women in particular and for the black community in general. The contributions of the foremothers of womanist theology, Katie Cannon, Jacquelyn Grant, and Delores Williams, have made it possible for black women in the twenty-first century to continue to build upon the historical cornerstone laid by such courageous and determined women as Sojourner Truth (1797–1883), Frances Ellen Watkins Harper (1825–1911), Anna Julia Cooper (1858–1963), and Ida B. Wells-Barnett (1862–1931). The foundational work of these earlier black women was based on the central idea that, "Black women have historically thought of themselves as beings of inestimable dignity, despite the systematic dehumanizing practices perpetrated against their personhood."[1] But it was not until 1979 that activist and writer Alice Walker first introduced the term "womanist" stating, "Womanist" encompasses "feminist" as it is defined in Webster's, but also means instinctively pro-woman.

> An advantage of using "womanist" is that, because it is from my own culture, I needn't preface it with the word "Black" (an awkward necessity and a problem I have with the word "feminist"), since Blackness is implicit in the term.[2]

Expanding on the term womanist and placing it in the context of the African American Christian experience, Linda Thomas defines womanist theology this way:

> Womanist theology is critical reflection upon black women's place in the world that God has created and takes seriously black women's experience as human beings who are made in the image of God. The categories of life, which black women deal with daily (that is, race, womanhood, and political economy), are intricately woven into the religious space that African American women occupy.[3]

Understood in the context of a theological and ethical reflection that seeks to critically examine and critique the deleterious effects of racism, poverty, violence, classism, and heterosexism, womanist theology is one of the many liberation theologies that developed in the early to mid-1980s and as such assumes a position of justice, inclusion, equality, and compassion. Like the other liberation theologies that have emerged, womanist theology also seeks to give words to the particular, that is, the lived experience of black women in the United States, while holding on to the universal elements of that same experience. By keeping this tension between the particular and the universal, womanist theology was also a critique of the false universalism of the white feminists of the first wave of feminism, who claimed their experience as the experience of "all" women even though in reality it was the lived experience of white middle-class women. Womanist theologians dared to claim their particularism and in so doing gave their lived experience a cultural/social/racial location that resonated with black women because it took seriously their context, their language, and their identity as black and female. Yet womanist theology also makes this claim:

> womanist theology demands a God talk and God walk which is holistic, seeking to address the survival and liberation issues of [all] women, men, children, workers, gays and lesbians, as these relate to local and global economies and the environment.[4]

This claim to universalism becomes even more significant as womanist theology in the twenty-first century finds itself situated in a world of changing demographics, where there is greater cultural and linguistic diversity than was true twenty-five years ago. Womanist theology is today

272 DAISY L. MACHADO

surrounded by the emerging theological voices of other oppressed and exploited racial-ethnic women, who are no longer living overseas but are living and participating in life in the United States. Many of these communities, unlike the African American community, have a large immigrant population group whose lived experience and realities have necessitated the emergence of a new theological discourse. As a Latina historian of North American Christianity living in the U.S. borderlands, that in-between geographical and social location where Latinos remain the "eternal other," I believe that now more than ever womanist theology must continue to develop, uphold, and intentionally engage in the universalist claim it has made. The need is for womanist theology to stay open minded and not ignore but rather intentionally seek to enter into conversation with the varied theological production of Latinas that has occurred in the last fifteen years. The need is for womanist theologians and Latina theologians to find ways to more clearly articulate the dialectical relation between the particular and universal found in the theological production of both communities. If womanists have been asking and reflecting upon the issues of black women's survival in the face of so much hardship and indignity, and if womanists have been using "memory [as a] vital [tool] for revisioning communal and social transformation that is healing,"[5] as Karen Baker-Fletcher claims, the next issue to be examined is how are Latinas also surviving and what memories and voices from the Latina experience can become the universals needed to bridge the experiences of black and brown women. How can the learnings of Latinas, their reflection and analysis of their lived experience, help to inform and expand the theological work of womanists? In thinking about these questions the fundamental concern for me is how can womanists and Latinas promote justice *between* women of color? How can womanists and Latinas join their voices to speak out against the detrimental issues faced by *both* our communities, such as youth violence, domestic violence, sexual abuse and exploitation, public health, education, abuse of alcohol and drugs? How can womanists and Latinas together reflect upon and together challenge the social sexual ideology of patriarchy? And finally, how can the lived experiences of Latinas inform womanists so that they now reflect upon realities that may not be their own but have to do with the collective good of other women of color, such as immigration, border violence, sexual trafficking of women, farm worker women and children?

The reality has been and continues to be that the voices of all racial ethnic women living in the United States have been silenced, ignored, dismissed, and devalued. That is why I think that Latinas and womanists have before them the opportunity to impact the national discourse on race and gender. Some questions I think need to be considered are: How can the particular experience of historically excluded women, in this case blacks and Latinas, be woven to retell a more inclusive and honest national story? How can womanists and Latinas work together to promote a new historical imagination that will acknowledge and lift up the struggles for justice and equality that have been a part of the universal experience of both black women and Latinas living in the United States? How can Latinas and womanists provide a new vocabulary for the national discourse on race that will not only acknowledge the presence and history of Latinos in the southwestern United States since the eighteenth century but also reexamine that history and create a space for the telling of a new national story about race in the Americas in which black and brown women are present and active?

The idea of creating a space in which women of color can do this important work of critical/reflective theological analysis is essentially an act of resistance. It is an act, which involves creating an alliance between womanists and Latinas as "they are looking to extend their resistance to forge effective opposition to all forms of domination for the 'collective good.'"[6] But in order to do this we must know more about our particular history, our particular struggles, our particular lived experiences and then juxtapose those learnings with the shared or universal reality of how black and brown people have confronted the powers of domination found in white society, powers that have continually tried to marginalize, disempower, and depoliticize our communities. We must not allow our not knowing to be an excuse for not coming together to seek the well-being of all members of our communities. Historian Emma Pérez challenges women of color living in the United States to engage in what she calls *strategic essentializing*, and I would like to conclude my reflection on the future of womanist and Latina theologies with Pérez's challenge.

> It is by *strategic essentializing* that we are able to create an important practice against the hegemonic ideologies that define us in ways to silence us and control us. *Strategic essentializing* . . . is a powerful way to find the decolonized spaces among ourselves. It does not provide a final destination, but a journey by which we may find our "multiple identities" so necessary in the fight against colonization. It is the fight . . . for our own definitions and our own decolonizing spaces.[7]

It is my hope and vision that womanists and Latinas will together forge those decolonizing spaces of which Pérez speaks so that our theological production not only will be more collaborative but also will continue to have relevance in the larger struggle for justice and the collective good that is still so very needed in our communities.

## NOTES

1. Rufus Burrows, Jr., "Womanist Theology and Ethics," *Encounter* 59, 1–2 (1998): 160.

2. Ibid., 160–161.

3. Linda E. Thomas, "Womanist Theology, Epistemology, and a New Anthropological Paradigm," *Cross Currents* 48, no. 4 (Summer 1998), web access www.cross currents.org/thomas.htm, p. 2.

4. Ibid., 6.

5. Karen Baker-Fletcher, "Tar Baby and Womanist Theology," *Theology Today* 50, no. 1 (1993): 30.

6. Teresa Córdova, "Anti-Colonial Chicana Feminism," in *Latino Social Movements*, ed. Rodolfo D. Torres and George Katsiaficas (New York: Routledge, 1999), 31.

7. Ibid.

# Chapter 20

# What's the Theological Equivalent of a "Mannish Boy"? Learning a Lesson from Womanist Scholarship

## *A Humanist and Black Theologian Response*

## *Anthony B. Pinn*

For some time now I have found the blues appealing, something about the aesthetic of that genre, but also something about the general worldview that I find hauntingly tragic and attractive. While I am drawn to the talents of numerous artists, Muddy Waters has captured my attention, particularly "Mannish Boy," and has held my attention many an evening. But what is this "mannish boy," perhaps someone with hypersensitivity to the ways in which the body receives and gives pleasure.

> I'm a hoochie coochie man
> The line I shoot will never miss
> When I make love to a woman,
>     she can't resist[1]

To be a "mannish boy," I believe, is to be positioned between adulthood and childhood—moving between assertions of responsibility to expressions of a narrow focus on strong individual want. Yet, it also involves an unfortunate attempt at invisibility, not of the body *per se*, but of the body's moral and ethical possibilities and obligations. That is to say, it seeks to ignore, or render invisible, the male's obligation to move the body in ways that are ethically and morally sensitive and productive. Within the context of the blues, this perspective is most commonly and graphically presented

with respect to the libido—the body as sexual. Regarding this, one finds
Muddy Waters noting that

> Now when I was a young boy, at the age of five
> My mother said I was gonna be the greatest man alive
> But now I'm a man, way past twenty-one
> Want you to believe me baby,
> I had lots of fun.[2]

In the lyrics to this song Muddy Waters demonstrates the manner in
which identity formation involves a psycho-social dimension. He places
the bio-chemical reality of the body in the context of the mind, wrapped
around less tangible but no less real dimensions of existence—desire, frustration, joy, happiness, discontent, and so on. And this attempt at identity
formation is shaped to some degree by the social arrangements and assumptions that also impinge upon the body as bio-chemical reality. The
language for this process might be considered the erotic—complex arrangements of relationships, but within the blues like "Mannish Boy" it is
dwarfed into a more limited grammar of sexual relationship: the libido as
worldview. How does one define meaning and come to grips with a world
that belittles? For the mannish boy the answer connotes the joyful placement of the body, and the recognition on psychological and social levels of
the pleasure involved. The mannish boy flaunts the workings of the body
that is despised often. In this case, the black male body does not swing
from a tree as the ritual substance of lynching; rather, in crude terms, it
celebrates its prowess through the pleasure its "wood" gives.[3]

While black males can legitimately claim to being oppressed within the
context of the United States, male-ness has also entailed certain forms of
privilege including a limited ability to render their bodies invisible in certain regards. Granted, practices such as profiling clearly indicate that the
black (male) body is never completely free from observation; yet, there
remain ways in which the black male body can be moved through the
world with a limited obligation to observe certain moral and ethical responsibilities, particularly with respect to interactions with black women.
This ability to shadow human interactions involves invisibility.

I want to label this epistemological and ontological oddity—the type
of invisibility—the "mannish boy" phenomenon. It is this male relationship to the world that at least in part accounts for the positioning in negative ways of women with respect to themselves and community. Perhaps,

in part, this is what Zora Neale Hurston meant when referring to black women as the "mules" of the world. And perhaps this ability to remain un-detected is noticed and signified in the subtle brilliance of Alice Walker's "Mr. ——," on so many occasions in *The Color Purple,* simply "Mr. ——" as the identifier of Celie's husband.

In the first instance, Hurston, I believe notes the manner in which the bodies of black women are "fixed" and understood in terms of service given (what Delores Williams might note as the meta-reality of surro-gacy); while others, including black men to some degree, have bodies that are more ambiguous. Walker, who is well aware of Hurston's analysis of African American women's alterity, outlines the various ways in which even privilege within the context of discrimination (such as the benefits of male-ness for racialized men) allows for the body to take on a "shadow" existence—to be somewhat ghost-like in that its "weight" is deniable. *That is to say, its social meaning is bracketed for a time.* Yet, in both cases it seems clear that invisibility of the black male body allows for moral and ethical slippage. Aren't, for example, Walker's "Mr. ——" (sometimes Albert, from *The Color Purple*) and Hurston's Tea Cake (from *Their Eyes Were Watching God*) in this sense "mannish boys"?

With this said, and in light of my training as a theologian, I cannot resist asking a question: What is the theological equivalent of the "man-nish body"? That is to say, are there ways in which this ability to disappear the black male body has shaped black theological discourse in particularly harmful ways? Put yet another way, has black (male) theological discourse, the project I participate in, acted in bad faith with respect to its moral and ethical outlook because black male theologians have conducted their work as "shadows"? The obvious, and correct, answer is: "Yes."

I ask these questions, and provide an answer in the affirmative, in large part because of implicit and explicit lessons I have learned from Womanist scholarship.[4] Although this should be an obvious statement, Womanist scholarship urged me to recognize that I have a body, and that this body is in fact gendered. In the same way that white privilege entails the ability of whites to think of only the "Other" as being raced, male privilege (even in its limited form as experienced by black men) entails a similar option for "not-ness" or invisibility (a dimension of invisibility I should like to say was ignored in Ralph Ellison's *Invisible Man*). Such willful ignorance on my part, I was beginning to learn, did damage to my ability to theolo-gize in complex ways; and it also influenced my pedagogical options.

I made certain assumptions and embraced particular unacknowledged privileges that accompany the male body—such as an assumption that one is entitled to comfortably occupy "space." And with respect to pedagogy, whether I acknowledged it or not, my physical presence in the classroom sent nonwritten and nonverbal messages to my students. My body provided information that affected the manner in which my students received and processed the knowledge I attempted to impart. But I often ignored this reality.[5]

With my first encounter of Alice Walker's definition of "Womanist," I was challenged to recognize the means by which the unacknowledged assertion of the black male body affects the manner in which black women experience the world. With respect to my scholarship, it became clear that a proper articulation and vision of "liberation" had to entail the exorcising of the black male body, the acknowledgment of its "weight" and presence. In its most pressing form this realization meant knowing that it is not enough to acknowledge sexism as a dimension of oppression experienced within African American communities.

While black male theology of liberation has acknowledged and attempted to exorcise its more demonic (in the Tillichian sense) features, problems remain. Black theology, for example, has failed beyond a few exceptions to critique and offer an alternative to the hyper-masculinity promoted in some Christian circles as a way of combating the destruction of the traditional model of familial existence.[6] By so doing, black theology fails to take advantage of an opportunity to extend its vision beyond an updated version of the cult of domesticity. There is no doubt that this epistemological stance fosters a theological posture that misreads African American communities and their "needs," the nature of their oppression, in that it views these communities through a lens of heterosexual male-centered existence. I am not suggesting the complete obliteration of "male-ness." Rather I am suggesting that there must be ways to add complexity to it and to place it in relationship with other modes of encounter with the world. Jacquelyn Grant's *White Women's Christ, Black Women's Jesus* and Delores Williams's *Sisters in the Wilderness,* for example, required me to acknowledge the manner in which my very be-ing as a male entailed a certain language and grammar that in itself placed restrictions on my theologizing.[7] These limitations revolved around a tension at times, and a paradox at other moments, in that I, like my colleagues, argued for an existential theology, a black theology as a body theology. But what I typically presented was a not-body theology. As Hortense Spillers and Toni Morrison have noted with great insight, the flesh tells stories, and as Mary

Douglas remarks, the body is a symbol of the social system. I am unwilling to say that my socially constructed and reified existence as "male" means a hopelessness with respect to my position as oppressed–oppressor. Redemption is possible for even those who move through the world carrying the weight of the male body. Yet, these three theories—presented by Spillers, Morrison, and Douglas—of the body when recognized, and combined with the insights of Womanist scholars, demand a need for sensitivity to the ways in which the existence of the male body (my body) as coded, as a symbol of the social system, involved a type of theological double-talk.[8]

Womanist scholars, through the development of a complex and intellectually sophisticated theological methodology and theory of experience that is interdisciplinary in nature, have challenged traditional theological formulations. This critique highlighted the manner in which black theological discourse, dominated by males, entails the passive acceptance of privilege that does damage to efforts toward liberation. This damage involves the, again passive, assumption that the black male body (keep in mind what Spillers, Douglas, and Morrison say about the body) is normative.[9] That means a certain set of symbols, signs, and a fixed grammar shape theological perspective and argumentation.

In a sense, the movement of the black body sets the proper posture for theological engagement. What results, Womanists have convincingly demonstrated, is a failure to take seriously, to really take seriously in a way that changes deeply the mode in which scholarship is conducted, alternate modalities of experience—sexism, heterosexism, and so on.

In addition to the ways in which Womanist scholarship has surfaced (through what I would refer to as a hermeneutic of archeology) African American women's experience as theological sources or data, there is a more theoretically and methodologically centered consequence of Womanist work.[10] This second, theoretical and methodological, challenge posed by Womanist scholarship has pushed on me a growing awareness of the incomplete status of my theological formulations, through an effort to maintain the invisibility of my body.[11] If I am sensitive to the socio-cultural, psychological, and political implications of my physical presence, even in the ways in which I think and teach theology, it is likely that theological formulations will take on a more nuanced, a more complex, a "thicker" meaning.

In a sense Womanist existential sensibilities push theologians to entertain the possibility of transforming black theology into a proper body theology. In this way it moves in the direction of discourse that is genuinely concerned with the implications of existence (and meaning) present in the physical body, mining the body for its theological import. So doing involves the ability to construct theology that does not seek to avoid or ignore the body, but rather theology that is done through sustained contact with the body. This seems the theological implication of the Womanist appreciation for "roundness," highlighted in Alice Walker's definition of the term. Such an understanding of theology's connection to the physical world holds intriguing potential for doing black (male) theology in ways that push beyond its methodological provincialism and theoretical xenophobia.

It is conceivable that black theology, following the *best* of the Womanist tradition, will give the notion of liberation greater depth and epistemological balance, in that it becomes a sense of free movement that appreciates the flesh rather than simply attempting to ignore it or assume that only male bodies matter.[12] This entails the death of the "mannish boy" and the birth of a more complex and more deeply connected human—one who appreciates, in Alice Walker's words, a yearning for "survival and wholeness of entire people, male and female."[13]

NOTES

1. Muddy Waters, "Mannish Boy," *Blues Straight Ahead.*
2. Ibid.
3. "Wood" is used as a euphemism for the penis, and more frequently as a euphemism for an erection.
4. I refer to formal engagement both through conferences and reading (and teaching as best I can) on Womanist scholarship, as well as the gracious ways in which Womanist scholars such as Katie Geneva Cannon, Stacey Floyd-Thomas, and Cheryl Kirk-Duggan have shared their insights and critique through more informal conversations. I have also learned a great deal through my work with Melanie Harris, on whose dissertation committee I served. In this short essay, however, I concentrate on my formal engagement with Womanist scholarship.
5. For my thoughts on pedagogy as it relates to the body see Anthony B. Pinn, *African American Humanist Principles: Living and Thinking Like the Children of Nimrod* (New York: Palgrave, 2004), chapter 9. This pedagogical issue has also been highlighted in a Wabash-sponsored seminar, organized by Lynne Westfield of Drew University, in which I participated.

6. Dwight Hopkins's recent work, an example of which is in *Loving the Body: Black Religious Studies and the Erotic*, ed. Anthony Pinn and Dwight Hopkins (New York: Palgrave, 2004), pushes for a new sense of masculinity.

7. Jacquelyn Grant, *White Women's Christ, Black Women's Jesus* (Atlanta: Scholar's Press, 1989); Delores Williams, *Sisters in the Wilderness* (Maryknoll, NY: Orbis Books, 1993).

8. I have given some attention to body awareness in recent publications. See my essay in Pinn and Hopkins, eds., *Loving the Body*, and Pinn, *African American Humanist Principles*, chapters 5–6.

9. See G. M. Gonzalez, "Of Property: On 'Captive' 'Bodies,' Hidden 'Flesh,' and Colonization," in *Existence in Black: An Anthology of Black Existential Philosophy*, ed. Lewis R. Gordon (New York: Routledge, 1997), and Toni Morrison's "The Site of Memory," in *Out There: Marginalization and Contemporary Cultures*, ed. Russell Ferguson et al. (Cambridge, MA: MIT Press, 1990).

10. In addition to the Delores Williams text already noted, good examples of this attention to black women's experience as theological sources include Katie Geneva Cannon, *Womanist Ethics*; Karen Baker-Fletcher, *A Singing Something*; Emilie Townes, *Ida B. Wells*; Marcia Riggs, *With a Steady Beat*; Cheryl Townsend Gilkes, *If It Wasn't for the Women*.

11. My text on theory of black religion, *Terror and Triumph: The Nature of Black Religion* (Minneapolis: Fortress Press, 2003), is one of my more substantive attempts to wrestle with this issue. It is an effort to develop an understanding of black religion's nature and meaning through continued awareness of the manner in which black bodies carry and shape perceptions of the world and our relationship to the world.

12. This is not to say that Womanist scholarship is without its own shortcomings. I do not want to romanticize Womanist work; it has its own issues, when one considers that the debate between Cheryl Sanders and other Womanists in the 1980s remains significant (see *Journal of Feminist Studies in Religion*). Yet, within the context of this short essay, I have in mind the limitations of black theological discourse pointed out by first-generation Womanist thinkers such as Jacquelyn Grant (see James Cone and Gayraud Wilmore, eds., *Black Theology: A Documentary History* [Maryknoll, NY: Orbis Books, 1979]), as well as women who predate the formal development of Womanist theology such as Pauli Murray (also see *Black Theology*). Within the context of black theology, Victor Anderson pointed out this problem with respect to the limiting effect of ontological blackness for a sense of "cultural fulfillment" that does require surrender of one's individual inclinations for the sake of blackness as the community unifier. See *Beyond Ontological Blackness* (New York: Continuum, 1995).

13. Alice Walker, "Womanist," in *In Search of Our Mothers' Gardens: Womanist Prose* (San Diego: Harcourt Brace Jovanovich, 1983).

# Chapter 21

# Lies above Suspicion: Being Human in Black Folk Tales
## *A Black Liberation Theologian Response*

## *Dwight N. Hopkins*

### *Gifts from Womanist Gardens*

Several dimensions of womanist studies in higher education and faith communities (i.e., church, mosque, temple, shrine, etc.) impact my way of developing theology, as a second-generation black theologian.

Womanist sister scholars and faith leaders continue to propose the critical demand to keep liberation of and justice for the poor, the working class, and other marginalized communities at the center of all talk about God and gods. This proves a revolutionary stance at the dawn of the twenty-first century. Now with one white supremacist imperialist power roaming the globe, it takes profound theoretical astuteness, deep faith commitments, loving compassion, and abundant courage to suggest an alternative and better world is possible. Contrastingly, most churches in the United States resume ritual practices without heeding the prophetic calling to speak truth to power. In a word, Christian churches, in the main, continue to witness in support of monopoly capitalism, white power, patriarchy, and heterosexism.

Likewise, the white power that dominates the formal academy in North America gives the surface appearance of denying that all education (whatever side one takes in the false debate between theology and religious studies) situates itself in support of systemic civic positions. But, in fact, one cannot exist on earth and teach in U.S. schools and somehow produce so-called objective research detached from real people, institutions, and public policies. Every single theological school, seminary, divinity school, and graduate religious studies program exists to support and promote the foundational economic, political, military, and cultural way of life in the United States. More specifically, as long as we, black religious scholars, pretend that we are individuals thinking on our own, that we have made it on our own, that it's chic to adopt the latest thought fad, that we have the right to detach from church and community movements; as long as we shy away from relying on the theories of our mammas and our papas and the religious institutions that helped us get over, we remain minstrels for the white academy as it gives us exclusive backstage passes to our own black face or white face performances.

This is when and where the womanist scholars enter. They inspire my intellect. They weave a web of holism, an integrated vision of nondualism, encompassing, among other things, gender, class, race, sexual orientation, ecology, religious studies and theology together, faith and rigorous "objective" scholarship together, academy and church and community together, individual healing with radical transformation of U.S. structures, and the aesthetic.

Furthermore, *holism* in methodology and cosmology coupled with *faith* in a justice and liberation power beyond the human realm connect to their intentional *self-naming* as intergenerational African American women. We observe a sense of historical sweep and continuity among the womanists. That is why, for me, they self-consciously use the terms first-, second-, and third-generation womanist scholars. They teach me that structural and individual conversions in the United States will more likely result when black religious scholars work toward relating to previous scholars, who put up the scaffolding for the house of our thought and witness. Contrary to this long view of the house that our parents and ancestors built, today's North American culture thrives on historical amnesia and instantaneous microwave individualism. But the womanists know where they come from and to whom they are linked.

Here, too, womanism cuts against the grain of people who believe they advance in the academy by themselves, by the brilliance of their individual intellect, by the accolades given them for being the first or only "Negro." And, therefore, they feel that they are not part of anything and have the right to start their own "academic" trend or simply to clarify an "interesting" idea in one's head. It is a curious phenomenon that the black thinkers who pursue this path of "I have a right to think detached in the academy" actually are very communal. They submit to the marching orders of the European Enlightenment and command instructions from the majority of white scholars in the United States who form this politically correct regime. The unannounced norm is that a person can act like he or she is thinking in the isolated womb of the academy without an umbilical cord to the outside world as long as the individual thinker does not challenge the ruling status quo in the academy. More curious perhaps is that the dominating voices (i.e., the small group of true powerbrokers) in the academy self-consciously realize that the role of education in U.S. society is to propagate the dominant race and class in that society. They know that this thing, at the plumb line foundation, is about the supremacy of elite Europe and its diaspora. By definition, the U.S. academy, at its highest level, displays a preferential option for white patriarchal power.

Still, womanists indicate how to maneuver in the academy given dire circumstances and one's own negativities and insecurities. They teach us that, yes, power resides in class formations and in-between class structures. But, at the same time, wherever there exists domination, possibilities for survival and resistance always abound. As long as we believe in a God who can "take a crooked stick and hit a straight lick" and as long as we "keep on keeping on," spiritual and material demons do not have the last word. Therefore, womanists' theoretical work and their sheer bodily presence suggest ways of being joyful and affirming in the academy. They raise the bar of intellectual pursuits. This is what their (our) mammas did when the latter picked cotton, worked as domestics, entered industrial jobs, used Vaseline as a medicinal cure-all, conjured success out of segregated schools, became the first to get college degrees, broke into politics and exclusive professions, held our churches together, stayed with some black men too long, and worked successfully with red, brown, yellow, and white brothers and sisters. Their faith in God and the future of their children helped them to hold on and forge ahead even when they thought they couldn't hold on anymore. African American female scholars quilt their being in the academy—take a little stitch of this and thread it with that and craft a canopy that is big enough for all races and ethnic communities to get under and learn from. In this manner, the academy becomes a vibrant give-and-take of ideas that matter.

In fact, the womanists are for power, but power from below, true democratic power and ownership by the majority. It's the type of power and joy that "man" didn't give and "man" can't take away. It's the power of our people's old time religion: God will fight your battles, but in the meantime you carry a Bible in one hand and defend yourself with the other; because God helps those who also help themselves. I see this power blossoming in the mothers' gardens of womanists with their categorization and redefinition of Alice Walker's four-part womanist definition into a womanist epistemology governed by (1) radical subjectivity, (2) traditional communalism, (3) redemptive self-love, and (4) critical engagement. These four multicolored interpretations move my being to continue to do anti-oppression, liberationist scholarship and practice as an advocate of *womanism*.

In this essay, womanist approaches move me to draw on the lies of African American folk tales (i.e., power from below) to pursue *holism* in methodology and cosmology, coupled with *faith* in a justice and liberation Power beyond the human realm and to connect to an intentional *self-naming* as an intergenerational black theologian. I find a large part of my being here in these folk tales and in this heritage. And so for the rest of this essay, as one way of learning from the womanist garden as well as from my own mother's and grandmothers' gardens in Richmond and rural Virginia, I will explore some lies above suspicion to discover being human in black folk tales. What can black people tell us (in the academy, church, and broader public) about the doctrine of theological anthropology?

### Lies for Being Human

One of the major forerunners for womanist thought and practice are the writings and life of Zora Neale Hurston, the daughter of a black Baptist preacher. Therefore, learning from both the gifts of womanist approaches in religion and society and the thought of Hurston, I'd like to advance the notion of "lies" from Hurston as a conceptual lens into constructing a contemporary theological anthropology. From 1928 to 1930, Hurston engaged directly in research among the black working class and impoverished communities of Polk County, Florida. The result is her classic *Mules & Men*. The theoretical beauty of these compiled folk tales resides in their revealing and forging the positive self-referential nature of black folk's communal self. In other words, neither a useless victim syndrome or slavish subservience to white scholars, black folk tales, here, blossom into radical subjectivity, traditional communalism, redemptive self-love, and critical engagement. These stories or lies represent the world that blacks created, even though they are sane enough to recognize that white humanity does exist on earth. (In this regard, they symbolize the method of the creative genius of another pioneer of womanist epistemology—Toni

Morrison. Morrison's brilliance continues to draw on the wealth of experiences primarily from black working peoples' own angelic and sinful natures.)

And so, to get at being human in black folk tales, we have to plunge ourselves into the murky waters of some black lies. For instance, in a Florida community, Hurston runs across a group of black men congregated on a store porch. One fellow cries out, "Now you gointer hear lies above suspicion." Lies are stories or tales delivered with verbal dexterity. They embody the art of living or how to be black in America. This intellectual and practical dynamic requires cunning and flexibility. As another speaker beseeches his colleagues, "We got plenty to do—lyin' . . . Lemme handle a li'l language long ere wid de rest."[1] Lies make a point with ethical import and visionary mandate for the human condition. Fact and fiction blend because the poor realize that truth incarnates in the folk who live out reality.

## Four Paradigms, Themes, and Spiritualities

The lies in black folk tales offer us a flower garden of potentialities for theological anthropology—that is, responses to the question: What has God created us to be, think, believe, say, and do in this world? At least four paradigms come to mind: the trickster with the theme of reversal and a spirituality of human flourishing; the conjurer with the theme of nature and a spirituality of all creation; the outlaw with the theme of ambiguity and a spirituality of individual desire; and Christian witness with the theme of empowerment and a spirituality of compassion for the poor.

The *trickster* character acts out the notion of *reversal* where usually the weak protagonist deploys the weapon of wit to outsmart the physically strong owners of material resources.[2] This dynamic produces a spirituality of *human flourishing*. Br'er Rabbit is the paramount trickster protagonist in this black folk paradigm. The Tar Baby lie, for example, portrays Br'er Rabbit constantly stealing water or crops from Br'er Fox or Br'er Wolf.

Here the definition of human interaction intimates that the strongest should perform most of the work because they have monopolized most of the survival sustenance and technologies. And this skewed act has upset the balance of community within the jungle or the woods. The weak, on the other hand, are called to perceive reality differently. They imagine a vision of society in which the bottom strata have natural access to all that is healthy in life. The move to think and see from a more inclusive posture empowers them to pursue whatever they need by utilizing their instinctual mother wit and intentional intellect to overcome the incorrect circumstances created by the strong's focus on the individual self. Such reimagining enables one to risk a new present in order to have a better tomorrow. In the midst of dire circumstances, entanglement in the tar of life, the weak pursue hope.

Following the trickster in African American tales, *conjure* doctors are folk characters who call on elements from *nature* to either perform good or evil against another human being. Some claim that they receive these natural powers from association with the Devil; others cite the grace of God's direct revelation. Still others underscore their natural extraordinary gifts because they were born the seventh son of a seventh son with seven cauls covering their face; or another person purports that wisdom passed on from the elderly long deceased.[3] At any rate, the conjurer introduces a spirituality of all *creation*.

Conjuring depicts a humanity where equilibrium and disequilibrium are key for a comprehensive social interaction within culture. It stands as an aspect of theological anthropology because it draws on human mystical ties to the supernatural powers derived from nature and from the strength of the spiritual (God or Devil) worlds. To be human, in the fullest sense imaginable, derives from attending to the gifts of nature (i.e., animals, plants, air, water, and the earth).

Perhaps, at first glance, the third folk paradigm, the *outlaw* character, stands as the most egregious model for what it means to be a healthy human self. Usually, a male protagonist, this folk hero kills seemingly innocent bystanders, relates to women in a utilitarian manner, and, in general, creates chaos in community. Yet, these surface marks obscure the deeper appreciation that black working people and those living in structural poverty oftentimes derive from the *ambiguity* of outlaw or bad man toasts and ballads. The latter are crafted by and acknowledge a spirituality of *human desire*.

Yet, despite the profound ambiguities of the outlaw (such as Shine and Stagolee), the community extends compassion even to seemingly misfits and potentially harmful characters. Where the larger culture disciplines (even to death) such folk figures, the tough love of the folk, in contrast, embraces them and thereby manifests a certain practice of realistic and sober compassion. Here the paradigm of "badness"—the outlaw—suggests a grey area (accompanied by a thin line between heroic acts and criminality) in the understanding of human nature.

The fourth and final model for theological anthropology (i.e., the spiritual and ethical dimensions of a new humanity) appears with the *Christian witness* effecting *empowerment* and thereby yielding a spirituality of *compassion for the poor.* Two historical figures speak to this paradigm; and, though factual persons, folklore legend has jettisoned them into the realm of quasi myth. Both Harriet Tubman and Denmark Vesey suggest the revolutionary nature of prayer, a vocation of risks, the correlation of individual rights and privileges to the liberation of group status and communal empowerment, a biblical interpretation paralleling black folk with the oppressed Hebrew people, and global perspectives linking black Americans with the freedom of blacks worldwide.[4]

## A Christian Perspective on Being Human

As a Christian theologian (i.e., a conscious pursuer of the revelation of the spirit of liberation through Jesus Christ with working class people and those in structural poverty, and consequently all of humanity), I am simultaneously informed by non-Christian theological anthropologies working with a similar spirit. In the four folk paradigms, I have discovered that a normative characteristic of God or an ultimate vision is a common quest or journey on the part of the poor for communal life beyond capitalist restrictions. This spirit of liberation (as well as a spirit opposed to liberation) comes upon the human condition and in human nature through diverse means. Spirituality, therefore, is that which transcends the self, particularizes in a concrete but goes beyond a concrete, and carries positive and negative dimensions. Co-laboring with God's spirit, liberation becomes a move beyond harmful restrictions on the self and the poor and, consequently, a pointer to freedom practice.

Freedom, as a result, is to love the creative humanity of the poor as God loves the poor. This is the *imago dei* (i.e., image of God) incarnated in real flesh. It stands for human efforts to open up space for those once chained internally by psychological sin and externally by structural sin. More specifically, the first aspect of the image of God means awareness of *who we are* as human beings—imaging God by creating healthy life without restrictions and collectively owning all wealth on earth.

In conjunction with knowing who you are, being made in God's image is accompanied by a second aspect—knowing *whose you are*. Saturated with knowledge of whose you are, one knows that she is possessed by a spiritual calling to subordinate oneself to the service of others. Jesus walked this earth with that purpose in life.

Freedom, furthermore, flowers beyond acceptance of one's *imago dei* (i.e., image of God). A holding pattern of mere acceptance eventually withers the spirit's gift of God's image. Rather, the divinity works with us and loves us into carrying out this good news. In other words, the *imago dei* unfolds outward into the *missio dei* (i.e., the mission of God to the world). We are called to exhibit healthy humanity by recognizing divine image in others and sharing this liberation evangelism for others' freedom. And the four paradigms aid us to put more flesh on the bones of what we mean by freedom.

The *Christian witness* with *empowerment* gives us a spirituality of *compassion for and service with the poor*. These types of lies show us a spirituality that requires a self-love, love of others, including the stranger, love of God, and a love, based on justice, of the oppressor. The *conjurer* with *nature* teaches us about a spirituality of *all creation*. We, therefore, need to be attentive to revelation of power in directions (i.e., north, south, east, and west), elements (i.e., air, water, dirt, and fire), animals and plants, and time dimensions. The *outlaw* with *ambiguity* gifts us with a spirituality of *individual desire*, urging our direct assertion (of our unique identities, space, and voices). Individual desire embraces sensuality and sexuality of the body, where one also finds the attached brain. Finally, the *trickster* with *reversal* embodies a spirituality of *human flourishing*, leading to creativity, cunning, and balance.

So, my response to womanists' approaches to religion and society is to appropriate their emphasis on the voices of the margins, those from below. In the lies above suspicion of black folk tales, I discover a theological anthropology of hope for all humanity, where a better world is possible— of course, grounded primarily in right relations of balance and justice among all of the created order.

NOTES

1. Both quotes are found respectively in Zora Neale Hurston, *Mules and Men* (Bloomington: Indiana University Press, 1978 [1935 original publication]), 21 and 91.

2. Bruce Jackson, ed., *The Negro and His Folklore in Nineteenth-Century Periodicals* (Austin: University of Texas Press, 1967), 148–150. The article was taken from William Owens, "Folklore of the Southern Negro," *Lippincott's Magazine* 20 (Philadelphia, December 1877). Other versions of the Tar Baby cycle can be found in J. Mason Brewer, ed., *American Negro Folklore* (Chicago: Quadrangle Books, 1968), 7–9, originally published as "A Familiar Legend" in *The Hillsborough Recorder*, Hillsborough, North Carolina, on August 5, 1874. Also see Langston Hughes and Arna Bontemps, eds., *The Book of Negro Folklore* (New York: Dodd, Mead, 1958), 1–2.

3. Leonara Herron and Alice M. Bacon, "Conjuring and Conjure-Doctors," in *Mother Wit from the Laughing Barrell: Readings in the Interpretation of Afro-American Folklore*, ed. Alan Dundes (New York: Garland, 1981), 359–368. Reprinted from *Southern Workman* 24 (1895): 117–118, 193–194, 209–211. The stories in this article were collected in 1878.

4. Sarah Bradford, *Harriet Tubman: The Moses of Her People* (Secaucus, NJ: Citadel Press, 1961 [1868 original publication]), 24–25, 84, and 29. John Oliver Killens, *The Trial Record of Denmark Vesey* (Boston: Beacon Press, 1970), Introduction, 70, 161, 64, 13, 42, 43, and 62.

# Chapter 22

# Is a Womanist a Black Feminist? Marking the Distinctions and Defying Them

## *A Black Feminist Response*

### *Traci C. West*

My formation as a scholar whose writing and research foregrounds black women's lives and ideas has been deeply influenced by black feminist thought. My introduction to feminist studies occurred as a young adult, and I immediately fell in love with the subject matter. I have embarrass-ingly starry-eyed memories of being an undergraduate sitting in Michelle Wallace's living room listening to debates among black scholars. When I helped to arrange for bodyguards for Angela Davis's visit to my college, I vividly recall the excitement among my feminist women of color group that cosponsored her talk. I also recall quickly getting past my shyness when a black feminist scholar-poet led a session for this same women of color group on sexual self-pleasuring as a feminist act. Later, when I was a twenty-one-year-old seminary student, I will never forget sitting in the audience spellbound while listening to Audre Lorde read her anti–U.S. imperialism poetry, or carrying boxes of Alice Walker's new novel (*The Color Purple*) to a small book party for her at the Women's Theological Center where I was a work-study student. Her reading was awesome. The influential scholarly mentors who contributed to my internalization of black feminist thought additionally included several white feminist profes-sors, my only Latina feminist college professor, and feminist studies con-versation partners among my peers who were white, Latina, Asian, and black women.

My scholarly identity as a Christian social ethicist began later in my adult life and happened to coincide with some of the earliest moments in the emergence of womanist religious thought. I started my doctoral work in ethics only a couple of years after the publication of Katie G. Cannon's *Black Womanist Ethics*[1] (and happened to enroll in the same program where she had created this work). I took what must have been one of the first "Womanist Theology" courses ever offered in a graduate school program. It was taught by Delores Williams.

As a black feminist scholar/activist I claim womanist scholarship within my own work and womanist scholars as my mentors, and at the same time, I differentiate my scholarly identity and writing from this exclusively black community-based tradition of intellectual work. Frankly, specifying the boundaries between feminism and womanism in my work is of little significance to me, unless it furthers some form of woman-affirming social shift toward a more just and compassionate world, and gives special attention to those persons who are victimized by violence (sometimes lethal) that is too easily tolerated by the society, such as wives, prostitutes, lesbians, gay men, and transgendered persons.

I have a deep appreciation for the extent to which many womanists in religious studies have unapologetically articulated black women's subjectivity as the focal point of their scholarly and communal endeavors. These articulations have claimed a space in the field of black religious studies to validate the particularity of black women's historical experiences and their significance to the evolution of society. Beyond achieving validation, this claiming of space has expanded discussions and analyses of texts by and about black Christian women. It has located a canon of neglected existing material and created a canon to fill gaps in religious literature, thereby bequeathing a richer body of sources to later generations of researchers.

I am inspired by the womanist dedication to this canon building work, especially the drive to do "our own" work that is directly relevant to "our own" mothers, daughters, and lives in the church. This strategy focuses upon naming ideas in response to silences in prevailing cultural discourses and extends the dissemination of ideas beyond existing venues in the academy into arenas that have been utilized by other African American intellectual innovators, from black cultural nationalist Ron Karenga with the creation of Kwanzaa to black feminist Barbara Smith and the other women co-creators of the Kitchen Table Press. The unique commitment to black female subjectivity by many womanist religious scholars has entrenched within African American scholarship black woman-affirming analyses related Christianity and black church life within African American scholarship in a new and lasting way. Cheryl Townsend Gilkes exemplifies this commitment to subjectivity, stating, "African-American Christianity is not only a product of black women's presence but also of their active and assertive role in shaping the spirituality and ethics of black churches."[2] This commitment is also concretely practiced in the partnering of womanists with black liberation theology scholars (in the form of the Black Religious Scholars Group) to offer community events in black church settings in the host city of the American Academy of Religion annual meetings.

Even as I am inspired by the bold defiance of racism in the academy found in the emphasis on "our own" womanist work by, for, and about black communities, I feel compelled to reflect on the dangers of parochialism that might be inherent in this project. Shouldn't this kind of intentionally politicized scholarly work that intends to expose assumptions of race and racism avoid a notion of accountability that is exclusively tied to one's own racial/ethnic group? How is a conscious attempt to learn from nonblack authored and black community-centered theoretical sources made when studying black religion and lives? I am prompted to revisit my own scholarly inquiries that make black women's lives and ideas a priority and delineate how my feminist theory demands accountability to women's lives across racial/ethnic and even national boundaries. I am reminded that I need to make conscious revelations about how my training in a Euro-American-dominated academy is employed so that I do not risk cathartic declarations about a pristine "black women's" hermeneutic that cannot possibly be true.

Womanist redeeming self-love is expressed in scholarship that rescues black women from being limited to common, perverse Christian caricatures of the heterosexual sexual temptress or the inexhaustible, self-sacrificing servant of God and man. Such womanist scholarship will often also include protests that I greatly admire against the exclusion of women from pulpit leadership in most black churches, and against a historic lack of interest in church sexism by black religious historians, sociologists, and theologians. In a 1991 critique aimed directly at an AME church audience, Jacquelyn Grant wrote, "We have taken the God-given collective resources of women and we have buried them, only periodically digging them up in part to be used and sometimes even abused."[3]

While this womanist theme about inclusion demonstrates how love of self means protesting the decidedly unloving behavior of rejecting women's pulpit leadership in black churches, the question of which selves this self-love includes is brought into view. In particular, the exclusion of black lesbian leadership and devaluation of black lesbian identity in the church is frequently left out of womanist self-loving sociological critiques of religion and theological visions for change. Formative influences that shaped my initial understanding of feminism like Audre Lorde, Barbara Smith, Alice Walker, Betty Powell, Flo Kennedy, coupled with the existence of rabid homophobia in churches (not just black ones!), lead me to emphatically depart from any notion of self-love that does not include fighting for the affirmation of woman loving woman sexual love in church and society.

New movements are almost always plagued by the problem of working out how they define their membership. This characteristic is most evident in womanist expressions of communalism and critical engagement with other sources, particularly with feminism, and has produced elements that have been, perhaps, the hardest for me to absorb in my scholarly formation. For instance, my work on the experience of intimate violence against black women requires the privileging of support for their wholeness. It involves my adamant opposition to maintaining silence about black male violence against them, a silence that is too often demanded out of concern for what image of black people descriptions of this black male violence might invoke in the minds of white people. Because my allegiance to women's wholeness takes priority, the womanist commitment to the wholeness of the black community as an expression of its communalism would not necessarily be an essential goal for me. Also, my liberationist commitments to pointing out the problem of black male clergy who sexually harass women congregants, or my identification of state sanction for and church blessings of same-sex marriage as a civil rights cause blacks must champion, may generate divisiveness that violates womanist notions of black communal unity. I don't know.

I remember a major public academic event where a womanist speaker decided to celebrate the large number of feminists and womanists who were gathered together in the room by asking them to stand up. When the speaker asked the feminists to stand, I proudly popped up, as did one other black woman and scores of white women. As soon as I stood up, a black woman friend tugged at my arm and whispered something like, "Sit down, sit down, we aren't feminists, we're womanists." I remember being amused and puzzled, and wondering "Who says 'we' aren't feminists? When was this decision made and why?" This gesture by my friend was a warm, kind invitation to be part of "everybody's" current consensus about the identity of black women (religious academics). But, if there is such a consensus being promoted by womanists, how can they avoid the contradiction of circumscribing conformity and policing black woman-hood while claiming to free it from the bondage of too few acceptable forms? This kind of narrowing is also evident in the ways that some womanists have engaged feminism with the assumption that whiteness and feminism are indistinguishable, problematically erasing the contributions of a generation of black feminist foremothers. The challenge of engaging such concerns has helped me to develop intellectually, specifically to reflect more deeply on the communal needs of subjugated peoples for gatekeeping and about their tolerance of differences. As many feminist and socialist debates over the years have proven, the struggle to maintain a stance of radical inclusion is always the bane and benefit of progressive, identity-based intellectual movements. I feel privileged to have been able to learn from, participate in, and chart my differences with womanist religious thought during the initial years of its production.

## NOTES

1. Katie G. Cannon, *Black Womanist Ethics* (Atlanta: Scholar's Press, 1988).

2. Cheryl Townsend Gilkes, *If It Wasn't for the Women: Black Women's Experience and Womanist Culture in Church and Community* (Maryknoll, NY: Orbis Books, 2001), 10.

3. Jacquelyn Grant, "An Epistle to the Black Church: What a Womanist Would Want to Say to the Church," *A.M.E. Church Review* 106, no. 342 (1991): 56.

Made in the USA
San Bernardino, CA
21 May 2019